FRIDA RAMSTEDT

The Furnishing Handbook

Illustrated by Sofia Gustafsson and Sara Petterson
Translated by Peter Graves

PARTICULAR BOOKS
an imprint of
PENGUIN BOOKS

PARTICULAR BOOKS

UK | USA | Canada | Ireland | Australia
India | New Zealand | South Africa

Particular Books is part of the Penguin Random House group of companies
whose addresses can be found at global.penguinrandomhouse.com

Penguin
Random House
UK

Set in 11.3/16 pt Adobe Garamond Pro
Typeset by Jouve (UK), Milton Keynes
Printed and bound in Latvia by Livonia Print SIA

The authorized representative in the EEA is Penguin Random House Ireland,
Morrison Chambers, 32 Nassau Street, Dublin D02 YH68

A CIP catalogue record for this book is available from the British Library

ISBN: 978–0–241–64849–0

www.greenpenguin.co.uk

Contents

7

MATERIALS

8

TIMELINE

9

PLANNING MEASUREMENTS AND CONCEPTS

Take a seat

What does that actually mean? It can be interpreted in slightly different ways, of course, and you might just as easily say: make yourself comfortable or make yourself at home. Well-meaning invitations, but not necessarily achievable on every piece of furniture. Nowadays, many things are pleasing to the eye while being hopelessly uncomfortable to use. How has that come about, and what can we do about it?

In my first book I shared the basic principles of domestic interior design and the tricks of the trade used by interior designers and stylists. In this book, I have brought together various aspects of the knowledge and experience of furniture designers and makers that are important for us to bear in mind when buying furniture – furniture that is both good to look at and comfortable.

During the last decade, we've spent more money on domestic design than ever before. Not only do we acquire more things – and more expensive things – for our homes, but also more pieces of furniture that we haven't

tested first. And never before have we had so much to choose from: things from every corner of the world made available to us by the internet and e-commerce. In spite of this, we are given remarkably little reliable guidance as to what we should be thinking about when we buy furnishings, beyond what is fashionable in terms of colour and style in a particular season.

These days we often know more about which chairs we think are trendy than which we think are nice. And there are times when we have to double-check whether the chairs of our dreams are actually sittable on. Are they individual items of sculpture or are they comfortable? And in that case, for whom? What are the important things to look for when considering a piece of furniture and comparing it with alternatives in order to come to a better informed decision? Especially if we are serious about making our furnishing more personal: after all, we don't expect a particular style of jeans to fit every bottom, so why do we expect one and the same chair to do so? And, taking the long-term view, if we want to become better consumers, I am convinced that there is just as much need for us to increase our knowledge of this kind of question as to recognize the importance of choosing suitable materials and shorter transport distances.

What is pleasing to the eye and pleasant for your body are not necessarily one and the same.

Your Body is Your Yardstick

It's not just chance that makes comfortable furniture comfortable and uncomfortable furniture uncomfortable. In this chapter you will learn more about the measuring points that trained furniture designers have in mind when designing products. But also about the measurements of your own body that you need to pay attention to when trying out and assessing their work in order to decide which is the optimal match for you and your requirements. *Different folks, different strokes*, as the saying goes. And the folks are not just different, they come in very different shapes.

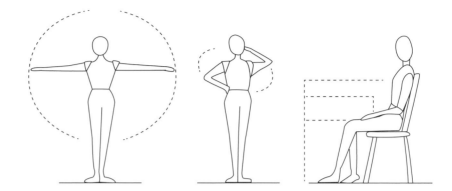

Anthropometrics

Our bodies are the yardsticks we always have with us, and it is from that perspective that we learn to judge and assess the proportions of the objects around us. Human measurements are also what is decisive when it comes to the fit and usefulness of the things we create. Statistical data about target groups provide furniture designers with their most important tool when designing a piece of furniture intended to be useful rather than just beautiful.

The science that deals with measurement of the human body and its proportions is called anthropometrics: the word comes from Greek *anthropos* (human body) and *metron* (measuring and the tools used for measuring). By taking the measurements of a sizeable number of people, a sufficient body of data is collected to enable us to work out the normal statistical distribution. Or, to put it simply, to get an idea of what the most common measurements are.

Standing still and moving

When measuring human bodies we make a distinction between structural data and functional data. The structural measurements are taken from fixed points of the body when it is motionless, whereas functional data is a measure of breadth of movement, of reach and of the space we need when we move around or carry out various activities. These functional measurements are sometimes referred to as dynamic, but the important thing is not simply to understand the definitions or the exact measurements, but to grasp the basic principles, both of which are important.

It is quite clear, isn't it, that we take up different amounts of space depending on whether we are walking or standing, or similarly, that we have differing abilities to reach a tall kitchen cupboard depending on how tall we are. So, on the same principle, it is hardly surprising that the same armchair is experienced rather differently by people with different physical shapes or sitting positions.

'It's the extremes that rule'

Anthropometric measures are used in order to facilitate the development of products that can accommodate as many variations as possible. That means that the aim is to come up with a product that offers a physical fit that allows a majority of the proposed target group to use the particular piece of furniture and design.

Traditionally, it is the size of the male that governs spatial requirements in housing – height and width of doorways, for instance. On the other hand, females, who generally speaking are shorter, are used to decide on reachability, i.e. what should be the maximum height of a shelf or hanging rail in a wardrobe to enable as many users as possible to reach it.

DID YOU KNOW?

Homo mensura: Protagoras's statement *'Man is the measure of all things'* was the basic principle of the furniture school started in 1923 at the Royal Danish Academy of Fine Arts. That is probably one of the reasons why twentieth-century Danish design classics have stood the test of time – and still do.

Important measurements for interior designers and furniture designers

You only have to look around you on the street to recognize that human beings come in different heights. And for each and every height there is any number of variations in physical shape. There are many books and manuals available to furniture designers to explain how best to design items of furniture to make them all comfortable. But not as many for us as their customers.

The following examples are just some of the measurement points that I have taken from the standard work *Human Dimension & Interior Space* (1979) by J. Panero. Their purpose is to help determine dimensions and to resolve technical and design questions. Knowing these measurements can be useful for all of us, as they will help us to read and understand the form and functionality of furniture.

Standing measurements

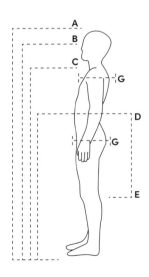

A. Stature
Metric used to establish standard measurements and minimum heights for everything from doorposts and doors to the height above head level for items such as ceiling lights and shelves.

B. Eye height when standing
This is used, for instance, to determine the optimal height for everything from privacy screens and picture hanging to the positioning of lighting. Even the shortest individuals in the household should be able to see out of the window and see their own reflection in the bathroom mirror.

C. Shoulder height and shoulder breadth
These help to determine the suitable breadth, shape and height of the backrest on sofas, armchairs and chairs. And, since most people's shoulders are wider than their hips, they are also used to determine the seating breadth necessary where several individuals are to sit alongside one another.

D. Elbow height when standing

This determines the standard height for counters and kitchen surfaces where people stand to work. It is also the standard for wash basins in the bathroom. According to the Consumer Agency book *Kitchens: Planning and Equipment* (1972), the elbow should be approximately 10 centimetres above the surface of the counter when the upper arm is allowed to hang down, while the lower arm is pointing forward. In *Human Dimension & Interior Space* (1979), the distance is given more precisely as 7.6 centimetres.

E. Knee height

Knee height is used, for instance, to determine the most suitable height for the seats of chairs and other seating furniture. It also provides guidelines for the design of tables, in order to prevent parts of the frame that support the table top banging against the legs.

F. Vertical reach

This is used to determine the standard measurement for the highest shelf height in kitchen cupboards, book shelves, display cases, wardrobes and hat and cap shelves.

G. Maximum body depth

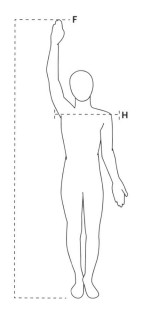

The maximum body depth is determined by measuring the horizontal distance from the foremost to the hindmost part of the body when viewed from the side: the foremost point is usually the chest, the hindmost is usually the buttock. This measurement might, for instance, be used to determine the minimum clearance necessary in tight spaces.

H. Maximum body breadth

This is the maximum distance across the body when viewed from the front. This measurement is used to calculate the minimum breadth necessary for everything from chair backs to doorways, but it is very easy to forget the need to take movement (functional measurement) into consideration, with the result that a space might feel constricted.

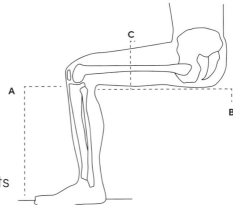

Sitting measurements

A. Popliteal height

The popliteal height is the distance, when seated, between the sole of the foot and the underside of the thigh behind the knee. This data is used to determine the appropriate height, shape and finish for such items as chairs and upholstered seating.

B. Popliteal length

This means the horizontal distance from the back of the lower leg/knee to the hindmost point of the buttock. It is used to determine the appropriate front-to-back depth of the seat for items such as chairs, sofas, armchairs and toilets. You can tell by just looking at them that many armchairs and sofas are far too deep, with the result that when you sit in them you have to sit with your legs outstretched.

C. Thigh clearance when sitting

This is the distance from the sitting surface to the top of the thigh. When designing tables, for instance, furniture designers make use of this measurement in order to avoid the user's legs colliding with the apron or sub-frame of the table. This measurement can also help you, as a customer, avoid mistakes or disasters: with the biggest member of your family sitting on a chair, measure the distance between the top-most part of his or her thigh and the lowest point of the surface or apron of the table. Is there sufficient space between the two, or do their legs knock into the table?

Seated hip breadth

How broad are your hips and backside when you are sitting down? It can provide useful guidance when you are considering chairs with higher sides or armrests as they may feel constricted if the inside dimension is too narrow.

Elbow-to-elbow breadth

With your arms by your sides, measure the distance between your elbows. This measure can be used to calculate how many people can be seated around a dining table while still having space to eat and use their cutlery. (Believe it or not, this is an easy detail to forget.) It can also be used to determine the size of the table top necessary for drawing or writing.

GEOGRAPHICAL DIFFERENCES

Without suggesting which is better or which worse, anthropometrical measurements make it possible for us to recognize that there are geographical differences with regard to people's sizes from one part of the world to another. Genetic and socioeconomic factors such as access to nutritious food and clean water have varied over the ages in different parts of the world, and such factors are believed to have influenced the size and average physical measurements of different populations.

Why should this matter? Well, it is of considerable importance to the furniture sector: ordering furniture and furnishings from other parts of the world can be problematic because measurements and standards may well differ from those we are familiar with. The end result may be that the pieces in our furnishing jigsaw simply don't fit together, or that the shape and scale of the furniture doesn't fully match your own physique.

The ergonomic balancing act

Did you know that your head weighs about five kilos? That means that we're balancing something like a small-sized bowling ball on our neck. Bearing that in mind, it becomes easier to understand that the calculations that go into well-designed furniture are an ergonomic balancing act.

Most people will be familiar from their working lives with the concept of ergonomics and its description of the interplay between the human and the tool. Ergonomics is a cross-disciplinary subject that combines biology, technology and psychology in order to prevent accidents and risks to health. Ergonomic knowledge has been particularly important in the office environment but, given the current trend for more and more people to work remotely, it's not too far-fetched to be considering the ergonomics of the home.

What do the ergonomics of your home look like? What kinds of stress do you put on your body in your home environment? Do you sit properly in your chairs? Do you sleep properly in your bed? How do you stand when you are working in the kitchen? Where is the lighting in your rooms and where is it aimed?

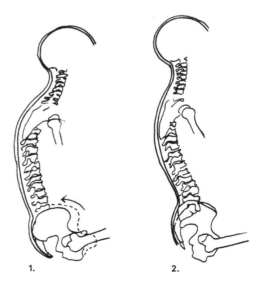

1. Furniture that hasn't been properly designed with human structure in mind can easily lead to sitting postures that skew the load on the body.
2. A well-designed piece of furniture should provide support for the natural curve of the spine.

For people who want to get straight to the creative phase of design, these may sound like dry questions, but I'm certain that in a couple of years' time you will be pleased that you kept your own well-being in mind rather than just focusing on the visual hormony in the room.

Most people go to a lot of trouble when selecting an office chair at work, but we don't put so much thought into how we sit when we are binge-watching a TV series on the sofa or spending many hours at the dining table during a long dinner. In the course of time both can cause backache or neck problems, can't they? Which is why I think it's a good idea to think about these issues even when purchasing non-work-related furniture: after all, we are likely to spend many hours using these things and may, over time, suffer stress injuries as a result.

The purpose of furniture in our everyday lives is to distribute the weight of our bodies so that we can relax without disturbing the natural S-curve of our spines. When we are sitting, the legs of the chair support most of our weight, so that the load is taken off our feet and knees. The muscles that aren't needed at that point can be relaxed. But poorly constructed furniture can lead to us relaxing one part of the body at the expense of others, so that, for instance, we end up compressing tissues, restricting circulation, pushing our hips forward into a position that causes a curvature in the back which, in turn, leads to neck strain to compensate for the curvature.

DID YOU KNOW?

The forward curvature of the human spine is called lordosis. Support for the lordosis should rest in the iliac crest region, which is roughly where you wear your belt. That is the area of the body said to have the maximum need of support when you lean back in a chair, if your back is to retain its natural shape.

Proxemics

In addition to physical measurements of size, there are theories that address our emotional need for space around us. It can be beneficial to remember this when planning furnishing. You should take account of the different spatial zones necessary, depending on how well we know the people around us and depending on the kind of activity being undertaken. Proxemics, derived from the Latin word *proxy* (near), is the technical term for this. It is the field of research that studies space and proximity between people and objects. Why should this be of any concern when choosing furniture? The answer is that the space allowed for seating on sofas, for instance, or the width of a table, does not simply depend on the amount of physical space needed, but also on the space we feel most comfortable with. In purely physical terms, we can easily find ourselves sitting too close for comfort to our neighbour on the sofa. And these comfort zones can vary between cultures – cultures are frequently described as high-contact cultures or a low-contact. The concept of *proxemics* was introduced first by the American researcher and anthropologist Edward T. Hall in 1963: he identified four zones that we might find helpful when thinking about furnishing. You don't have to be endlessly using a tape measure in order to take advantage of Hall's ideas: in my opinion, as long as you keep the approximate distances in mind, that is quite sufficient to enable you to come to more considered decisions.

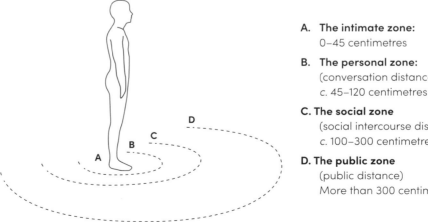

A. **The intimate zone:**
    0–45 centimetres

B. **The personal zone:**
    (conversation distance)
    c. 45–120 centimetres

C. **The social zone**
    (social intercourse distance)
    c. 100–300 centimetres

D. **The public zone**
    (public distance)
    More than 300 centimetres

The Emperor's New Furniture

For many years Scandinavian design has functioned proudly under the watchwords *form follows function*. We are internationally renowned for bringing aesthetics and ergonomics together, for our uncompromising uniting of artistry and construction technique. But, if we are honest with ourselves, can we still claim that to be true? Especially when we consider what the volume of sales tells us about the furniture we buy these days, or which furniture models are given most attention in the press and media. It's unlikely that anyone will dispute the fact that our interest in design and our investment in our homes has increased vastly during recent decades but, when it comes to furniture, has our knowledge of and feel for functionality and quality kept up with that development? Or has it declined?

Four different versions of the spindleback chair.

1. Classic (comfortable) 2. Artwork (sculptural)
3. Conceptual (experimental) 4. Commercial (rationalised)

Comfort, work of art, concept or cash cow?

It may perhaps sound strange, but you can't always rely on a chair being a chair, or even that it has been designed with comfortable sitting as its initial premise. There are, in fact, a huge number of different drives and ambitions behind the many forms and proportions of the furniture of today. Some are sculptures or art objects rather than furniture for sitting on, whereas others result from conceptual experiments by designers and producers more interested in putting their names or trademarks on the map than giving you a comfortable seat.

Some furniture has also been important as entry products and volume items – chairs, for instance, since they are often sold as sets. Anyone supplying chairs to a customer will most likely sell more than one and, with a little luck, a matching table and maybe even a suitable lamp to go with them.

All of a sudden we find ourselves talking about such large sums of money for the dealers, not to mention the regular payments on the consumer credit taken out to fund the purchase, that the competition for chair buyers not only affects the day's takings but can also make a serious difference to annual turnover, if you are able to win over enough customers. This can easily lead to the temptation to tamper with the ergonomics and human proportions for the sake of improved profit margins or aesthetic exclamation marks.

I do want to stress, however, that it doesn't have to be a case of either/or. Form does not have to be the converse of function – the ability to deal with that kind of dualism is surely the basis of a designer's professional skill. Nevertheless, it is surprisingly common for comfort to draw the short straw. That may be because designers don't usually become production managers – that function goes more often to buyers and economists or to people more versed in marketing strategy than carpentry.

The opportunity to test-sit on a piece of furniture in the shop rather than ordering it online can, of course, be of some help, but even so most things feel more or less okay if you only sit on them for a short time. Anyone who has been out hillwalking can testify that even a hard boulder can provide an unexpectedly comfortable seat. It is not until you have been sitting in a chair for some considerable time that you start noticing where it rubs, what its weak points are, how the different parts feel against your body after a couple of hours – all the important things you should have thought about before ordering half a dozen of them for delivery in the next month or so. Furniture produced for use in the public sphere has to fulfil some tough demands, whereas for a great deal of what is sold to private individuals, the requirements have been streamlined to the point that it no longer deserves to be called furniture. I've heard this phenomenon referred to as the design equivalent of the bread produced on TV *Bake-Off* shows: there is a great difference between how things appear and how they are experienced.

The more you learn about the essential features in the construction of a chair, the more obvious it will become to you how often artistic and conceptual factors – and above all commercial factors – are allowed to take precedence over comfort and utility.

Quality concepts for furniture

What is it that actually determines the quality of a piece of furniture over and above its aesthetic values? Here are a couple of points to bear in mind before we look more closely at the anatomy of furniture and analyse its component parts.

Utility value

What are the practical characteristics of the piece? How well does it fulfil its intended purpose? There are wide differences in the real utility value of the furniture sold today: many pieces are good to look at, but far from all of them are as functional as they should be.

Artistic quality

I read somewhere that the poetry of craftmanship is as important as the miracles of new technology. And I couldn't come up with a better way of putting it when it comes to identifying the artistic quality of a piece of furniture. Brilliant craftsmanship is not about taking shortcuts, but about the details that allow design to stand out from the crowd.

Purpose and context

Is the piece of furniture designed for the purpose you are intending to use it for? Take classic café chairs, for example. They are the result of industrialised mass production and have many qualities that are valued highly in a restaurant environment. Since they are compact, they allow many guests to be seated in a small area, and being light in weight they are easy to move around should there be a need to rearrange the tables. On the other hand, as far as seating goes, they are not really comfortable in terms of what we currently know about the ergonomics of sitting. This is not particularly important in a café, where we don't want customers to stay too long, but it's less desirable when this style of chair becomes fashionable in modern homes, where we may want to sit comfortably for long periods around the dinner table. When you take a piece of furniture from its original context and put it in a new one, it is frequently the new context rather than the object *per se* that is problematic.

Strength

How well does the piece stand up to everyday wear and tear? Some manufacturers carry out their own tests and estimate how long an item will last, and they are then able to offer guarantees based on normal usage for a set number of years. Other manufacturers make no mention of this – and hope you won't bother to ask.

Sustainability

How and where was the piece made? What materials were used and how were they transported? What effect did these things have on our common natural resources and on the people who work on the production line?

'The job of the furniture designer is to unite good functionality with expressive form.'

Erik Berglund, *Talking of Quality*

Safety

Is the piece of furniture safe? For everyone? Are there any weaknesses or faults in the construction that might lead to injury to people or damage to other objects? The regulations concerning such issues differ from country to country and it's easy to miss these differences when ordering items from overseas.

Made of the right material and skills

In the furniture world these days we hear a lot about sustainability, but it is mostly with reference to what the furniture is made of – the materials that have been used and how they have been harvested. Not so much about the craftmanship or skills that went into the construction and production. This in spite of the fact that comfort and finish are factors that have at least as much influence on how long we keep a piece of furniture or, perhaps above all, want to keep it. There is much to be looked into in this area – and much to be surprised by! Which is why I can promise you that you'll look at furniture with a new eye once you've read this book.

Can you imagine cars being reviewed in the same way as we see new furniture covered in the press? 'Manufacturer X has brought out a new model and it's available in ten different colours. The streamlined bodywork has been inspired by nature.' And over and above that? What's it like to drive? What's its top speed and its technical characteristics? What's under the bonnet and is there anything innovative and unique in its construction? What has the manufacturer done well – and what less well?

It would be unthinkable for a motor journalist not to follow up with a series of questions about functionality and technicalities at the launch of a new model, whereas media coverage of furniture and design rarely goes deeper than subjective judgements about the aesthetic qualities of a new piece and what inspired the designer. All this is in spite of the fact that, these days, many exclusive pieces of furniture or lamps might cost as much as a small car and, moreover, we use them at least as often and perhaps more.

But not everything in the furniture business is manufactured with a high degree of care, nor does it achieve a high level of quality. Quite intentionally! Some manufacturers are happy to take short cuts to keep the price down, and they are adept at concealing flaws, which makes it difficult for the consumer to evaluate quality.

Those of us in the furniture trade are expected to know intuitively how best to combine different modules, in spite of the fact that pieces of furniture are team players and it takes years of education to qualify as an interior designer. The delivery of the items we have perhaps waited weeks for can lead to endless headaches and feelings of frustration when we discover they don't fit in with the furniture we already have in our homes. But that issue is seldom addressed by current interior design, not even when obvious failures show up in the 'Life and Style . . .' genre of articles or TV programmes. (And when they do show up, they are usually passed over without comment.) What frequently happens is that we turn our backs on the errors, become dissatisfied and replace the furniture early, long before its physical life is over. Well, I think you can now begin to understand my frustration: given all this, I'm amazed that we don't demand much more from those who observe and write about interior design – what is at issue is much more than just describing the appearance of things and telling us where we can buy them.

Complaints to the National Board for Consumer Disputes in Sweden have increased in recent years and the reason, in my view, is that not everything on the market is up to a standard we consider acceptable.

The Consumer Agency recently tested children's bunk beds and concluded that only one of the seventeen tested was sufficiently safe. So there is a major problem with furniture, which, in spite of certification, safety regulations, EU standards and labelling of various kinds, is not properly constructed, but is nevertheless bought by us in good faith and makes its way into our homes.

Seating

Apart from our beds, seating of one sort or another tends to be the furniture with which we have most contact. A well-made chair, sofa or armchair that welcomes us after a long day can give us almost the same feeling as a warm embrace. It is a safe haven, offering a moment of rest and renewed energy. Life is too short to have to put up with sitting uncomfortably. In the following section we shall dig down into such things as sitting angles, seat tilt, finish and important contact points with the body, in order to simplify the process of sorting through the enormous range on offer and getting a better idea of the furniture you think comfortable – and why.

Chairs

Let's start with chairs – the most common things we sit on. The chair is reputed to be the furniture designer's ultimate test, the equivalent of the perfect sauce pairing for a chef. A well-made chair is a balancing act between form, function, proportions and strength. A blind person can often sense immediately whether or not a chair is a piece of truly skilled craftsmanship. The problem is that today's trade will not always permit us to sit on and test products, and the range of available styles is so huge that there is no way we can work our way through all the models.

Fortunately, it is quite possible to train your ability to read furniture and to understand the basic grammar of design, so that your body's sensory system is able, almost intuitively, to make a visual evaluation and come to an appreciation of what will – and will not – work for your own body.

The anatomy of the chair

In order to analyse a chair you need to break it down into its most important constituent parts. There are primarily three things that need to be analysed, separately, and in relation to one another: the seat, the back and the legs.

TIP!

Dan Gordan's substantial reference work *Svenska stolar och deras formgivare* (*Swedish chairs and their designers 1899–2013*) offers a photographic record of twentieth-century Swedish chairs and their designers.

THE ÅKERBLOM CHAIR

BENGT ÅKERBLOM (1901–1990) was a Swedish doctor. He thought the chairs currently on the market gave insufficient support to the lumbar region because the backrest was too high up. Furthermore, he considered that the seat and the back of the chair should not meet at a 90° angle – the backrest needed to lean slightly backwards in order to give better support to the back. Åkerblom also recommended that the seat height, standard at that time, should be lowered to allow the sitter's feet to rest firmly on the floor and thus avoid excessive pressure on the underside of the thigh. This would lead to enhanced blood flow to the legs and feet. As a result of lowering the seat height, he also thought the standard table height should be reduced in order to avoid stress in the shoulder region.

ON THE BASIS OF HIS ERGONOMIC PRINCIPLES Åkerblom had the architect Gunnar Ekelöf design a number of different chairs, which were then produced by various factories and marketed under the name *Åkerblom chairs*. Something like 120,000 Åkerblom chairs were sold between 1949 and 1958, 45,000 of them being exported overseas. Bengt Åkerblom's serious research interest in anatomy and ergonomics led him to graduate in 1948 with his doctoral thesis *Standing and Sitting Posture*. The curvature in the backrest, characteristic of Åkerberg's chairs, has become known as the *Åkerblom curve* and continues to influence furniture designers.

The seat

From childhood onwards we have probably been taught to sit still at the dining table, but in practice we seldom do so. An important factor that distinguishes good chairs from bad chairs is whether they allow us to change position from time to time. While sitting eating our meal, we need to be able to vary our sitting posture every so often, partly because we receive automatic signals from our internal organs (the muscle spindle system) telling us it is time to change position, and partly because we need to be able to move our arms and upper body in order to eat with the cutlery or to reach for a drinking glass on the table. A well-designed seat should relieve pressure and provide support without locking the body into a fixed position.

The seat should not be so deep that we are unable to rest our backs against the chairback. It should preferably be slightly shorter than the distance between the buttocks and the back of the knee, otherwise we would be unable to bend our legs and would find ourselves sitting like dolls with our legs sticking straight out or just dangling down. The front edge of the seat where it meets the back of the knee ought to be gently rounded like the lip of a waterfall, without any sharp edges that might press on or cut into the sensitive soft areas immediately above the back of the knee. Ideally, there should be two-fingers' breadth of free space between the front edge of the seat and the back of the knee in order to obviate the risk of pressure on the underside of the thigh where there are blood vessels and nerves near the surface. This is all to ease circulation to the legs during long periods of sitting and thus avoid stasis dermatitis in the legs. On the other hand, if the seat is too short, too tight or too narrow, it can press instead on the outer side of the thigh muscles and also cause discomfort when we remain seated for lengthy periods.

A chair with a sloping backrest should have the front edge of its seat angled upwards and, preferably, not be slippery: this prevents the sliding effect that can cause the lower body to slide forward and put the back in an uncomfortable position, particularly during lengthy periods of sitting, such as at a dinner party.

Finally, it is important to check the distance from the seat to the floor in relation to the distance between the sole of the foot and the back of the knee. (Read about popliteal height in the section on anthropometrics on p. 8.)

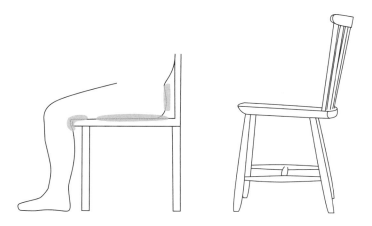

The design of the front edge, depth of seat and slope of seating surface often determines how comfortable a seat feels.

If the seat is too high, the soles of our feet will not reach the floor, but if it's too low our knees will be at an acute angle, more or less as when we go down on our haunches, which is not comfortable for any length of time.

Details about the seat to double-check

- That the size, design and contours of the seat match your buttocks.
- That the front-to-back measurement of the seat is not so generous as to stop you reaching the backrest, which is there to give proper support to your back.
- That the distance from the seat to the floor is just right. With padded chairs, remember that the apparent height and the height when in use can differ, so always measure the height of the seat when it is pressed down (i.e. when someone is sitting on it), and check that it fits under the table it is to go with. Bear in mind that heavier individuals compress padded seats more than lighter people – even though it is only a matter of a few centimetres, it can make a considerable difference and cause unnecessary strain on the shoulders and neck.
- That the front edge of the seat is gently rounded (waterfall-lipped), not sharp or angular.
- That the seat slopes slightly from front to back so that you don't slide forward or need to strain to stay in a comfortable sitting position.

The height and shape of the seatback, the slope of the back and the availability of lumbar support all affect how comfortable a chair will feel when you lean back on it.

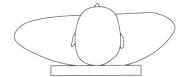

A straight back does not follow the body's curvature.

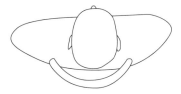

A curved back that is too tight might create uncomfortable pressure points.

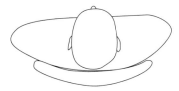

Try to find a chair with a back that fits your body yet is wide enough to let you change seating position.

The seatback

Chairs that have a slightly backward-sloping seatback are preferable because they provide a more comfortable sitting position at the dining table and because they offer support to the upper body while still allowing movement. The sloping back also opens the angle between the seat and seatback to a little more than 90°: this in turn opens your hip angle, which makes it easier for the blood to circulate.

The seatback must not be too high, too straight or too small, as these things can lock your body in position, cause you to push your jaw forward, or make it more difficult to change your sitting position. The seatback must be wide and stable enough to lean back against and sufficiently strong to take the weight of your upper body, otherwise you are effectively just sitting on a stool. I think of it as feeling as if you are wearing underwear that is too tight: the whole day can be ruined by a bra strap that cuts into your back, irrespective of how nice the rest of your clothes are.

Another important point to check is the vertical curvature of the seatback and the positioning of the lumbar support in relation to your back, (i.e. how far above the seat the support is) since that can affect how supportive the chair feels. If there is no lumbar support at all, your back will slump into the space and your posture will be bad.

Example of a chair design with a straight back and 90 degree angle between seat and back.

Example of a chair design with no lumbar support.

The seatbacks: points to double-check

- The slope of the seatback, as that will affect your sitting angle on the chair and open your hip angle to more than 90°.

- The height of the seatback, as that affects how much relief you feel in terms of upper body pressure. A seatback that is too low gives virtually no support at all; a seatback that is too high can affect your head movements and tend to cause you to lean forward.

- The size of the seatback and its horizontal curvature and design – these can affect how comfortable you feel when you lean back.

- The surface and structure of the seatback may feel comfortable or uncomfortable to lean back on. A shaped seatback or one with gaps may rub or press painfully on your vertebrae and can sometimes feel like lying on a bed of nails.

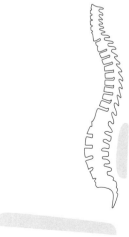

The form and position of the backrest in relation to the S-curve of the spine affects your feelings of comfort and relief.

After sitting for any length of time without a lumbar support 17 centimetres above the seat of the chair, there is a risk that the lower back will sag uncomfortably and begin to ache.

Whether a chair feels stable or unstable usually depends on the structure under the seat. How the legs are attached, whether they are linked together or not, and how the weight of your body is distributed, are all points that affect the stability of the chair.

The legs and stretchers

How firmly a chair is anchored to the floor depends on its legs and stretchers or central pillar. How many of them there are, where they are placed and at what angle all determine the chair's centre of gravity and how stable the chair will feel both when in use and not. You could turn the chair upside down to examine the corner blocks under the seat as they will usually reveal the quality and strength of the carpentry.

The legs: points to double-check

- The positioning and angle of the legs give an indication of the centre of gravity and whether there is any great risk of tipping. Completely straight legs are more sensitive to knocks from the side, whereas legs that are angled slightly outwards are better able to absorb these.

- If the backrest slopes backwards, the back legs should also slope outwards enough to balance the weight on the chair, especially the weight of the upper body when the chair is in use.

- Stretchers and stays are often necessary to achieve a stable construction, but they must not hinder a natural sitting position or any desired movements – in the process of standing up, for instance, we usually pull our feet back in under the seat. You can check that for yourself by standing up from a chair without armrests while pretending that there is no space to pull your feet back under you. It is very difficult to do this elegantly.

- Corner blocks beneath the seat can help to strengthen and stabilise the chair legs.

- Legs attached outside the seat indicate that the chair is stackable. Check that they don't protrude too far or are placed in such a way as to dig into your knees or thighs.

- What is the maximum weight the chair will take? The quality of the material used is vital to a chair's ability to take the weight of the human body. Chairs on sale in the USA frequently state their maximum load-bearing capacity and manufacturers of low-price chairs often post a lower capacity in order to guard against complaints.

- What is the total weight of the chair? Is it light enough for you to move with one hand while simultaneously being sufficiently stable to avoid the risk of tipping or being knocked over?

- Is the shape of the chair back easy to grip? This is important, for instance, when you are pulling the chair out to sit down or when getting up.

- Does the chair have a crumb gap (CG)? That is, is there a space between the seat and the back so that crumbs and bits of food can be brushed off without them lodging in the crease between seat and back? This is particularly vital in the case of padded chairs.

- Does the chair have a solid construction? Check how all the parts are fitted together, particularly the joints between the back, the seat and the legs. These are the points that carry the heaviest loads, shear forces and wear when the chair is in use. Check the construction of the chair to see whether it is repairable if damaged.

'A chair is a very difficult object. A skyscraper is almost easier.'

Ludwig Mies van der Rohe

Do the measurements fit in with other pieces of furniture?

- Height of seat in relation to height of table: the standard recommendation for this gap is 27–30 centimetres.

- Chair arms in relation to the table apron: is it possible to push the chair in to enable you to get closer to the table or do the chair arms prevent this?

- Space beneath the table: the recommendation is that there should be at least 63 centimetres clear space beneath the table to allow space for your legs and for the legs of the chair.

- The width of the chair in relation to the number of sitting places around the table and to the positioning of the table legs. The usual allowance is 57–60 centimetres per person, but padded chairs may be wider. Certain types of chair construction may knock into parts of the table or its sub-frame, forcing people to adjust their position to avoid the table legs.

- The footprint of the chair and the table. Do the stays and stretchers become entangled? Measure the chair at its widest point – the spread of the legs is often wider than the width of the chair back. Measuring the footprint is important to ensure that you recognize that the legs spread outwards beneath the seat and are thus wider than the widest part of the chair visible above the table top.

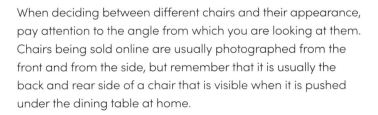

REMEMBER!

When deciding between different chairs and their appearance, pay attention to the angle from which you are looking at them. Chairs being sold online are usually photographed from the front and from the side, but remember that it is usually the back and rear side of a chair that is visible when it is pushed under the dining table at home.

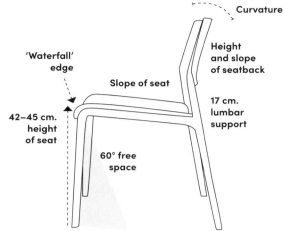

Curvature

'Waterfall' edge

Height and slope of seatback

Slope of seat

17 cm. lumbar support

42–45 cm. height of seat

60° free space

Have you ever tried to get up from a chair without moving your feet back in under the seat? Unexpectedly difficult, isn't it? That is why furniture designers avoid placing awkward stretchers on the front of well-made chairs: they leave 60° of free space below the seat.

Checklist: important measurements to fit the human body

- The recommended height of the seat above the floor is 42–45 centimetres. A chair that is too low will cause your pelvis to tip backwards and that will then make you round your back, causing a hunched posture that will give you aches and pains after a while. A chair that is too high will prevent your feet reaching the ground. You will feel as if your legs are dangling, and that causes an unnatural pressure below your thighs.

- The seat must not have sharp edges that rub against your body as you change position.

- Sitting stability begins with the pelvis. The weight should be concentrated on the ischial tuberosities (sit bones) since that means that the pelvis is tilted forwards and the sitting posture is stable. The front edge of the seat of a dining chair should, therefore, be a little higher than the back edge, otherwise there is a risk that the loading on the body will be crooked.

- On the other hand, when sitting on an office chair, the normal tendency is to lean slightly forward while working. The recommendation in this case is that the front of the seat should be lower than the back of the seat.

- The back of the seat should allow you space for movement and, preferably, not cover the whole back area down to the seat of the chair – if it does it limits the possibility of changing seating position and consequently locks the pelvis.

- If the seatback is high, it's important that it follows the vertical curvature of the back so that it doesn't lock the body into an uncomfortable posture. When it is too high, it forces the head forward and that puts strain on the back, shoulders and neck during lengthy periods of sitting. Nor, however, should the seatback be too low or so narrow that it cuts in or makes shoulder movement uncomfortable.

- The horizontal curvature of the seatback should follow the shape of the body and not be too tight.

- The seatback is not only there to serve your back. You should also check that it's possible to get a firm grip on it since, every time you pull the seat out to sit down, your hand has to take hold of the seatback somewhere.

- Normal elbow height above the seat is approximately 25 centimetres, so the arms of an armchair should not be either too high or too low relative to that. Arms that are too high will push your shoulders up towards your ears, whereas arms that are sloping or too low offer no support worth speaking of.

- To allow you to rest your arms on them, armrests that slope down towards the back are better than those that slope down towards the table. Armrests sloping in the wrong direction put a strain on your arms since they are having to counteract the force of gravity.

- The seat should be even and not have cavities that the soft tissues of the body can squeeze into.

- The seat must not be shaped in a way that cuts into the underside of the thighs during long periods of sitting.

- Padded seats lose their cushioning over time. Check the construction of the seat to ensure there are no parts (screws, joints, attachments and the like) that will cause discomfort when the cushioning loses some of its resilience.

A sloping armrest that allows your arms to slide forward will be less comfortable as this will create tension in your body.

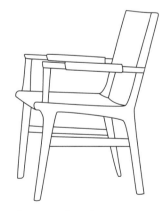

Armrests that slope backwards will be more comfortable and will provide a more relaxing position for your arms.

The weak points of chairs

- When moving chairs, we usually lift them by the chairback or drag them, so it's important that chairs are built to tolerate that treatment. The backs of padded chairs should not be too soft or puffed up because if it's not possible to grip them from above, we end up gripping them by the sides which, if done frequently, can leave marks or dents in the padding. Chairs with slim backs made of slender materials are likely to be sensitive to twists and uneven stresses when being moved and, over time, this may damage the joints and cause the seatback to become loose or wobbly. Chairs constructed from steel tubing can be difficult to grip and become slippery. Covered chairs can easily get stained if they are moved during meals.

- The legs, aprons and stretchers of a chair are subject to stresses and strains during use, not only when you are sitting on it, but also every time you stand up, sit down or drag the chair across the floor. If you know that your floor is not completely smooth (a tiled floor, perhaps?), you should select chairs with solid legs that give a bigger contact area between floor and chair and thus minimise the risk of the chair wobbling. The front legs of a chair frequently suffer more wear and tear than the back legs, because they have most contact with the floor when, for instance, we move the chair with just one hand.

- Chair legs made of curved wood can be deceptive. The legs can be unnecessarily sensitive to loads and stresses unless the bend in the curve runs in the same direction as the fibres in the wood. Pay particular attention to chairs in the bentwood style that have been saw-cut rather than steam bent, since the former may have cut through the fibres of the wood and consequently made them more liable to break under loads. Steam-bent furniture tolerates higher loading precisely because the load on the fibres follows the direction of the curve.

- Steel screws in bentwood chairs may work loose over time and enlarge the screw holes, making it impossible to re-tighten the screws. Check the tightness of screws regularly to ensure that they aren't working loose and enlarging the screw holes. The length and quality of the screws under the seat of steam-bent chairs are a good indicator of quality.

- Screws may need to be checked and re-tightened in wooden chairs that have the parts joined with metal brackets, since screws don't allow for the natural movements of the wood in the way that pinned and glued joints do.

- Chairs made of welded steel tubing can be weakened or deformed when holes are being pre-punched to facilitate final assembly by the customer. You should, therefore, avoid buying metal furniture in which the tubing appears to be the same size as the head of the screw. Also, check the welds carefully since cracks may occur after a period of usage or when the loading has been excessive.

- Chair seats may gather crumbs. The types of chair used in public places should preferably have gaps left between the seat and the chairback so that dust and crumbs can be brushed off.

- Sharp edges on upholstered frames can wear holes in the seat over time.

- The surface of chairs can be scratched by items such as buttons, zips and the studs on jeans.

- Vice versa: clothes – women's tights and other delicate materials, for instance – may be damaged by contact with sharp parts of the chair.

- The surface of the chair can be stained by the use of strong disinfectant or cleaning fluids.

- When assembling furniture at home, over-tightening of screws can damage the wood.

- Chairs may be damaged if they tip over. Chairs that have rockers or curved metal legs should have stoppers fitted in order to avoid the risk of tipping over.

- Stretchers beneath the seat can easily split or become loose if subjected to too much stress by, for instance, being used as support for the feet or as a kicking-off point when standing up.

- Screws and other metal parts can cause discolouration if they rust or erode. This is most common in proximity to salt water or with outdoor furniture when you live near the coast.

A FORGOTTEN PIONEER IN THE DESIGN OF FURNITURE

WHEN WE LOOK BACK at the history of design, we tend to focus on the iconic objects, on the classics that are still current today and consequently often remember the names of their designers. Erik Berglund was a rather more anonymous figure, who nevertheless had a considerable influence on modern design. He trained as a furniture designer and worked as Carl Malmsten's draughtsman before becoming an academic and devoting the greater part of his career to furniture research. He was a pioneer in terms of furniture design.

NOWADAYS, AS FEW as five successful years can lead to a designer achieving international recognition. Erik Berglund devoted five decades of his career to studying and communicating knowledge about the function, durability and sustainability of furniture, focusing especially on the measurements and proportions of furniture designed for sitting. In spite of that, he remains relatively unknown to the majority of Swedes, which is a pity as his contribution to modern understanding of furniture is without parallel. His books and the fundamental principles he outlined are still in use today by trained designers all over the world. The Swedish Furniture Institute and the whole business of standardising the manufacture of furniture in Sweden in the middle of the twentieth century may have initially been regarded as questionable, but, in retrospect, the question we should be asking ourselves is whether we would still be enjoying our current good reputation were it not for the debates and lively discussions about design that took place at that time.

IN 1945, ERIK BERGLUND WAS EMPLOYED as an illustrator by the art historian Gregor Paulsson. A little later he became a study supervisor with the Swedish Crafts Association (now Swedish Design), where he organised study circles and arranged exhibitions all round the country to promote knowledge of art and design.

IN 1948, BERGLUND CARRIED OUT the first Swedish study of the function and functionality of furniture. The aim was to improve and standardise Swedish beds and bedroom fittings.

DURING THE YEARS 1950–1960 Erik Berglund and Tryggve Johansson set up the Colour Centre under the aegis of the Swedish Crafts Association and organised 'living circles' and courses on 'the Natural Colour System' both within Sweden and abroad. The Colour Centre laid the foundations for colour education in Sweden and for what later became the Scandinavian Colour Institute.

IN 1953, WITH BERGLUND'S INVOLVEMENT, a Furniture Committee was set up within the Institute for Informative Labelling, the aim being to develop methods for defining and reporting on the technical quality of furniture. The laboratory for testing furniture proved very successful and was recognized even outside Sweden – the Swedish methods are still in use in many places.

IN 1967, THE FURNITURE INSTITUTE was set up. Partly state-financed, it was a joint initiative of the Swedish Crafts Association, the Cooperative Union, the Trades Union Confederation, and the Confederation of Professional Employees, along with IKEA and the University of Arts, Crafts and Design, and its aim was to develop new methods of testing, a standard for the design of government offices, and a methodology for product inspection – Möbelfakta, a Swedish labelling system for furniture.

ERIK BERGLUND WAS APPOINTED MANAGING DIRECTOR and head of research and he was able, under the umbrella of the Furniture Institute, to further develop the testing that he and Brita Åkerman had been working on since the 1940s. During the eighteen years he spent as MD, he was involved in the production of a thousand or more studies of various pieces of furniture and was also the joint author of some sixty reports. In 1984 he stood down in order to be able to focus on his research. The Furniture Institute celebrated its twenty-fifth anniversary by moving from Stockholm to Jönköping in the hope that proximity to the major producers in Småland would re-energise the enterprise: the result, unfortunately, was quite the reverse.

THE FURNITURE INSTITUTE DID NOT LAST LONG in its new home and three years later it was closed down. But its work had not been in vain. The insights gained from its activities still reverberate in the design field and live on in many of the aspects that raise the quality of life in Swedish homes.

Advantages and disadvantages of different seats

Solid wood seats

+ Wooden seats reflect body heat and tend to feel more pleasant since the temperature of the body is quickly transferred to the surface of the wood, unlike those with metal components which can feel cold.

+ Wooden seats can be easily maintained, rubbed down and repainted.

− Wood can be affected by changes in temperature and humidity: damp can lead to swelling, and heat to drying and shrinkage. You should avoid placing wooden chairs close to sources of heat, such as radiators and fireplaces, as this may cause cracking.

− The colour of wood can be affected by sunlight. If your dining table and chairs are located by a window, you should remember to change them around at intervals in order to even up colour changes.

− Depending on how the surface has been treated, wooden seats may be liable to staining. Spilt liquid and pieces of food should be wiped off immediately as liquid left lying on the seat may penetrate under the surface and cause staining that is then difficult to remove.

Woven seats

+ The advantage with chairs that are woven, usually with cord made from jute or twisted paper, is that they are significantly lighter and easier to move around than chairs with solid wooden seats.

+ Rather than being rigid, corded seats have a natural flexibility that follows your contours and which many people find more comfortable.

− Cording is a craft that calls for precision if the final result is to look even and elegant. Given cheap and cost-cutting means of production, however, on close inspection the finish often leaves a good deal to be desired. The cording on a wishbone chair demands about an hour's concentrated work and the employees in Carl Hansen's factories in

Denmark are offered regular massage sessions to keep their bodies in shape. Do low-cost producers show the same level of consideration for their workers?

– Over time, corded seats can sag, thus becoming less comfortable and needing regular re-cording. It is quite possible to do this on good-quality chairs, but it is not so easy on cheaper models, where the structure of the frame may not be strong enough to allow re-cording.

– Corded seats often make a slight creaking noise and may even sound a little like flatulence when you move. That, of course, can be embarrassing in certain situations.

– If you wear a skirt or shorts, corded seats may leave marks on your skin.

– Corded seats are more difficult to wipe clean if, for instance, someone spills porridge on them. (I'm speaking from personal experience.)

Rattan seats

+ Rattan is a natural material that breathes and allows for air-flow.

+ It weighs very little, so it's easy to move a rattan chair with just one hand.

+ It is relatively simple and cheap to re-cover rattan seats yourself. Rattan can be bought by the metre.

– It is sensitive to localised loads, e.g. standing on the seat.

– Rattan is a natural material and, with time, it can become brittle. This can be avoided by moistening the material at regular intervals.

– Rattan should not be placed in the sun or close to sources of heat.

Plastic or shell-shaped seats

+ The shape remains stable over time.

+ The material is easy to wipe down and to keep clean.

+ These chairs often weigh less than similar wooden or metal models.

− If the sitting angle is too wide and the material slippery, it can feel rather like going down a slide.

− Seats made of plastic do not breathe and may consequently feel unpleasant in contact with the body, especially in hot climates or environments. The feeling of sticking to the chair is particularly noticeable if you have a good deal of skin exposed and in contact with the seat.

− Plastic chairs can suffer scratching and abrasions from sharp edges, but also from buttons and studs on your clothing.

− Shell designs with high sides may be too tight around the thighs and make movement difficult.

Padded seats

+ These are often more comfortable for long dinner parties.

+ Chairs with padded seats and backs can help improve the acoustics of a room.

− Padded seats are easily stained and more difficult to keep clean.

− Always test these seats by sitting on them! It's difficult to judge a padded chair with your eyes: what is lurking beneath the covers, and what does it feel like to sit on? If the seat is hard or uneven, you won't want to be sitting on it for long periods; and if it's too soft, it may be difficult to stand up from or easy to sink down into an undesirable slouch.

Metal

+ Chairs made of metal often stand on runners (like a sledge), which gives them a springy feel when you sit on them. It also makes them much less noisy than four-legged chairs when you move them around a dining table. It is possible to lock chairs of this kind together with special clamps so as to form straight rows in lecture rooms and the like. These are some of the reasons why you often see sledge-base chairs used in public spaces, such as schools and restaurants.

+ Metal chairs are often stackable and, usually being lighter and more resilient than wood, they can be stacked higher.

– Metal chairs may feel cold against your skin.

– If damaged or worn, metal chairs are often more difficult to repair at home.

Network and wired (in all materials)

+ Because of the perforations in the seat, these chairs are lighter than other kinds.

+ The perforations allow air to circulate, which is good in hot environments or climates.

+ They make a room feel more spacious than a room with padded chairs.

– If you don't own one of these chairs, you will certainly have sat on one at an open-air café on a warm summer day. You plonk yourself down unsuspectingly and in no time at all your flesh is bulging through the gaps and then, when you stand up, you take the chair with you in the form of a criss-cross pattern of indentations on your thighs. The seats of this kind of chair cut into human flesh as much as, if not worse than, the netting on a joint of meat. If you are going to sit for any length of time, use a cushion to avoid discomfort.

Stiletto chairs

How is it possible for a wooden floor to suffer more damage from a human being in stiletto heels than from being walked on by an elephant weighing several tons? It's not simply that elephants rarely get invited to parties, it's all about the size of the contact area of the heel with the floor. The narrow point of the stiletto heel concentrates the weight of the whole body on an area of less than a square centimetre, whereas the elephant's much wider feet spread the load over a bigger

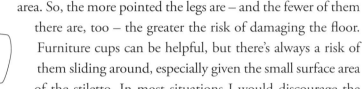

area. So, the more pointed the legs are – and the fewer of them there are, too – the greater the risk of damaging the floor. Furniture cups can be helpful, but there's always a risk of them sliding around, especially given the small surface area of the stiletto. In most situations I would discourage the purchase of stiletto chairs if you are at all concerned about getting ugly marks and dents in your varnished or softwood floor (pine, for instance). It's worth bearing this in mind out on the terrace, too, to ensure that your garden furniture doesn't leave ugly marks on your new wooden decking.

Stackable chairs

Stackable chairs can be stacked one on top of another with a minimum of three chairs. The stack is usually built up from the front and leans forward. There are other types of stackable chair, such as those that lean back and form a vertical tower (Sven Markelius's orchestra chairs, for instance), or versions that stack from the side. There are also versions, such as Åke Axelsson's Gästis chairs, in which the stack builds around its own axis. The simplest kind of all is the folding chair, with a seat that tips up so that it can be pushed together horizontally. Irrespective of which variety you choose, there will always be slightly different stresses and loading on the chairs when stacking them rather than when sitting. It's worth bearing this in mind when buying so that you can check that the quality of the chairs is up to the standard you want.

Is it easy to take a chair from the stack or do the legs get tangled? Check that the materials that come into contact with one another are compatible and won't get scratched by screws or other protruding parts on the chair above or below in the stack. A stack of five chairs is usually fine, but a stack of more than eight is unusual unless they can be located on a dolly for stability. If you purchase stackable chairs for public use in Sweden, they will have undergone rigorous testing for stability; stackable chairs for use at home, however, are not always so carefully designed and thoroughly tested.

HAS IT OCCURRED TO YOU THAT . . .

. . . Windsor chairs, where the backrest is made of wooden spindles, take a good deal longer to wipe down than a chair with a smooth back? Worth thinking about if you have small children likely to spill food.

The story of a modern chair

We've already mentioned the fact that a really comfortable chair can be the starting point for a long career as a designer, but the fact that a stubbornly uncomfortable model can do the same is demonstrated by Jonas Bohlin's exam project, 'Concrete'. It was premiered at the University of Arts, Crafts and Design graduation show in 1982 and was the start not only of Jonas Bohlin's own professional career, but also of Swedish Post-Modernism, a new and freer era of Scandinavian design following on from decades devoted to standardisation and testing for durability. 'Quality lies in the eye and heart, not in the buttocks!' is what Sven Lundh, MD of Källemo, is said to have exclaimed when he saw the chair for the first time. 'Concrete' was then produced in a numbered run of 100, just as if it were a print.

But shouldn't we be able to rely on a chair being a chair? Where do we draw the line between art, craft and furniture? My own view is that such a line doesn't really need to be drawn. Wherever you find originality you find delight, whereas no one gets any joy from cheap rubbish! And that is precisely where we encounter today's problem area: our great concern is not about original art being produced in limited editions, but about the shamelessly low-quality items being mass-produced by manufacturers.

A more immediately current turning in the history of Swedish design is a development in the design industry that gathered pace during the happy-go-lucky 2010s. These days many businesses include furniture among their wares, regardless of whether their real business is groceries, clothes or retailing automobile parts, but few of them count furniture designers among their employees. That, in my opinion, has had a very significant effect on the range, quality and price structure in the sector – in a way that is anything but positive.

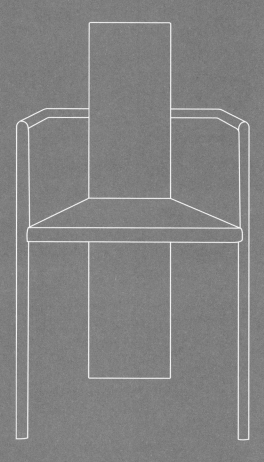

Jonas Bohlin's chair 'Concrete' marked a radical turn in the history of Swedish design. Up to that point the sector had been dominated by scientifically based product development, but this was the start of a new way of looking at furniture design and also at furniture as art objects.

Stools

Stools are considered one of the oldest forms of furniture for sitting on and they were in use as early as ancient Greece. In technical terms, what distinguishes them from chairs is that they have neither backrests nor arm supports. There are also stools that can be folded up, i.e. folding stools.

As well as providing something to sit on, stools also function as occasional tables, bedside tables or side tables to stand alongside armchairs in your living room.

Regardless of the purpose you have in mind when buying a stool, it's important that it has the right dimensions in order not to wobble or tip you, or whatever you might have placed on it, onto the floor. In the following section I shall point to a few of the things you should think about before buying a stool.

Seat height

The recommended seat height is 42–45 centimetres, that is, the same height as a chair. The recommended heights for bar stools and bar chairs is dealt with in a separate section on page 56.

Shape of the seat

The seat should be big enough to have room for your bottom – or for your foot if you are intending to use it as step. There are many 'creative' seat shapes these days and not all of them are genuinely compatible with the human body, so Point Number One is to check whether the shape and size of the seat suits your bottom.

Curvature of the seat

To be comfortable, a stool, like a chair, should have a rounded edge where it comes in contact with the back of your knees. And since a stool is backless, the edge should be rounded off around the whole seat – either that, or it should be quite clear which is the back and which the front.

The stretchers meet the legs at different heights (the usual pattern).

The stretchers meet the legs at the same height (very unusual).

H-pattern strutting does not need a height difference.

Legs

Stools are usually either three-legged or four-legged. They vary in stability and tip-resistance depending on the angle and positioning of the legs in relation to the seat. Legs angled slightly outwards will lower the centre of gravity and make for a more stable stool. Stools made of slightly heavier material have greater stability than stools made of lightweight materials, particularly when the legs are lighter than the seat. Different legs affect the load-bearing capacity, so pay attention to how the legs of the stool are strutted.

To ensure maximum strength, the stretchers between the legs of the stool do not usually meet the legs at the same height – strut-holes drilled at the same height in a leg remove too much wood and consequently weaken it. In exceptional cases this is solved by angling the end of the stretchers and joining them within the leg, but this requires high craftsmanship, absolute precision, high-quality timber and very strong glue. ('Miss Button', Jonas Lindvall's bar stool made for the furniture producer Stolab, is an example of this.) Another solution is to have H-pattern strutting.

Stackability

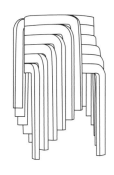

Many stools are stackable, which makes them ideal from a storage point of view. The positioning and construction of the legs to optimise stackability can, however, affect their comfort. Staffan Holm's three-legged stools, Spin, form a spiral when stacked, becoming a decorative detail in their own right and making storage in a cupboard unnecessary. So, before you make up your mind, make sure you check for both sittability and stackability.

Stepladder stools

Many Swedish homes have stepladder stools – that is, stools with a ladder construction and often with a handle cut into the upper part to make them easy to move. Stepladder stools can be used as extra seating when needed, and also as a step up when you want to reach a high shelf or cupboard. Make sure the steps are deep enough for you to have secure footing on them and that the rise between the steps leaves enough room for your foot and lower leg. And check that the cut-out handle is big enough for your hand to grip the stool properly when you want to move it.

Tips when buying stools

- Test the stool by sitting on it. And not just by sitting still: be more active, try leaning forward to a table as if eating or, if you are thinking of keeping the stool in the hall, try bending down as if tying your shoelaces.

- The lower the centre of gravity of the stool, the more stable it will be.

- Stools that can be adjusted for height by rotating the seat up or down often feel less than stable in their higher positions. Before buying, try out the stool at all possible heights rather than just the height it is in the showroom.

- Wobble the stool from side to side to check how firm it is and whether it is stable on the floor. Three-legged stools will always be stable, irrespective of how even or uneven the floor is: as the mathematicians say, 'three points define a plane'.

- Take care when using a stepladder stool with high side pieces. If you stand on one end of the step, the whole stool may become unbalanced and tip over.

- When buying a stepladder stool, check the width and slope of the steps and how smooth the surface of the steps is: you want to avoid the risk of slipping or tripping.

- Since stools have no backrest to catch hold of, you usually move them by gripping the seat. What does it feel like when you lift it and carry it? Can you get a good grip with just one hand or do you need to use both hands to move the stool sideways without dragging it across the floor?

A HIDDEN CLASSIC

The stepladder stool, the housewife's stool as it's sometimes called, is a hidden classic of Swedish design, some 700,000 of which are reckoned to have been sold over the years. The stool functioned partly as a seat for the housewife, who at one time might find herself spending a good eight hours a day in the kitchen, and partly as a set of steps when she needed to get at things from a shelf or cupboard that was out of reach. The Lindqvist
Brothers AB in Motala are thought to have been the first to produce it in Sweden, but they never patented the idea, with the result that another Swedish company, AWAB (Anderstorps Werkstad AB), produced a very similar version, which is why you will find two virtually identical stools with different labels.

Bar stools

Bar stools, as the name suggests, are a common kind of seat in bars and restaurants, where guests may want to sit but nevertheless want to stay at about the same height as staff and standing guests. Even if you don't have a real bar in your house, bar stools can provide you with some extra seating for occasional use around a kitchen island or other workbench.

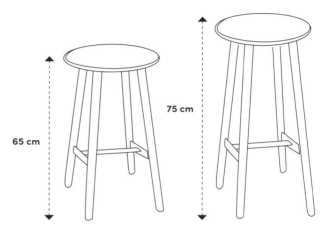

65 cm

75 cm

Seat height

Bar chairs and bar stools are usually made in two standard heights, 65 or 75 centimetres. One of the most common mistakes when buying bar stools is to buy stools of the wrong height, the result being that you are either too low to reach the top of the bar or so high that there's no room for your thighs. Which size you decide to go for will depend on the height of the table or bar counter at which the stools are to be used. Those with seats at 65 centimetres are usually the best choice for tables, benches or kitchen islands with work surfaces for domestic work, whereas those with seats at 75 centimetres are for higher bar counters or for kitchen islands with what interior designers like to call a wing – that is, a raised and protruding counter. There are also some models of bar stool that offer the possibility of raising or lowering the seat according to need.

Backrests

The difference between bar chairs and bar stools is that the former have backrests and the latter are stools but with longer legs. The backrests on bar chairs come in endless varieties, everything from short vertical extensions of the seat to normal, solid seatbacks. A good starting point is to check whether the backrests on the bar chairs you like really do provide lumbar support, if that is what you are looking for. Otherwise, they are not much more than decorative details and make very little difference to your sitting position. There are times when the design of the backrest, whatever its actual purpose, has details that make the seat less comfortable. Always test a chair in a variety of seated postures – straight-backed and upright, leaning forward onto the bar, leaning back, slouched, and also moving your arms actively as though eating a meal or reading the morning paper.

Contact with the counter top

When choosing a bar chair and its back support, as well as the comfort of the seat, you need to think about the actual counter top and whether its edges are rounded off. If you are going to have a bar chair that is pushed in against a sharp-edged counter, it is essential that the chair back be sufficiently robust to withstand wear and tear. A plastic chairback, for instance, continually pushed in hard against the sharp edge of a counter, will eventually begin to cause notching. Backless stools that slide in under the top of the counter are probably a better option, either that or bar chairs with their backs covered with soft but durable textile.

Legs and stretchers

When buying bar stools and bar chairs it's important to remember that they should have a cross strut capable of supporting your feet. It functions firstly as a step when you are getting up onto the stool and then, since stools are usually too high for most people's feet to reach the ground, you need the strut to provide purchase when you want to change position or step down. Given the stresses and wear involved, particularly when the stool is in a location where the users are wearing shoes, the strut needs to be capable of sustaining considerable force. It must be made of strong and durable material, and seated soundly into its joints if it is to take the full force exerted by adult leg muscles without breaking. The shape and joints of wooden support stretchers and the welding of metal stretchers can give some idea of the risks of wear and tear over time.

Leg space

When we were estimating how many sitters can fit around a dining table, our prime consideration wasn't the size of the chairs but how much elbow room should be left between one person and the next. The same is true with bar chairs and bar stools: 60 centimetres per person is a good guideline, though people frequently squeeze up a bit closer than that since we aren't talking about long dinners or lengthy sessions. But what has to be borne in mind when calculating the space necessary between bar stools is that they are usually designed with legs that slope outwards in order to lower the centre of gravity and increase stability, and this means that the footprint of the stool is bigger than the area of the seat. In this situation it is easy to miscalculate and place too many stools too close to one another with the result that their legs get tangled when people move them sideways in order to make space to sit on them. So, in the case of bar stools, seat area and elbow room are not the only factors to take into account: the width of the footprint will determine how many stools you have space for to avoid things feeling too confined and crowded around the table.

Different seats and their materials

The choice of seat style on bar stools and the material they're made of is not just a question of aesthetics, it's very much a matter of comfort and the risk of wear and damage.

Wood A wooden seat reflects back the warmth of the body of the sitter, which means that it usually feels more pleasant than other, colder materials.

Metal Bar stools with metal parts feel colder against your body and backside than other materials.

Plastic Easy to wipe down and keep clean. Resistant to damp and food spills. Will survive in environments that experience temperature changes, such as conservatories. Plastics may, however, be susceptible to scratching, and shell-shaped seats are slippery with certain kinds of clothing. When choosing plastic, remember that the material does not breathe and can feel sweaty and sticky against bare skin if you sit there for any length of time in hot weather.

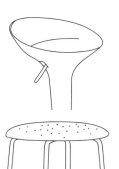

Fabric A fabric seat is softer and cosier, but – depending on the particular material – it is susceptible to staining. If you often wear shorts or a skirt, you should avoid fabric as it can easily feel sticky against your skin.

Leather A leather-covered bar stool gives a feel of exclusivity and develops a fine patina over time. Be careful with sharp objects and accessories such as the buttons on jeans and zips, all of which can make nasty marks. Synthetic leather is a more affordable alternative to leather and will tolerate rougher treatment.

Webbing or linen strip seats These offer a soft and well-ventilated seat, but they do tend to sag after a while and might need tensioning after a couple of years.

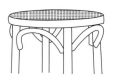

Cording or rattan In material terms, corded seats are often better value than, say, solid wood or leather, but cording them neatly is very time-consuming, so always check low-priced versions extra carefully. Corded seats can leave marks on your backside and can feel uncomfortable for individuals who are less padded in that area. It's not difficult to see the differences in quality of finish and tautness in the more exclusive versions than in low-budget models. A corded seat can be easily damaged by pressure put on a small area by, for instance, an overweight individual with something hard like a mobile telephone in their back pocket. And you can't stand on them either.

Advice if you are buying bar chairs

- Bar chairs and bar stools must be of the correct sitting height relative to the height of the counter. As with ordinary chairs and tables, a distance of 27–30 centimetres between the seat of the chair and the counter or table top is recommended. A less favourable distance will soon make itself felt in your neck and shoulders.

- If the bar chair is height-adjustable, check how well the mechanism works. Over time, cheaper chairs frequently stick and get stiff so that raising or lowering the seat can sometimes feel like sitting on a rocket.

- Seats that are adjustable for height are sometimes also swivel chairs. Check that it is possible to lock the chair into the position you want, so that you don't constantly have to be resisting the rotation of the seat.

- Avoid seats made of materials that are too slippery. You don't want to be constantly sliding off or slipping down. That quickly becomes uncomfortable.

- Since they are backless, bar stools can usually be pushed right in under the countertop when not in use. This gives you more free floor space, particularly good to have in smaller rooms.

- Bar stools and bar chairs with seats that are over-large when measured front to back mean that you will end up either sitting too far from the worktop or too far from the backrest. Having to lean forwards can – depending on the construction of the stool – affect its stability so that you feel it might tip over.

- Bar stools with a sledge base make less noise when you move them across the floor, and they can feel more stable when you change your sitting posture. But watch out for sledge bases that are too rounded as they may tip over backwards unless fitted with safety blocks.

- Always sit on the stool to check stability. Does it tilt or creak when you shift your sitting position?

- In order to reach the floor, short people often have to hop or slither down from tall stools. How well does the stool tolerate the wobble caused by hopping down off it and how well does the front edge of the seat take the wear of sliding off it? Are there parts of the stool likely to be damaged by these movements?

'Perfect seating is an art, but it shouldn't be. Making furniture to sit on should be produced with such skill that sitting on them doesn't need to be an art.'

Bruno Mathsson

Benches

Bench seats can be useful in many kinds of rooms: at the table in the kitchen to make room for several people; as seating in the hall for people to use while putting on their shoes; alongside the bath in the bathroom in order to play with the children while they're in the bath; as an extra surface to put things on while having a bath yourself; as somewhere to sit in the garden, especially against a sunny wall.

Regardless of where you intend to use it, all benches need to be tip-proof, stable and not saggy in the middle when you sit down. It is important for the bench be wide enough to accommodate your bottom, otherwise it will feel like sitting on a railway track. It is useful for there to be enough space beneath the bench to draw your feet back and stand up without needing support for your upper body. You can compromise on this last point if the bench is for occasional use only, in which case you could choose a bench with storage or a shelf for shoes under it.

Here are some worthwhile guidelines and measurements to help you avoid buying the wrong bench and having to return it, particularly if you are buying online or buying a vintage item where the older standard measurements don't necessarily agree with current ones.

- The seat height of a bench should be roughly the same as a dining chair, that is 41–45 centimetres. The height of the seat can be at the lower end of the scale if the bench won't be placed at a table.
- In order to allow for comfortable sitting without straining your neck or raising your shoulders, there should be 27–30 centimetres space between the seat and height of the table top.

The length of the bench should be matched with the length of the table and the placing of the table legs. This is to prevent the bench hitting the legs/stretchers of the table and to avoid the sitting position being a little too far out.

- The sitting surface needs to be about 40 centimetres across to be comfortable for your backside and thighs. A narrower seat will tend to cut into the thigh muscles and be uncomfortable to use for any length of time, whereas an over-wide bench can lead to an unnatural sitting angle.

- To estimate the number of people you can accommodate on the bench, reckon on leaving about 60 centimetres of space per adult (including elbow room).

- Ideally speaking, the front edge of the bench should come slightly in beneath the table: if it doesn't, it is likely that some people will have to lean slightly forward, with the risk they will get backache after a while.

HAS IT OCCURRED TO YOU THAT . . .

... benches are not really suitable for use at dining tables where people are likely to spend a lot of time since sitting upright without a backrest quickly becomes uncomfortable.

... sitting on a bench with a group of other people can be awkward for a woman wearing a skirt, particularly a narrow skirt, since it's difficult for her to swing her legs over the bench. If that individual is sitting in the middle, the others will have to stand up to let her out.

... benches with legs that slope slightly outwards are, like similar tables and stools, usually more stable and less likely to tip over.

Office chairs

The decision about good ergonomics in the home office often comes down to the choice of chair. Depending, of course, on what your work involves, a good chair designed for long periods of sitting can frequently allow you to get away with a much simpler choice when it comes to the table.

A good office or desk chair must provide you with lumbar support and either be adjustable or be exactly the right height relative to the table you work at. In the course of a long working day, you will feel the need to change your sitting posture at regular intervals, so it's important you choose a chair that will allow you to do so and thus avoid aches and strains.

The following are a few of the factors to be taken into consideration when deciding between different types of office chair.

Adjustable back

Make sure you choose a chair that follows the natural S-curve and supports the lumbar part of your back, thus ensuring that you don't end up with a posture like Gollum. To take the strain off your back while doing deskwork, the chair should be in contact with the inward curve of your lower back and, to enable you to vary your position now and again, the chair should have a back that is adjustable both for height and for angle. This permits you to raise or lower the back when you want a break, to lean back, to read through a document, or talk on the telephone. An adjustable model will also allow you to change the height of the seat if you need to.

 TIP!

Office chairs and desk chairs should stand on five castors in order to be stable at all angles, since the centre of gravity and loading changes when, for instance, we lean over or stretch to reach something. Many models do not have that many wheels, so it is worth checking.

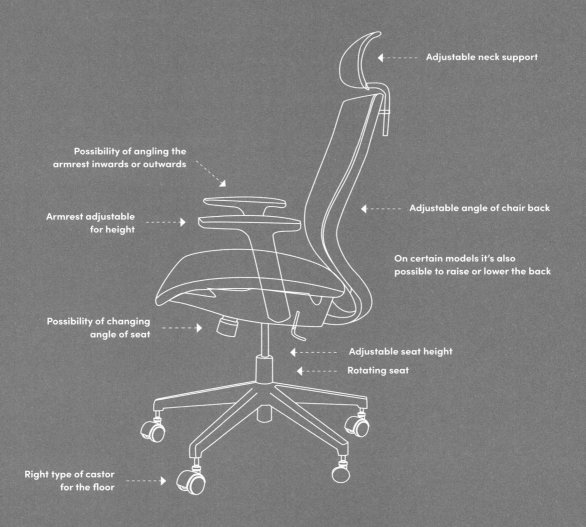

Adjustable neck support

Possibility of angling the armrest inwards or outwards

Adjustable angle of chair back

Armrest adjustable for height

On certain models it's also possible to raise or lower the back

Possibility of changing angle of seat

Adjustable seat height

Rotating seat

Right type of castor for the floor

Is it possible to change the angle of the seat?

Check that the seat of the chair is a good fit for your own body: it should feel neither too big nor too small, when measured both front to back and crosswise. If the seat provides support for the whole of your thigh or rather more than that, it's likely to become uncomfortable after a while. Bear in mind that there should be a palm's width of space left between the front of the seat and the back of your knee: blood vessels and nerves lie very close to the surface in that area and, if they are subject to pressure for any length of time, it affects the blood circulation to your legs and may cause swelling of your lower legs and feet. On the other hand, with a seat that is so small that only half of your thigh is supported, the front edge of the seat will tend to cut into the thigh muscle.

For preference, choose a chair which has the possibility of changing the angle of the seat. The ideal position, when working at your desk, is for the front edge of the seat to be a couple of centimetres lower than the back edge (in other words, the opposite to what you want when sitting in an ordinary chair). This will help hold your lower back and neck in an ergonomic position. Also, avoid desk chairs that are shell-shaped or slippery.

Is it possible to change the height of the seat?

Ergonomists are careful not to make general statements about the optimum height for seats since the posture of the whole body needs to be taken into consideration. You should be able to sit with the soles of your feet flat on the floor, your upper body at a height that allows you to reach the keyboard without bending your wrists and to view the screen at the correct level in front of you. Somewhere between 41 and 45 centimetres between the floor and the seat is the usual rule of thumb. If you invest in a desk chair adjustable for height, the chair will provide longer service either in your home or with someone else who has a different desk from the one you own.

Is it possible to adjust the armrests?

If you have enough space for it, a desk chair with armrests is a good choice. If the armrests are adjustable for height and side movement, they will offer maximum support for your arms and for the muscles in your neck and shoulders.

When buying a chair with armrests, always check that the arms will fit under your desk without colliding with the desk drawers or apron.

Can the chair swivel on its base and castors?

Assuming that you have sufficient space, select a chair that has castors and swivels on its base. That means that it's the chair rather than you that does the work when you need to turn round for something on the shelf behind you or move along the desk. But don't forget the floor covering: castors are liable to catch on the edge of rugs and you may need covers to protect the floor. Check that the castors on your chair can be changed depending on whether they are for use on a hard floor or on a soft, fitted carpet.

The seat material

Once you've gone through all the above points, it's time to think about the material of the seat. And not just from the point of view of appearance: different coverings can make one and the same chair feel very different in use.

Leather is durable and develops a lovely patina, but it's usually a bit more expensive and it doesn't breathe so it may feel sweaty after a while. Leather can creak and groan and make noises when you move. Fabric coverings tend to be softer and usually less pricey than leather, but they can bobble and tear if you get the wrong sort: you want samples not just for colour choice but so you can feel them and test for quality. Bear in mind that the office furniture you are sitting on for eight hours a day is likely to show wear faster than other covered seats in your home, so it needs to be really hard-wearing.

Wear and tear is often concentrated on certain parts of the chair: it might be worth spending a little extra on Martindale abrasion and pilling testing as well as on colour fastness if you are looking for a long-term workmate. (There is more on furniture coverings in the section on sofas.)

Netting or mesh covering has an airier feel about it and, given that the material is perforated and can be seen through, it makes the chairs seem neater. A good choice if you are equipping a small space as a home office, but it is more difficult to keep clean and to repair if it gets torn.

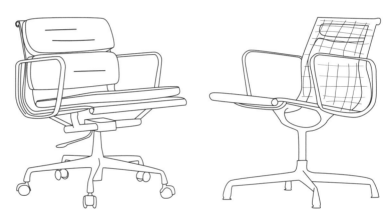

Desk chairs with padded seats are softer and more comfortable to sit on, whereas mesh chairs are better for air circulation.

Saddle chairs, as the name implies, are chairs where you sit astride as when riding a horse. They encourage a better posture and make it less likely you will let your back slump down. The shape of saddle chairs is also said to be good for the circulation of blood in your legs and gives you more freedom of movement than a standard desk chair.

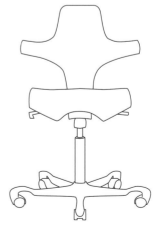

Colour

Lastly, we come to the factor that many people start with: the colour or shade of the covering. My advice is the same as my advice for ski clothing – avoid black and white, particularly on desk chairs where the covering cannot be washed. On white covers, dirt shows up immediately, both on the seat and on the seatback just from ordinary daily contact, from fingers that have picked up newsprint from the day's paper or from printouts. The trouble with black is that – in addition to the risk of fading – dust, hairs, fluff, dandruff and everything else shows up just as obviously on black as on white. Grey and other intermediate shades on the colour chart are usually preferable. Depending on whether you want the chair to blend in or to make a statement, you can work with contrasts or chameleon effects to draw the eye towards your chosen focus point in the room.

TIPS FOR BETTER ERGONOMICS

- If you do your work on an 'ordinary' chair, it might be worth investing in a cushion you can attach to the chairback to function as the kind of lumbar support provided by a desk chair.

- If your screen is too low – if you spend long periods working on a laptop, for instance – your upper body and neck is likely to slump down. It would be worth your while to get hold of a laptop stand that allows you to raise your eyes and achieve a better posture.

- There are also triangular seat cushions available with the back end thicker than the front part, so that your posture is adjusted to leaning forward slightly.

Sofas

The purchase of a sofa is a major investment, both literally and figuratively, partly because it's the item of furniture that takes up most space in our homes after the bed, and partly because its technology costs so much to produce that it's expensive to buy. It is also said to be the piece of furniture that most of us – during our waking hours – spend most time on, which means that sofas suffer a great deal of wear and tear over their lifespan. So it isn't out of place to do some serious research before splashing out. The problem is, how to distinguish between the good and the bad when it comes to upholstered furniture? In this section I shall attempt to tease out the visible and the invisible differences in quality between the various alternatives.

The seven S's of buying a sofa

Before going into detail, and so as not to miss anything essential, here are some quick tips to have in your back pocket when looking for a new sofa.

- Size: how much space do you have available and how many people do you need to seat?
- Sitting habits: how do you sit and use the sofa on an everyday basis?
- Strength of frame: quality, price bracket, how long will it last?
- Stuffing: choice of upholstery material, softness, comfort.
- Servicing: choice of covers and time needed for upkeep.
- Style: aesthetics, cut and shape.
- Saturation: colour, shade, contrast with room.

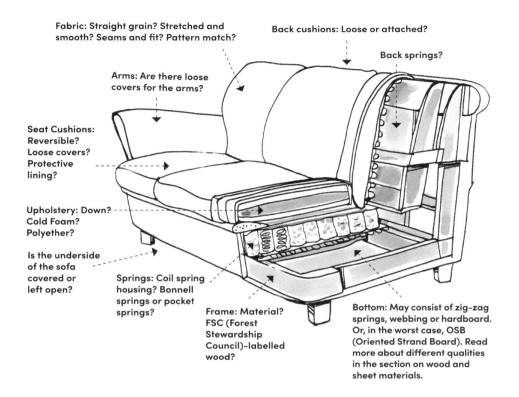

Fabric: Straight grain? Stretched and smooth? Seams and fit? Pattern match?

Back cushions: Loose or attached?

Back springs?

Arms: Are there loose covers for the arms?

Seat Cushions: Reversible? Loose covers? Protective lining?

Upholstery: Down? Cold Foam? Polyether?

Is the underside of the sofa covered or left open?

Springs: Coil spring housing? Bonnell springs or pocket springs?

Frame: Material? FSC (Forest Stewardship Council)-labelled wood?

Bottom: May consist of zig-zag springs, webbing or hardboard. Or, in the worst case, OSB (Oriented Strand Board). Read more about different qualities in the section on wood and sheet materials.

The anatomy of the sofa

Frame

When choosing a sofa you should start with what lies under the surface, the basic construction. The frame may be compared to the human skeleton, it is the foundation on which all the rest is constructed. The frame of quality sofas is usually made of solid wood. Since the frame is not immediately visible to the eye, this is the part that low-price manufacturers economise on, thereby shortening the lifespan of the sofa and making it more difficult to resuscitate in the future when it's in need of repair. The most basic models might even be structured around a frame of OSB board or chipboard, neither of which offer much by way of comfort or durability.

Another point to check is to make sure you can't feel the frame through the upholstery: there must be no sharp corners and edges that could wear through the coverings. To avoid this, manufacturers frequently cover the frame with a thin layer of padding or foam, and that makes it difficult to assess an upholstered sofa when it's standing in the shop at the point of sale. An advantage of buying a model of sofa with a frame that is partly or completely visible is that it's possible to properly examine what you are getting and assess the quality before you buy it.

Tips to help you assess the quality of the frame

- A simple way of getting some idea of the quality of the frame is to take hold of one of the front legs and lift the sofa just a little. If the leg on the opposite side does not lift off the floor, it means that the frame is bending or twisting under pressure and that is likely to imply that the sofa may well sag with usage.

- Always ask the staff in the shop about the construction of the sofa. If they are unable to answer your questions, the message is quite clear – you are in a shop that is not committed to quality.

- The weight of the sofa can give you some indication of the solidity of the frame. A sofa with a frame made of solid wood is always heavier. You should also get down and look under the sofa: the underside of more basic sofas is often left uncovered and it may be possible to see what the frame is made of.

- If solid wood is at one end of the quality scale and sheets of chipboard at the other, there is a range of quality between the two. Some sofa frames are constructed of welded metal, others of plywood. Plywood frames may vary in quality depending on how many ply the board is, but – on the whole – plywood is more resilient to knocks and wear than chipboard. With plywood you can re-tighten screws that work loose over time, whereas with chipboard this proves impossible, which means that you have to move the screws and make new holes. In addition to that, the more basic varieties of chipboard don't tolerate damp and there is the risk of them swelling and becoming deformed in damp environments.

Springs

In the days before I learned more about upholstered furniture, I assumed that it was the feather and down cushioning that determined the comfort of a sofa, but in fact it is more often than not the layer beneath that that decides the issue. Does the sofa have springs and, if so, what kind of springs? (Not all sofas have them – the cheapest sofas often have cold-cured foam throughout, with polyether on the chipboard.) The main springs in a sofa lie in the frame beneath the cushions, so check that the sofa has some sort of resilient, damping layer on top of the webbing layer – this may, for instance, be zigzag springs, Bonnell springs or pocket springs.

Zigzag

Zigzag springing consists of a wavy zigzag of steel wire that runs from one edge to the other of the frame. Sometimes there are also rubber bands stretched between the rows of zigzags and this distributes weight between the zigzag springs, leading to more even loading and increased comfort.

Bonnell springing

This consists of a series of spiral springs, tied or hooked to one another.

Pocket spring

In pocket springing, each spiral spring is fixed within a pocket of material so that the loading comes more onto the individual spring. A compressed spiral does not have the same effect on its neighbour as happens in Bonnell springing, which means that it is possible to adjust the tension in different parts of the sofa to increase comfort. Individual springs can have different numbers of coils and the more coils a spring has, the more resistant it is.

You'll find more information on springs in the section on beds since the springing in sofas and beds follows the same principles.

Upholstery

The usual padding for sofas is cold foam and polyether, which is, of course, a petroleum-based plastic and something of a problem for the environmentally conscious consumer since it is usually fossil-based. There are also various qualities of foam plastic. The heavier the padding, the better.

Cheaper sofas usually have a layer of foam between the frame and the cushions. More ambitious designs of upholstered furniture work with layers, as when making a tart. The bottom layer, directly on the wooden frame, consists of a harder layer of foam, on which there lies a softer layer and then, on top of that, comes the softest layer. Taken together, all this provides cushioning and a greater degree of comfort: on a sofa constructed in this way it is impossible to feel the wooden frame however hard you press.

In order to create even greater comfort, more advanced sofas have a number of layers of polyether glued together in one and the same cushion so as to make it softer at the back edge and firmer where it meets the back of the knees. Making them in layers also enables them to achieve the same slope and angle as chairs, with the back edge lower and the front edge higher. This is the reason why it is not possible to move the cushions around on corner sofas – the part that lies in the corner is layered like a fan so that the front edge is firmer than the softer part that meets the backrest of the sofa. If the sofa is to have reversible cushions, it is impossible to create the slope in the polyether: this provides some indication of the level of comfort to be expected. Apart from cold foam, there are a number of producers whose sofas are made of natural materials, the core materials being natural rubber and natural latex with an overlay of down.

Cold foam

In the manufacture of foam, polyols are added. Cold foam contains one type of polyol and polyether another. Generally speaking, cold foam is of slightly higher quality than polyether.

Cold foam comes in many different qualities, so it's worth checking the values of the sofas you are looking at. Density is measured in kilograms per cubic metre (kg/m³). High density means that the sofa is slightly harder to sit on, but also that it is more durable. Softer sofas may be comfortable initially, but can feel shapeless after a while – and they are not as hard-wearing. Cold-foam cores can have foam values from 55kg/m³ down to 20kg/m³, but the extremes are rarely preferable, neither from the comfort nor the durability point of view. A good guideline is that the padding should have a volume weight of 30–35 kilos for it to last over time.

Polytex and Moltex

Polytex and Moltex are materials manufactured from the ground-up and shredded remnants of foam production bonded with glue under high pressure. Since it is a waste product, the density and hardness can vary depending on the material that was currently available.

TIP!

Within most countries in the EU the production of foam for use in furniture must follow the REACH regulations. Make sure that the parts of the sofa you're thinking of buying carry some kind of eco-labelling such as Ecolabel and OEKO-TEX100. Sofas imported from other parts of the world may follow different regulations with regard to the chemicals used in their production. For example, flame-retardant foams, which may contain substances that are less then desirable. However, these treatments might be compulsory in certain countries with different fire regulations.

Ball fibre and wadding

Also known as synthetic wool. Wadding is looser in consistency, whereas ball fibre – as the name implies – is wound into a ball, which gives it a more stable form. However, both need to be puffed and fluffed up at regular intervals to stop them collapsing. Wadding is most often used to pad the actual frame, whereas ball fibre is more common in envelope cushions.

Down/duck feathers

These are used for the filling of seat cushions or loose cushions. Real down is significantly more expensive than feathers and comes in a variety of grades from enterprises with varying levels of animal welfare. The lower quality contains many hard particles, whereas down is a specific type of feather located closest to the skin of the bird and it is much softer. The term 'down' is frequently used inaccurately for what isn't really down. It is also possible to buy recycled feathers. Make sure you read the labelling carefully and ask questions in the store.

Down

Down and feather filling is incomparably more comfortable to sink into, but it tends to cost rather more and to demand more care. Feather and down-filled cushions and loose cushions can lose their filling if they aren't sealed tight. Back cushions and pillows with loose filling should be constructed in compartments or sections so that the filling remains distributed evenly over the whole cushion and doesn't all end up at one end. Down does have a tendency to form clumps in one place, making the cushion uneven. The walls of the compartments help keep the filling evenly distributed and make it easy to plump up the cushions after use. To achieve the maximum level of comfort, there is a varying quantity of filling in different compartments so, for example, the bottom edge of a back cushion will have more down filling than the top edge in order to provide lumbar support when leaning back. In the case of the seat cushions, more down is put in the compartments you sit on and less in the parts of the seat cushion that meet the back cushion – this also ensures that the cushions meet neatly without forming a bulge where they touch. In order to conceal the

Feather

walls of the compartments, quality manufacturers may cover them all with a layer of down. Down is sometimes mixed with other materials to help it hold its shape and make it easier to plump up.

Horsehair

Horsehair is a natural material derived from the manes and tails of horses and cattle. It is processed to make it frizzy and fluffy and suitable for use as filling. Refer to the section on beds for further information on the use of horsehair as filling.

Sofa covers

The choice of covers for your upholstered furniture is primarily a matter of taste and preference, but if you are having trouble navigating your way through all the alternatives, it may perhaps be helpful to have some quality guidelines to narrow down the range. What are your priorities?

Covers may be fixed or removable, even if the cushions are fixed. If the covers are removable, there should be an inner lining over the padding so that the fabric of the covers does not suffer unnecessary wear. When you move on a sofa, the fabric covers move and the inner lining shields it from friction wear caused by the cold foam.

The top fabric is, of course, the one you choose, the inner lining being the less visible layer between the fabric of the covers and the

DID YOU KNOW?

It is not good for a leather sofa to be allowed to stand within 30 centimetres of a radiator or any other source of heat. That is one of the reasons why leather sofas often have artificial leather at the back – it makes them easier to position in the room and also makes them cheaper to produce.

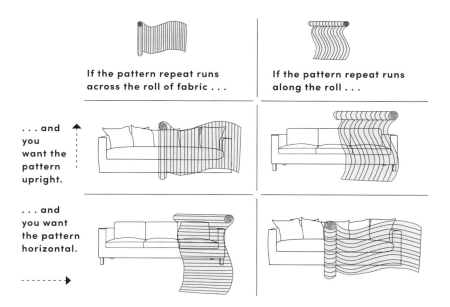

If the pattern repeat runs across the roll of fabric . . .	If the pattern repeat runs along the roll . . .
. . . and you want the pattern upright.	
. . . and you want the pattern horizontal.	

When buying or re-covering a patterned sofa, think of the direction the pattern repeat runs on the roll of fabric so that the direction will be as you want it. Which direction will be nicest depends both on the width of the fabric and the size of the sofa cushions.

padding. On better-quality sofas, the inner lining is cotton stretched over the padding, whereas on cheaper, more basic models a felt-like, non-woven fabric made of 100 per cent polypropylene is used.

Any discussion of sofas demands a language all of its own. It's worth becoming familiar with some of the following terminology in order to be able to interpret product descriptions. And you can read more about polypropylene and textiles in general in the section on materials (pp. 227–81).

Martindale test

The durability of the covers of a sofa is measured using the Martindale test. This tests the abrasion resistance of a fabric by oscillating steel discs across the fabric and counting the number of oscillations before the fabric breaks: the more oscillations the fabric survives, the better.

Grades of pilling

How susceptible to pilling a particular fabric is can be measured by pilling tests. There is a five-point scale that classifies the resistance of upholstery covers to wear and tear.

1. A lot of pilling across the whole surface of the fabric.
2. Clearly visible pilling across most of the fabric.
3. A moderate amount of pilling, mainly on the most exposed areas.
4. Very little pilling, often not noticeable.
5. No pilling at all.

Fade resistance or colour fastness

Furniture fabrics can be sensitive to sun and UV light. Colour fastness is measured on a scale of 1 to 8, where 8 is best. For use indoors, 4–5 is the norm. This is most relevant in the case of dark or patterned fabrics since fading rarely occurs evenly across the whole sofa: it will be most marked on those areas exposed to most sunlight and there might possibly be no fading at all where scatter cushions have been lying.

Dry-rubbing colour fastness

What is the risk of staining being caused by contact between one fabric and another even though neither surface is damp or wet? Will the sofa covers shed colour when you sit on them? It's also worth considering whether your clothes might stain the sofa. If you choose white covers when you know that you or one of the family always wears blue jeans, the combination is not really very wise.

Wet-rubbing colour fastness

This assesses the risk of the covers' fabric shedding colour when rubbed against damp surfaces such as wet trousers. It is measured on a scale of 1 to 5.

Shrinkage

Will the covers change size when you wash them? Shrinkage or any change of dimensions is obviously important when you purchase a sofa with covers that you want to be able to wash.

Cigarette test

This is a standard laboratory test to determine whether a piece of fabric or leather will withstand the heat of a lighted cigarette without bursting into flame. If the answer is yes, it only means that the fabric is fire-resistant, not that it will not show burn marks.

Sofa cushions

The seat and back cushions of a sofa.

Envelope cushions

Decorative scatter cushions that are not back cushions.

Bolster

A sausage-shaped sofa cushion.

THINGS TO THINK ABOUT!

Linen is not suitable for the covers of sofas that have sharp edges at the corners or arm rests. The danger is that, over time, the fibres in the fabric will wear through at these points and leave you with holes.

If you choose patterned covers, the stitching and the matching can give an indication of the quality. A meticulous manufacturer will always ensure that patterns match and that they meet precisely on all parts of the sofa. Less meticulous mass–producers rarely have the profit margins to offer the same finish.

The sofa's underclothes

Not all sofas are covered underneath with a bottom cloth and, as a result, dust can easily get in and build up around the springs, possibly leading to problems in the long run. The presence or absence of a bottom cloth can, in itself, be an indicator of quality. In the case of more basic models, you can often see straight into the innards of the sofa, or there may just be a piece of thin, plastic gauze, similar to the fleece you might use to cover the plants in the garden.

Sofas of a slightly higher quality sometimes have an openable bottom cover, with Velcro or a zip to make it easier to get at the insides to carry out repairs. More exclusive models of sofa may even have logos printed on the bottom cover. Ever since discovering this fact, I've taken to inspecting the undersides of sofas rather than completely ignoring them. It doesn't take a great deal of effort to do so since all you have to do is to take a quick photo of the underside with your mobile phone while you are sitting on the sofa.

Depth of the seat

The seat depth of a sofa is measured from the front edge of the seat to the point where the back cushion meets when both seat cushions and back cushions are in place. What we're dealing with, then, is the usable seating area. In other words, the measurement isn't taken from the front edge of the frame to the back of the frame, nor from the front edge of the cushion to the loose cushions since that space can vary depending on the positioning and size of the soft parts. The back edge of a sofa, just like the back edge of a chair, should be softer or lower than the front edge. In the case of cheap sofas, the padding in the cushions can create the opposite effect when the padding forms lumps and bulges in the middle while thinning out towards the edges.

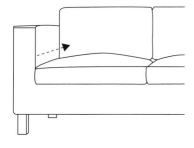

Height of the seat

The height of the seat is measured from the floor to the highest point of the seat cushion. Remember that cushions will be compressed when you sit on the sofa, depending on how soft the filling is and how much the sitter weighs. Consequently, static seat height may differ from dynamic seat height. A heavy person will compress the cushion more than a light person, and the two individuals will thus experience the height of the seat rather differently.

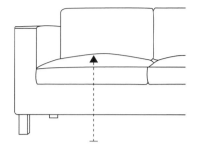

Angle and height of seat back

How much the back of the sofa slopes indicates whether you will be able to sit upright or half-lie on it. The greater the inclination of the back, the stronger the back of the sofa needs to be to take the weight of your upper body. And the greater the angle of inclination, the deeper the seat needs to be and the shorter the distance from the floor to the seat, if your legs aren't to be waving in the air. The height of the back in the sitting position is not the same thing as the overall height of the sofa: the height of the back is not always stated, but should be measured from the highest point of the seat cushion to the top of the back support. In the case of sofas with wavy or camel-shaped backs, the measurement should be taken from the highest point of the seat cushion to the lowest point of the back support.

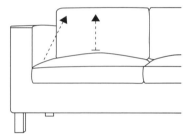

How many can the sofa seat?

When you are buying a sofa, you are probably not thinking too much about how many it will seat – after all, the majority of retailers market their sofas according to the number of seats they have. But how can you check that the retailer's statements are correct? Or, how can you make a rough estimate yourself, when buying a second-hand sofa? You can't always decide by simply counting the number of seat

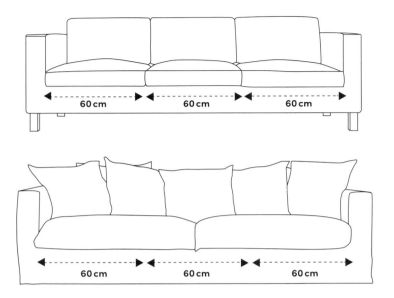

Measure the breadth of the sofa from the inside of one armrest to the inside of the other. If the edges of the sofa are not straight, measure between the innermost points of the armrests in order to get an idea of how many people it can seat.

cushions. Some three-seater sofas do have three cushions, but there are others with one, two or four. It is largely a question of design. So, to play it safe, assume as a rule of thumb that an adult needs approximately 60 centimetres of space, including elbow room.

Depending on the width of the seat cushions, the filling in them and the gaps between the cushions, some of the sitting places may well be unusable. So do check that the whole sofa is comfortable to sit on: a three-seater can easily become a two-seater if no one is willing to sit in the middle because they are likely to sink down between two cushions and find their back or their backside coming into contact with something hard.

And it's not only a matter of how many you can seat, but also how many you want to seat. Do you remember the section on proxemics? Have a look back at it. It's one thing to squeeze up close with the family for a Friday evening snuggle, but you probably won't want to sit quite that close when you've invited guests you are less familiar with. It's worth bearing that in mind when calculating the number of people who can be accommodated on one particular sofa rather than another.

Breadth of the armrests

The broader and higher the arms or side pieces of the sofa are, the less sitting space is left from the total breadth of the sofa. If the overall measurement of the sofa is 186 centimetres and each arm is, let's say, 20 centimetres wide, the quickest of calculations shows that it's unlikely to provide very comfortable seating for three adults even if the retailer chooses to call the particular model a three-seater. Wide armrests are good for people given to half-reclining or leaning against the edge of the sofa. Narrow armrests with minimal padding tend to be uncomfortable for people who like lying on the sofa, resting their heads on the armrests.

TIP!

As well as being decorative, scatter cushions can also be used to adjust the depth of the seat: those who want to sit in a more upright position can stack them up behind them and those who want to lie back can simply move them.

Useful tips when buying sofas

- How much space in the room is actually available for the sofa? Don't simply go from the length of the wall and that of the sofa, remember the depth of the sofa and all the protruding parts. Don't forget about plinths, skirting boards, radiators, windowsills, electrical sockets and the necessary clearance for door and balcony doors, as well as for furniture with doors, such as TV cabinets, bookcases, china cabinets and sideboards.

- How much space is free in front of the sofa? The more the back slopes, the more space is needed in front of the sofa since your legs will stick out further.

- How much wear and tear will the covers tolerate? Somewhere between 15,000 and 25,000 Martindale is usually the recommended minimum guideline for sofas in private houses.

- How much fabric pilling is likely? A pilling measure of 4–5 indicates good resistance for everyday use.

- What is the volume weight of the seat cushions and the back cushions? 30–35 kg/m^3, is the recommendation for a sofa that will be in daily use. If the cushions are any softer, they will quickly lose their puff.

- How much time and effort are you prepared to put into the upkeep of the sofa? Down cushions have to be shaken and puffed up regularly to prevent the down getting lumpy and losing its bounce.

- Last but not least, will the sofa fit into your house? Literally and metaphorically! Measure all the passageways and obstacles – everything such as the width of the outside door and the clearance in the hall when the door is open, the distance between your outside door and the neighbour's hedge, the stairwell, narrow corridors and anything else the sofa will have to pass on its way to the room in which you want to place it.

General advice on washing sofa covers

Always follow the advice given on the label on the sofa covers. Here are some further tips worth considering.

- If the covers have to be distributed over several machines or washes, make sure you use the same wash programme and detergent as this will give you a more even result. The point is that the same fabric may run or pill differently if washed at different temperatures, with different detergents, on different programmes, with the result that what started as a single-coloured sofa is no longer single-coloured after washing.

- Avoid bleaches and fabric softeners, and do not dry the covers outdoors as there could be a risk of differential fading in sunlight.

- Give the covers a thorough shake before putting them in the machine. Ideally, turn them inside out and remove bits of down and other things trapped in the corners, which may cause discoloration in the wash. I'm speaking from experience when I say that washing machines don't like pieces of feather and other padding material.

- To prevent the fabric shrinking, ensure that all zips are zipped up and all buttons buttoned up before washing.

- Covers should be laid out flat to dry at room temperature. Unless the suppliers' instructions say that it's okay, do not tumble-dry covers, as there is a risk of tearing or spoiling them.

- Remember to replace covers before they are completely dry. They should not be so wet that it risks damaging the filling, but they are easier to replace on the cushions if the fabric is still slightly damp.

Common complaints about sofas

- In reality, the colour and material does not match the illustrations shown in catalogues or online. This is particularly the case with light colours – white, grey, beige and green.
- The cushions are hard and uncomfortable.
- The sofa quickly loses its bounce and becomes shapeless.
- The finish of the stitching and seams is poor; various parts don't match up properly; the fabric rubs against sharp edges of the frame of the sofa.
- Pattern match is poor.
- The backrest is far too low and, when you lean back, the edge catches you, which can be or become painful.
- The sofa lacks depth so that you have to sit upright, as on a chair.
- The sofa squeaks and creaks.
- The fabric soon shows wear and becomes pilled.
- The legs feel weak and wobbly when several people sit down at the same time.
- The cushions ride up at the edges and make uncomfortable ridges between them, which means they actually provide seating for fewer people than the shop claimed.

CPU

Do you remember the CPU – Cost Per Use – strategy mentioned in my *The Interior Design Handbook*? Cheap sofas are usually only cheap at the point of purchase. If you disregard the price label, cheap furniture can prove quite expensive in the long run as you will probably need to change it sooner than if you'd bought a better-quality product that is more durable and can also be repaired and re-covered several times.

HOW DO YOU SIT?

We don't always dare try out sofas in the shop in the way we actually use them at home. Do you recognize yourself in any of the following positions?

Don't choose a sofa that is too deep. If you do, you'll end up sitting like a doll with your legs sticking straight out in front of you.

Choose a sofa with cushions that will take loading on the front edge without losing their form or their bounce.

Do not choose a model with arms that are too narrow or too low. Or, worse still, has no arms at all.

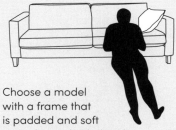

Choose a model with a frame that is padded and soft at the front edge below the seat cushions. This will give your back more comfortable support when you are sitting on the floor and leaning back.

Sitting on the arms is not to be recommended, but children and teenagers tend to do so when you are not looking. If you know that the sofa will be used by unruly occupants, avoid models that have very flimsy arms.

If you are one of those people who eat on the sofa or perch on the front edge (or if you live with someone who does), choose a sofa with washable covers. Remember, too, that you will overload the front edge of the seat cushion when you sit and lean forward while eating on the sofa; in this case, make sure you do not choose a model on which the seat cushions protrude beyond the frame as they will have a tendency to slide down and lose their shape.

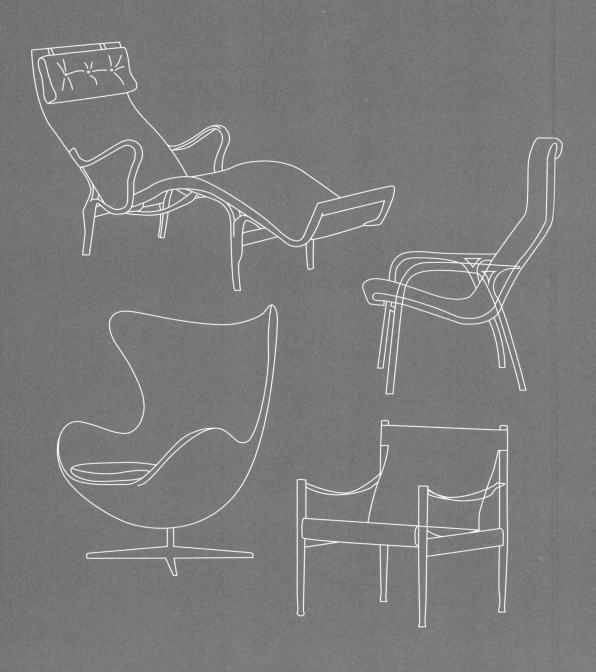

Armchairs

'Can you recommend a nice armchair that will match with the sofa in our living room?'

A common enough question, but difficult to answer without knowing how the questioner will be using it.

Is the armchair to be part of a suite of chairs, comfortable to socialize in and chat? In that case, you won't want to be half-lying backwards so that the others, more upright on the sofa, end up staring right up your nose. Will the armchair be facing the television and mostly be used for watching films or TV series? In that case, you probably won't want a hard-padded model in which you have to sit upright with a straight back. If you like settling down and relaxing with a good book, you'll be looking for a comfortable reading chair, in which case it's important to choose a style that provides support for your neck, as you will frequently want to lean back to take the weight of your head off your upper body.

Having an armchair that matches your most common sitting posture (or your most desired posture) is far more important than having a chair that matches your style. Not that one need exclude the other: it's just a case of learning the visual language of chairs as well as their design language and then you'll be on the right road.

When interior designers set about combining items into seating groups, the angle of the seating is an important factor, but for private individuals searching for armchairs online the selection is haphazard and there is no guidance as to the depth of the seat and the rake of the back.

Armchairs can be divided into subgroups depending on sitting position and the angle at which the chair places the sitter. The following are some of the distinctions made:

- Chairs with arms/club chairs
- Armchairs/lounge chairs
- Reading armchairs/ resting armchairs
- Lie-back armchairs

Guidelines for armchairs

For sitting in a more upright position, it's best if the seat of the armchair is not too soft: if it is, you'll be risking ending up in a tense posture reminiscent of squatting or doing squats in the gym. Also, when the depth of the seat is too great, smaller people may be unable to reach the backrest and consequently have to choose between having their feet on the floor or sitting with their back against the backrest and their legs sticking out.

With more sloping armchairs it's important that the slope of the back and the height of the backrest follow each other. If the angle of the back is more than 30 degrees, you will need neck support to take the weight of your head. And, if the chair is to be comfortable, the depth of the seat will also need to be longer.

In the case of deeply reclining chairs designed for resting or lying down, the height of the seat needs to be lower if the user is to be able to rest their feet on the floor. If the chair is too high, your legs will end up dangling in the air, which not only feels uncomfortable but can also stress the thigh muscles. (A footstool is helpful in this case.)

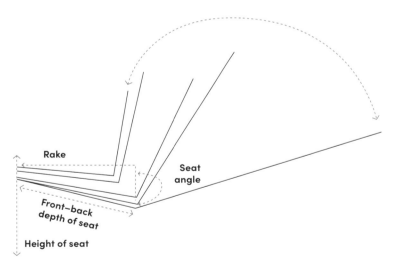

Different seat angles for chairs and recliners, showing how the height of the seat, the angles of the seat, the depth of seat and the rake should change in relation to one another. The greater the rake of the back, the lower the seat needs to be to allow the feet to remain in contact with the floor. The illustration is taken from the book *Bostadsplanering* by Björn Klarqvist.

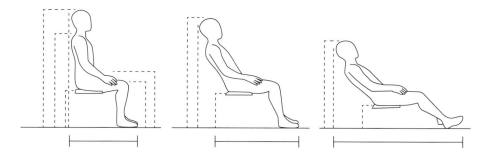

The more a sofa or armchair slopes back, the more space is needed for your legs and feet in front of the chair or sofa. If space is limited, it's important to bear this in mind when checking the amount of space available for different models.

- An over-soft armchair and backrest makes greater demands on your stomach muscles in the process of sitting or getting up. Worth bearing in mind, for the elderly (and for women who may be pregnant or have recently given birth or had a caesarian).

- If the distance between the arms of the chair is tight, you are likely to feel locked in and unable to adjust your sitting position. This can feel uncomfortable when, for instance, you are watching a long film.

- When buying an armchair with a padded seat, check the positioning of the seat buttons. Depending on the location of the buttons in relation to your body and also on how hard the padding is, the buttoning may create uncomfortable nodes on the seat of the chair. Always test a chair by sitting on it and noting the position of any buttons that may rub or press against your bottom or back.

- Older people tend to sit slightly more upright in armchairs as it is then easier for them to get up. It is important that the arms of the chair are solid, firm and easy to get a good grip on.

SOMETHING TO THINK ABOUT!

The arms and backs of armchairs can give you some idea of how easily they can be moved around when you are doing the housework or changing the room: the softer and deeper the armchairs are, the more difficult it is to move them. Arms made of wood or metal are usually easier to get a firm grip on than padded arms.

93

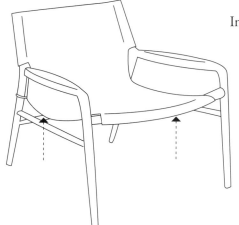

In the case of armchairs with seats made of stretched fabric or leather, you are likely to feel the parts of the frame made of wood or of steel tubing pressing against your body when you sit down. Always check the shape of the frame and the positioning of the supporting tubes, particularly, for instance, where they can cause pressure behind the back of your knees. Seats of this kind tend to become 'steeper' with time, as the fabric stretches.

Inspect the seams of the armchair

In the case of padded armchairs, don't forget to inspect the stitching and the upholstery, particularly on the arms and on the back. The piping should be straight and even, but it's important that it lies close to the fabric rather than standing proud, which is a sign of the fabric being too taut – fabric that has been overstretched is likely to wear more rapidly and, with time, may split. Also check that the upholstery lies straight-grained and does not run at an angle across the seat. On well-made furniture, the grain runs straight along the front edge of the armchair, unless there is some deviation for decorative purposes. (It is usually easy to see whether it is a matter of style or of carelessness.)

'For me, pieces of furniture are like people. They should have character and personality, but they ought not to scream about their individuality.'

Kerstin Hörlin-Holmquist

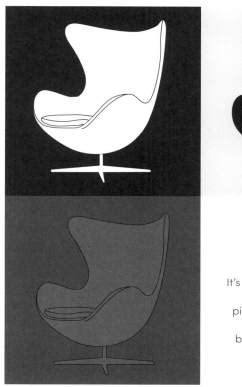

It's not only the choice of colour that determines the effect a piece of furniture has, it is also how it contrasts with the background or fits the context in which it is to stand. Read more on visual effect in *The Interior Design Handbook*.

Fit in or stand out?

Do you want your new armchair to fit in or to stand out? Depending on your choice of colour and lightness in relation to the wall behind it or to the rest of the furnishings, the chair will stand out more or stand out less. It's worth considering whether you want the chair to act as a focal point in the room or simply to blend into the background.

Rocking chairs

Throughout the ages, people have used rocking and swaying to help them relax. And that's equally true whether it's a matter of getting children off to sleep, or of easing pain or calming your thoughts.

Seeing the rocking chair as a kind of adult rocking cradle is, in fact, by no means wrong, since one of its forerunners is said to be the bed on rockers the Shaker movement used to build for their older members. At its very simplest, a rocking chair is just a chair on rockers that allows the user with the right technique to gently sway back and forth.

There are many different designs of rocking chair. The back may be high or low, it may have arms or no arms, the stretchers may vary, as may the length of the runners on which it rocks. The very earliest version is said to have developed in the United States in the eighteenth century, but the idea quickly arrived in Europe and, these days, rocking chairs are in use the world over.

The rocking chair is credited with many benefits to health. The rhythmic movements are said to promote circulation and help the lymph system, ease pains and have a calming effect. Within the 'care of the elderly' programme, rocking chairs are often used as aids for those with dementia or anxiety problems.

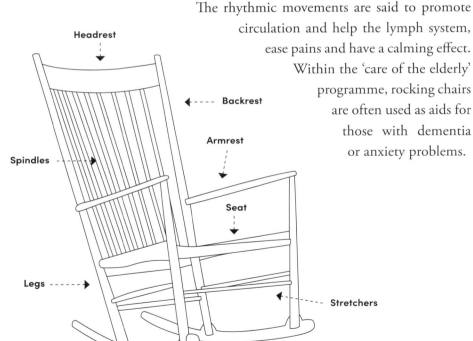

Headrest

Backrest

Armrest

Spindles

Seat

Legs

Stretchers

Rockers

The anatomy of the rocking chair

Seat height

The height of the seat on a rocking chair is slightly lower than on an ordinary chair. This is so that – even though the slope of the chair back is considerable – your feet can still reach the ground and make rocking easy.

Point of balance

All rocking chairs have a point of balance. Where exactly that is on each chair will vary depending on the construction. You can identify it by noting the contact point between the chair and the floor when no one is sitting on it. If you draw an imaginary vertical line upwards from the point of contact, it will pass approximately a fist in front of where the chest of an average adult sitting in the chair would be.

A good rocking chair should take the load off your back. If the balance point of the chair is not far enough back, you will constantly have to be pushing back with your legs and feet in order to find the best angle to relax your back, which is counter-productive in that it leads to lower-body stresses instead.

DID YOU KNOW?

The American President John F. Kennedy was a great enthusiast for rocking chairs, so much so that he is said to have had no fewer than fourteen of them, several of them specially made for him. One of them even went with him in Air Force One when he was travelling. The point was that the rocking chairs helped his back problems. Even now, the Appalachian Oak Rocker is still known by the nickname the Kennedy Chair and, for a time, the Swedish spindleback chair factory in Nässjö produced a model named after the president. It's said that a rocking chair was the only piece of furniture he took with him to the White House from his office in the Senate when he became president.

Footstool

By using a rocking chair with a footstool, your body can achieve what the Americans call the zero gravity point. By raising your feet, your back automatically assumes a more open angle, which straightens out the lower part of your back. Furthermore, the positioning of your feet at the same level as your heart creates a sense of virtual weightlessness which allows you the most profound relaxation. Furniture designers actually refer to this point as 'rocking perfection'.

Tips when buying a rocking chair

- Watch out for backrests that are completely straight, both laterally (no rounding) and horizontally (no curvature). An ergonomic rocking chair will give support to the natural S-curve of your back, but since all bodies are different, it's a case of finding the particular model that matches your body and its needs. It should provide support for your lumbar region and room for your shoulders. If the backrest does not suit your body, try loose cushions along with a neck cushion that can be attached or tied to the headrest. Or choose a different model!

- A rocking chair with a very low back and with long rockers can have an excessive backward tilt and fail to provide support for your head and your back. This can cause you to tense up, resulting in aches in the shoulders and neck.

- The length and curvature of the rockers affect the nature of the rocking. Short rockers produce more abrupt rocking. Less curved rockers generate very little movement and tend to produce a jerky rhythm.

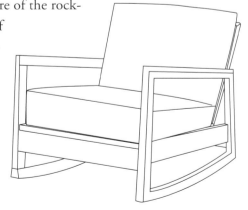

- In the case of rocking chairs, the quality of the stretchers and joints is absolutely vital to the stability of the chair. Since they are designed to be in motion, the various components and joints are subject to more stresses than with ordinary, motionless chairs, so always check the stays, stretchers and joints with great care. The way the parts have been assembled will often give some indication of the quality of the chair. (Read more about this in the section on materials and wood.) Cheaper, mass-produced rocking chairs are rarely of the same quality as more handcrafted models.

- Armrests that are too narrow can easily become uncomfortable. Rounded armrests may make it difficult to rest your arms on them without your arms sliding off. When you are rocking, you hands want something to hold on to, so check that the front ends of the armrests finish in gently rounded curves rather than sharp edges that will cut into your forearms. What you should look for are armrests that are sufficiently wide and roomy for you to rest your forearms, elbows and wrists without them sliding off or being cramped.

- Always avoid rocking chairs with a spindle that runs centrally down the middle of the back: a centre strut like that will inevitably rub on your spine. Competent designers ensure that the back stretchers are positioned to be each side of the spinal column.

- Does the chair creak? That can be difficult to determine when buying a chair via an online auction of antiques, but it can be upsetting to discover later that half your relaxing experience is disrupted by creaks. It will cost you nothing to ask the question before you buy.

DID YOU KNOW?

Charles and Ray Eames produced a rocking version of their classic, moulded-plastic shell chair. It's said that all new mothers at the Herman Miller factory in Michigan were given such a chair as a gift, so that they would have a good chair in which to nurse their babies.

Tables

The Swedish word for table, *bord*, is derived from the old Germanic word for board – *boroa*. Before humankind became sufficiently civilized to place the board on stands, it seems that a wooden board was simply rested on your knees when you wanted to eat or work at it. These days, there are any number of varieties of table to go along with other furniture: dining tables, side tables, writing tables, bedside tables, just to name a few. In the follow-ing section, you will discover more about this piece of furniture, which the vast majority of us have in our homes.

Dining tables

If the kitchen is the heart of the home, the dining table must be its aorta, the main artery. It's where the family gathers most frequently to top up its energy with breakfast, lunch, dinner and snacks, as well as to socialise, do homework or to have a quiet read of the newspaper.

A good, solid dining table makes mealtimes more pleasurable, but there is much more that determines our experience of comfort around it. What follows is some advice to assist you in deciding on which table to choose for one or more people to dine around.

Parts of the table

A dining table consists of a table top that usually rests on an apron, which is a jointed frame with legs at each corner. Longer tables may have a central stretcher to support the middle of the table top between the aprons. A table with absolutely straight legs that are located at the outer edges demands a higher standard of construction overall if the table is to be stable. According to the laws of physics, if the table legs slope outwards slightly, the table will be more resistant to impact. To check how well a table resists knocks and bangs and how quickly vibrations fade after impact, you can carry out an impact test by pushing the table from the side and observing how it reacts. An unstable table takes some time for the tremors to fade, whereas a more stable construction is difficult to disturb.

The table top

Take a close look at how the table top is constructed. Solid wood tops are usually made up of a number of parts glued together or with tongue and groove joints. When the wood dries, it may warp or split. Tables that are mass produced or made too quickly may show traces of glue. If the table top is veneered, take a close look at how the veneer has been put on. (There is more about veneers and various patterns in the section on materials on pp. 242–5.) The weight of the table top will vary depending on what the veneer has been glued onto and that may not be visible in illustrations, so always check the product description if you are buying a table online.

Table tops made of solid wood can vary enormously in terms of quality, depending on the variety of wood used and also on how well the manufacturer knows and has taken account of its properties. Since wood changes in response to temperature, humidity and seasonality, the aim is to produce a table top liable to as little change as possible in order to avoid any splitting and warping. Study the pattern of the annual growth rings at the end grain of the wood: if the growth rings in the end surface are vertical (vertical grained), you can be virtually certain there will be no splitting. If, on the other hand, the growth rings show as flat sawn, the table top will be considerably less likely to hold its shape over time. (In the chapter on materials, you will find a more thorough explanation of why this should be.)

Table tops made of materials such as stone or concrete tend to be extremely heavy and consequently make greater demands on the construction as a whole.

The apron

Heavier table tops are usually mounted on an apron or on a leg stand of various materials. Since wood has a tendency to expand or contract across its width rather than along its length, the fixings or the attachment points

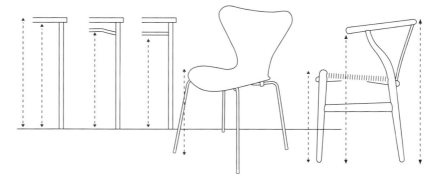

Having chairs that match the table is not just a matter of aesthetics, it's also functionally and ergonomically important. A table with an apron that hits the arms of the chair, particularly if the chair arms protrude the same distance as the front edge of the seat, will prevent you sitting comfortably. This is why the arms of well-designed chairs are often set back slightly.

of the apron on a wooden table are often a challenge and mark the divide between mass-produced products and quality products. The simplest and cheapest furniture has metal brackets whereas better quality tables often have concealed fixtures such as countersunk screws or pegs.

The size of the apron beneath the table top will affect your choice of chairs to go with the table. This is partly because of the height of the seat and the free space you need to accommodate your thighs, and partly because of the possibility that chairs with arms will bump into the apron of the table.

The legs

The recommended height for a dining table is 72–75 centimetres. The length of the legs themselves may, however, vary depending on the thickness of the table top and the apron. In addition to individual legs attached at each corner, there is an abundance of alternative types of legs and stretchers to choose from.

Slightly sloping legs are generally more stable than straight legs, though legs mounted on runners or stands also tend to be fairly resistant to tipping as they have more contact with the floor.

In physics, the centre of gravity is an imaginary point on which the total weight is concentrated. The centre of gravity of a piece of furniture should be as low (i.e. near the floor) as possible in order to prevent the piece toppling over in use. The centre of gravity of a table, however, is not constant. When in use and laid or laden in different ways, there can be no guarantee that the centre of gravity remains in the same place. A heavy pan placed close to the edge of the table, someone leaning forward with their elbows on the table, or someone supporting themselves on the table top when standing up – all these can cause the table to wobble.

How much sideways movement will the legs or stretchers of the table you are considering tolerate? After all, the forces affecting a table in use are not always vertical forces. What happens when the table is nudged sideways by children playing or by someone squeezing past or by getting knocked by a different piece of furniture.

If the table is standing on an uneven surface (uneven joints between floorboards or raised tiles or a thick rug, for instance) then it is possible that not all of the legs of the table are able to make proper contact with the floor: you need to think about that possibility when choosing an appropriate design of legs and their dimensions.

In the case of circular tables, a single central pedestal leg may be sufficient, but that's unlikely to work with square or rectangular tables as any uneven loading can easily cause the table to tip over.

Illustrated below are examples of various table-leg types.

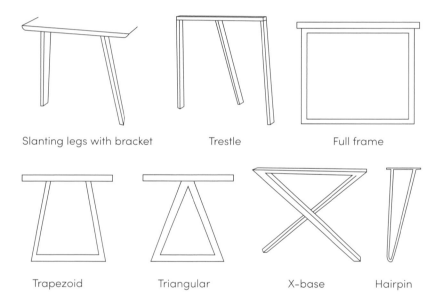

Slanting legs with bracket   Trestle   Full frame

Trapezoid   Triangular   X-base   Hairpin

TIP!

A round table with three legs will stand firmly on the floor even if the surface is uneven.

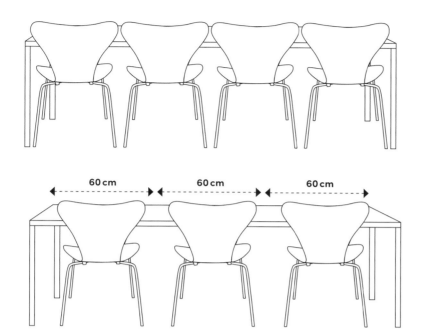

It is not the number of chairs that determines how many people can be fitted in at a dining table, it is the width of the upper body of an adult, plus the extra space necessary to allow movement.

How many people can you fit at a table?

How many individuals are in your household, or what is the maximum number of people you want to invite to dinner? You can work out the space you will need by using a standard measurement based on allowing an elbow-to-elbow space of 60 centimetres per adult. Measure the length of the table and divide by 60, but remember to take account of the shape of the chairs and the width of their armrests. And allow sufficient space for the diners to sit down and stand up without difficulty.

This is why the staff who lay the long table for the Nobel dinner measure out the space with such precision. And it's worth mentioning that for festive occasions, such as weddings and formal dinners, it may be necessary to allow a little extra space for the style of clothing worn. (The same may be true for outdoor parties when guests may want to keep their coats on!)

Table legs, chair legs and human legs – they all need space under the dining table. Always double-check all your measurements before spending your money on expensive furniture.

Positioning of the table legs?

How many people you can fit around the table will depend on the positioning of the table legs. Badly designed positioning can restrict the 60-centimetre allowance by, for instance, causing some individuals to bang their knees or being unable to get close enough to the table for comfort. This is a common mistake with manufacturers who have rationalized their production in order to minimize price and transport costs at the expense of functionality and user-friendliness.

Are you considering a table with a central pyramid? In which case, check that the pyramid works with the chairs you are thinking of getting and isn't so wide that it prevents the chairs being pushed in.

TIP!

Small, circular, three-legged tables may make it difficult for two people to sit right opposite one another because the table legs may get in the way of the chairs.

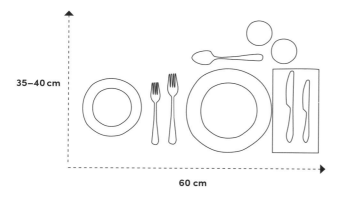

35–40 cm

60 cm

Space for place settings

Each diner needs space on the table for a plate, glass and cutlery. The usual estimate is 60 x 35–40 centimetres per setting per person, but since the size of our dinnerware and ordinary tableware has increased since the standard measurements were set, it is worth measuring the size of the plates and glasses you actually use at home and then have a table-laying test. Since there are many different ways of setting a table, whether for dinner parties or for everyday meals, it makes sense to work it all out with the dinnerware you already have – or are thinking of getting. If you don't yet have a table and chinaware at home, make a mock-up on the floor by marking out the size of the table with masking tape and cutting out plates, bowls and serving dishes from pieces of paper.

Space for dinnerware, jugs and serving dishes

The wider the table, the more room there is between diners on each side. Modern bowls and pans are bigger than those of fifty years ago, so, if you know that you usually lay and serve the food from the middle of the table, make sure there is sufficient space for you to do so.

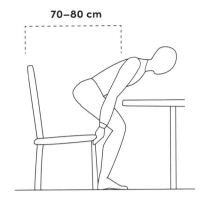

70–80 cm

Space in the room

Bear in mind that the table needs to stand at least 70–80 centimetres from the nearest wall so that people can sit down and stand up without banging into it. Eighty centimetres is the recommended standard, but you can get away with 70 centimetres if space is tight. If the dining table is in the kitchen and close to work units where you need to open oven or dishwasher doors, the usual guideline is to allow 120 centimetre's space.

Table shape and fit?

We are quick to criticize the clothing industry when fashion dictates such tight fits that it's impossible to breathe properly, or when trendy clothes are so skimpy with material that they scarcely cover your backside. Shapes of that sort are not only uncomfortable to wear, but they also exclude anyone and everyone with a body that won't fit, and that leads to frustration and bad moods for a host of people. Discussions about such issues are far from unimportant – unfortunately, however, they simply don't get aired in my own field of interior design.

Why are no questions being asked about the incomprehensible shape and fit of today's furniture and design trends? It often seems that the designed interiors we are inspired by were made for people as skinny as paper dolls. Many of the combinations of tables and chairs don't even go together. How must it feel for people who have to avoid a restaurant because they simply can't fit into the chairs? Or for the people who decorate their homes according to the current trends only to discover that it doesn't then match their own furniture. Of course it's great to have a charming home that brings you numerous likes on Instagram, but what good is that if there isn't enough room for your own body or for your partner's long legs and feet? That sort of striving for effect – and the waste of resources that goes with it – both creates completely unreasonable design ideals and is likely to lead to irritation and frustration amongst the many others who are perhaps inspired to do the same. 'But at least it doesn't affect my health . . .' is what you may think now. But who knows? In my opinion, the kind of furnishing ideals that are currently dominant in the social media are no good at all for our bodies, in particular for our backs.

Older tables and new chairs?

Combining traditional rustic tables with modern chairs is very trendy at the moment. I'm not saying that it can't work well – I've actually got an old trestle table in our conservatory. But you do have to remember that furniture makers in those days used different methods to make tables stable, and nineteenth-century furniture was not designed to function along with today's anthropometrics and modern standardized chair sizes. So it's important to check the table's stays, stretchers and measurements before you splash out. What does the underside of the table look like? Can you actually use your chairs with the table? If there is a strut running centrally the length of the table, there won't be a problem, but if stretchers are mounted as a frame between the four legs, they make it impossible to push the chairs in and no one gets to sit comfortably. However well chairs and table may match stylistically, if their legs crash into one another it simply won't do.

SOMETHING TO THINK ABOUT!

When you are planning your layout and doing the measuring, remember that a dining table never comes alone. The width of the chairs and their armrests and anything that cannot be pushed right under the table will increase the surface area necessary for the dining suite.

Common shapes of table tops

Rectangular

This is probably the most common shape in Swedish homes. Since each table setting demands a space of 60 x 40 centimetres, this shape seems to be the natural one for tables with enough space for two or more to sit alongside one another.

Oval/Elliptical

The advantage with oval tables is that people sitting around the edge of the table can get a better view of those sitting in the middle than they would get at a rectangular table.

Racing track/D-shaped ends

This is a rectangular table shaped like an athletics track, with each end curved like a big D. Since it is more expensive to round off corners than to leave them straight, this will usually affect the price bracket. The curves do, however, give a more finished appearance and also cut down on the number of sharp corners in a room that may already have plenty of them.

Boat-shaped

This table top takes the shape of the hull of a boat. It has the same advantage as the oval shape – people around the edges can easily have eye contact with other diners. The downside – as with the oval – is that it costs more to produce.

Round

Round dining tables are unbeatable in the social sense in that everyone sitting round them can make eye contact with all the others. Everyone can join in the conversation and no one needs to feel left out. Usually, however, round tables for more than two people take up more room, since you have to leave space to pull out chairs all the way around the table.

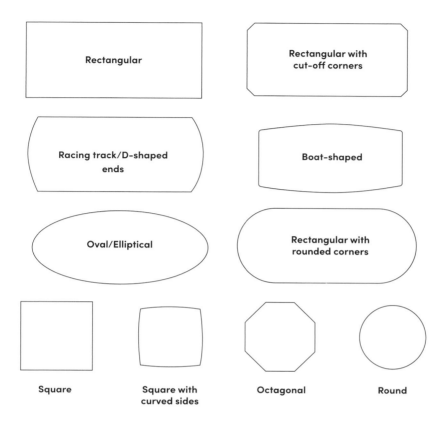

Rectangular

Rectangular with cut-off corners

Racing track/D-shaped ends

Boat-shaped

Oval/Elliptical

Rectangular with rounded corners

Square

Square with curved sides

Octagonal

Round

Square

Splendid – or impractical – depending on where you place it. As with a round table, a square table means you have to leave space to pull out the chairs all the way around the table. There are social advantages, but square tables do take up more space.

Square with curved sides

This shape was common during the 1950s and 1960s. The curved sides give the table a gentler shape, but can be a bit of a problem if you use table mats since straight-edged ones won't work here. And tablecloths made for straight-edged tables tend not to lie smoothly.

Rectangular with cut-off corners

Rather more pleasing than the square shape. The cut corners are frequently combined with leg embellishments.

Octagonal

An unusual shape, most often seen in more formal surroundings.

Extendable tables

One way of providing occasional extra seating for special occasions is to buy an extendable table. This makes it possible to have a table of a size that suits your everyday purposes while still allowing the possibility of hosting larger parties.

TABLECLOTHS AND TABLE MATS ON ROUND TABLES

Finding ready-sewn round tablecloths for larger tables can be a bit of a problem, although it's usually possible to order larger round tablecloths from well-stocked suppliers.

You can, of course, sew your own tablecloths, though the majority of fabrics sold by the metre are usually 140–150 centimetres wide. If your round table is bigger than that, it is important to look for patterns/textiles double that width so that you don't have to have a join in the fabric.

Do you use table mats? Round and oval tables are not really compatible with straight-edged table mats since the corners of the latter can stick out beyond the curves of the table top.

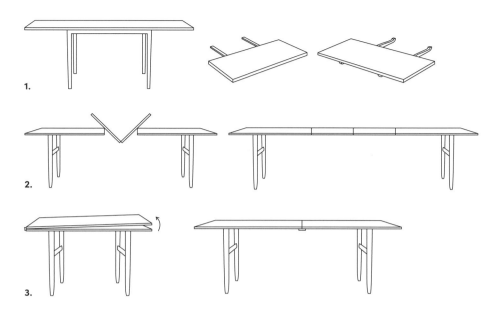

Three common types of extension

1. The table has extension leaves that can be added to the ends of the table.
2. The table can be pulled open and extension leaves added in the centre.
3. The table top is double and hinged in the middle, allowing it to be opened out.

Check how changing the table affects the positioning of both chair legs and table legs. It may be that, while leaves increase the size of the table top, the positioning of the legs or stretchers makes it difficult to find space for chairs to fit in under the table and allow diners to sit comfortably. Not every furniture manufacturer bears this in mind and, of course, they can have no idea about the dining chairs you possess. This is an important point for you as consumer: you don't want to buy a table that extends only to discover that it is actually no use to you.

End extensions lengthen the table by hooking on an extra leaf at each end. The advantage of this type is that there is no groove in the middle of the table.

Central extensions are added to the middle of the table by drawing apart the two halves of the table top and dropping in one or more extra leaves.

Folding tables

Gateleg, drop-leaf and draw-leaf tables are all varieties of table that can be varied in shape with the help of gatelegs and drop-leaves in order to vary the size of the table top. The drop-leaves may be angular or rounded, and the construction of the supports varies depending on the model and on the year of construction. What is common to this type of table is that they have a fixed middle section with drop-leaves on one or on each side. Older models frequently have drawers in the middle section and these were used to store cutlery and other domestic utensils. When the table is in the unopened position and depending on how much of the table top protrudes, these drawers can take up a good deal of the seating space around the table. (Check back to earlier parts of this chapter for more about the measurement of chairs and tables.)

Because of their construction, folding tables can – when unopened – function as a kind of sideboard. But given that the leg construction of older models rarely suits modern chairs that are designed for ergonomic sitting, I would not recommend any of them for everyday use as dining tables. However, I certainly don't mean that you should simply throw them out: they may leave a lot to be desired from the functional point of view, but they can be attractive pieces of furniture and give a great deal of pleasure. They are not usually very stable when unopened and they are rarely of the right height in relation to our modern standards for chairs; moreover, the drawers and table legs frequently take up the space your legs need under the table. For all that, they can be decorative and still be useful as an extra table in smaller kitchens with the right décor.

If, however, you are on the lookout for an older folding table, check that the table top and the leaves are more or less straight. Over time wood has a tendency to warp and it may become impossible to sit at the table. Also, double-check that the table has some kind of locking mechanism to prevent the open leaf falling down if the table is knocked or pushed. The metal fixtures on gateleg tables get worn over the years, so check the quality and stability of the hinges and whether they are replaceable before you spend your money.

MI 901 GATELEG TABLE BY BRUNO MATHSSON

In 1936 furniture designer Bruno Mathsson launched his brilliant further development of the traditional gateleg table, which had existed in Swedish homes ever since the seventeenth century. When closed, the table top on his Mi 901 measures no more than 23 centimetres, but it becomes no less than 280 centimetres when fully opened up. Moreover, the table can be extended or closed by a single person. When the American magazine *Everyday Art Quarterly* wanted to illustrate an article on Swedish design during the 1950s, they did it with just a single picture of this wonderful piece. And, incidentally, it is still in production.

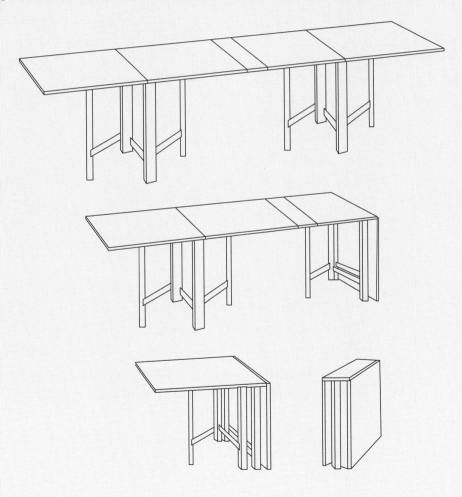

Build your own dining table

Anyone who is reasonably practical can build their own dining table. Avoid pressure-impregnated wood or timber that has been treated with anything unsuitable to dining. Even though you won't be eating straight off the table (hopefully, you've actually got dishes!), the surface may come into contact with foodstuffs and, consequently, with you, the diner. And don't forget to rub down the underside of the table. Many people focus on the top surface because it's obvious to the eye, but forget that the underside will also be in touch with the diners and any splinters and uneven patches can cause damage both to the individual and to clothing.

Tables for children

The height of tables for children depends more on the height of the child rather than on its age, but since growth tends to run at a standard rate, guidelines for children's tables more often follow age groups rather than body height. According to Seth Stem's 1989 book *Designing Furniture – from Concept to Shop Drawing*, the standard table height for children from 3–6 years is 56 centimetres and the height of their chairs is 32–33 centimetres. The book also states that children need 51 centimetres breadth per person in order to sit comfortably.

Common complaints about tables

- The table top is too easily marked and stained by cutlery, glasses, plates or pans being dropped. It should be possible to put things on a table without making ugly marks and scratches. If you are buying on the internet, make sure you read other people's comments carefully.

- The table feels unsteady and shakes when several people sit at it to eat.

- The table top gets stained by strong cleaning fluid and disinfectants or gets scratched by pieces of jewellery and bracelets.

- If a glass of water is left standing on some surfaces, it leaves a mark that is impossible to remove.

- Sunlight causes wooden table tops to fade, so if you leave a cloth runner on during your holidays it will leave lasting marks.

- Legs and so on are damaged. When you are dragging a table across uneven floors (rather than lifting it), remember that the vibrations may damage the joints and frame. In the worst case, legs may work loose or even snap off.

- The table did not look like the online illustration. That happens with lacquered and painted tables as well as with glass tables. Glass tables may look different in daylight to the way they look when flashlit. In other words, there's nothing unusual about photographs of glass tables looking different online than they do in reality.

VISUAL WEIGHT

Two dining tables of exactly the same size can appear very different in terms of bulk and weight depending on how they contrast with the room they are in. The colour and material of the table in relation to its surroundings will determine whether it appears to be bigger or smaller. And even if the surface area is the same, the frame and legs alone may well make it appear neat or clumsy.

This is important in small rooms, where you want to avoid the feeling that the room is over-furnished. But it can also be really worthwhile in open-plan arrangements where you may feel the need for something with more visual weight to provide balance in an open, spacious room.

Coffee tables

In terms of construction, coffee tables are very similar to dining tables, but their size and function differ, of course, since they need to fit in with lower-level seating. The following are some important points to think about in order to avoid the frustration that comes from buying the wrong thing.

Table tops and designs

As a general rule of thumb, the coffee table should not be wider than the sofa it stands in front of. The recommended maximum width is two-thirds of the sofa, with a minimum width of 50 per cent of the sofa. There will otherwise be a risk that the pairing appears out of proportion – either too big or too small.

As to the shape of the top of the coffee table compared with that of the sofa, interior designers take the view that pieces of furniture should relate to one another but not be twins. They try to avoid placing two identical shapes next to one another, as that will tend to turn the sofa group into a single unit and consequently impair the traffic flow. On the other hand, the sofa and coffee table should relate to and complement each other in terms of colour, shape and material. A sofa that has squared-off edges may well fit in with a rounded or elliptical table, whereas sofas with rounded shapes and finish can be balanced with a coffee table with square corners in order to give the whole group stability. Interior designers strive to create a sense of dynamism in the sofa group. Combining a rectangular, three-seater sofa with a rectangular table top of precisely the same height as the seat cushions seldom works as well as choosing a nest of two round tables of different heights and sizes.

TIP!

If the shape and size of the coffee table is such that it can't be reached by everyone sitting on the sofa, you can add to the arrangement by having small side tables on each side of the sofa.

Height

How high should a coffee table be? Opinions vary on this: plus or minus 10 centimetres measured from the top edge of the seat cushions is the usual guideline, but avoid lining them up exactly. Higher tables are an advantage if you frequently eat or have snacks while sitting in the sofa as they allow you to eat without having to bend double. Lower tables are usually more suitable when they are paired with sofas designed for leaning and lounging back since, in that case, your head will be at a lower level. But low coffee tables are not really advisable if you have small children who are likely to climb up on them or fiddle with any ornaments you've put on the table.

Space for your legs

It's easy to focus on appearance and design when choosing coffee tables and consequently forget about things that aren't so obvious, especially when you are sitting down, i.e. your own legs and feet! The more backward sloping the sofa is, the more room you need to allow for your feet out in front. Check this for yourself wherever you are sitting at the moment: the further back you lean, the further forward your feet will move in order keep your body in balance. (And the lower you will need to sit in order to keep your feet firmly supported on the floor.)

How does this affect your choice of coffee table? Well, unless you have unlimited floor space in your sitting room, a backward-leaning sitting posture means that you will need a coffee table with sufficient space under it to allow room for your feet. If not, the coffee table will have to be moved forward to allow you to sit comfortably, but that means that more and more floor space is eaten up. This is why solid coffee tables, mirror cube tables and ottomans are, in practical terms, so difficult to place. All of this is worth thinking through if you want to end up with a sofa group that it is comfortable to relax in as well as looking nice.

Advantages and disadvantages of different coffee table tops

Glass

Advantage: If you have limited space, a table with a glass top is excellent as it gives the room a more spacious feel than a solid table top. The glass will also reflect light, which will brighten up the room and, again, make it feel more spacious. And any patterned rug you have under the table will also be more visible – if you own an oriental rug, for instance, you wouldn't want the central pattern or medallion to be hidden under a big table, would you?

Disadvantage: Fingerprints and marks show up immediately. If you have sticky fingers, you'll be forever cleaning the marks off. The colour of glass can often have a hint of green as a result of the iron in it – this is not always obvious in online photographs of the products since glass tables come out differently in daylight and artificial light. The effect may actually be even more marked in the home, depending on the lamps and lighting you use. Always make sure that the table you select is made of toughened safety glass. Read more on this topic in the section on glass on pages 280 and 281. Toughened glass is more expensive, but the extra cost may well save you, your children and your pets from some nasty accidents.

Wood

Advantage: The grain and irregularities in the surface give wood a natural and unique life of its own. It also gives the acoustics of the room a very different sound to plastics or stone. And wood reflects back the warmth of the body and is warm to the touch.

Disadvantage: The surface patterning in wood may not be to the liking of people who want uniform colours. Depending on how the surface has been treated, wood may demand more care. As a material, wood changes and adapts to the moisture ratio in its surroundings and you should therefore be cautious about using it in places where there is a risk of major changes in temperature and moisture. (Environments such as conservatories, mountain cabins left unheated through the winter, and swimming pools come to mind.)

Chrome

Advantage: Shiny, and the reflection lights up a room with many dull surfaces.

Disadvantage: Picks up and takes on the colours in its surroundings. If you are unlucky, it may also create distorting and dazzling reflections, depending on the angles from which the lighting or the daylight from the windows strikes it.

Stone

Advantage: A solid, authentic and timeless material.

Disadvantage: The edges are vulnerable to knocks and, at worst, it can easily be chipped. Has sharp corners for children not yet able to walk properly – in fact, it's rarely suitable if there are children around. If you're fond of having parties and eating, it doesn't make a good table surface since it easily picks up rings or water stains. Some sort of covering is a must.

Concrete

Advantage: Good value for money compared with stone. Fairly resistant to wear and tear. With time and use, it develops a nice patina.

Disadvantage: If the surface hasn't been treated, coloured liquids can easily cause unattractive stains.

Laminates, melamine and the like

Advantage: Light in weight and consequently easy to move when doing the housework or moving the furniture around. More resistant to surface stains. Often good value for money. Available in organic designs and many variations.

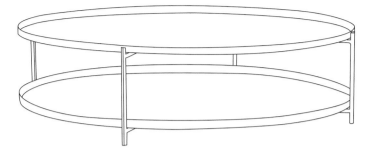

Coffee tables with shelves so close to the floor that the vacuum cleaner can't reach under them are likely to be a nuisance when doing housework as you have to move the table to get at the floor surface.

Disadvantage: Easily scratched. Any damage is difficult to repair. If you or anyone else in the family is given to putting your feet on the table, it's quite likely to skate off across the room.

Common complaints about coffee tables

- Unstable legs, supports and sub-frame.
- Surface sensitive to stains and scratches. White surfaces may be permanently stained by coffee or wine.
- Surface and legs are different colours (particularly in the case of wood or veneer). Also applicable to side tables, where the appearance of the table tops can sometimes be very different from one another.
- Risk of tipping over. The construction of the table is unsafe for small children.
- Some tables can be awkward to lift or move when cleaning or changing the furniture around.

TIP!

Are you or your partner in the habit of putting your feet up on the table? Shameful! But, joking aside, before you choose a table, check its stability and the strength of the table top, as well as the weight of the table: after all, you don't want one that slides away when you put your feet on it. And avoid glass tables – they don't like uneven point loading.

Small tables

As well as larger tables, small tables can be useful around the house and they can make a room feel more comfortable. I'm thinking, for instance, of small occasional tables that go alongside sofas and armchairs, hall tables and half-moon tables in the corridors, sideboards and buffet tables and so on – all of which fulfil practical needs around the home. What the tables are designed to be used for is, of course, the basis of the specifications, but let's for a moment run through some of the most common types and some of the points to consider with regard to construction, complaints and weak points – regardless of whether you are buying new or second-hand.

Occasional tables

Small occasional tables to go alongside chairs and seats are often called side tables or small tables. The rule of thumb used by interior designers is that all the seats in a seating group should be able to reach a surface to put things down. So, in a social seating group, side tables can complement a larger coffee table in situations where the shape of the sofa or the positioning of the armchairs make it impossible for everyone to reach the main coffee table. The height of the tables will vary depending on manufacturer and style, but as a general rule an occasional table will be slightly lower than the arms of the sofa or chair it is to stand beside. This is to allow you to put things down on the table easily and so that the top of the table does not stick up above your shoulder height when you are sitting on the chair or sofa.

Nests of tables

Nests of tables consist of a number of small tables that will slide under each other. They used to provide a popular location for the wireless set, but these days they are more often used as occasional tables alongside sofas and armchairs. The great advantage is the flexibility they offer,

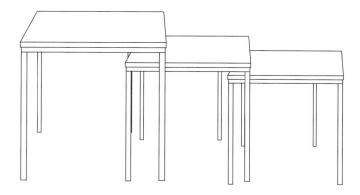

since each unit can be slid out or in to suit the space available or the needs of the moment.

Check that the various parts actually do slide under each other and that the different heights of table have a function and aren't just a gimmick. Cheaper versions sometimes fail to recognize the risk of protruding parts of the tables rubbing against each other, which can lead to scratches on the surface of the tables that go beneath the largest one. Some manufacturers attach felt pads to the underside of the larger tables in order to protect the surface of the smaller tables.

Half-moon tables

In the past, the half-moon tables we now use as side or window tables were not just used as occasional tables. By pushing together two half-moon tables you can form a full round table and, by putting in an extra leaf between the two, you have quickly made a dining table with space for more people to eat. These days, however, we usually see these tables as hall tables or standing in windows that don't have window seats.

Trolleys

Trolleys, drinks trolleys and tea trolleys used to be used for moving things from one room to another in larger houses. The bigger the wheels, the more smoothly they moved, even when they encountered obstacles like door-sills and rugs. That is probably why older drinks trolleys had such large wheels – it meant they could deal with uneven surfaces and transport glass bottles less noisily, which is worth bearing in mind if you are buying a trolley for practical mobility rather than just for the sake of appearances. Remember, too, that the trays need to have some kind of rim to prevent items on the tray sliding off when you move the trolley. A good general rule for the appropriate height of a trolley is 60–65 centimetres.

	Tea trolley	Rubber wheel	Metal wheel	Hard plastic	Brass /metal	Ball
Best surface	All round	Hard & smooth	Soft & carpets	Non-scratch	Best with cups	Doesn't roll
Load capacity	Medium	High	High	High	High	High
Roll resistance	Medium	Medium	Medium	Low	High	Low
Sprung	Medium	High	Low	Low	Low	Low
Noise level	Medium	Low	High on hard surface	Medium	High	High
Risk of marking surface	Low	Low	High	Medium	High	High

Are the wheels fixed or do they swivel?

- Wheels that swivel are good on small trolleys if you are likely to want to turn quickly in small spaces – they can turn in smaller spaces than fixed wheels.

- Wheels that swivel but can also be locked to prevent them swivelling while still allowing forward motion. These are good for trolleys used over uneven surfaces in that the wheels can be locked to allow the trolley to move in a straight line.

- A simple brake can stop the wheels rolling forward but still allows them to swivel.

- A full locking-system that stops the wheels both rolling and swivelling – this is good for holding the trolley on sloping floors such as bathrooms, for instance.

Advice on buying serving trolleys

- Think about the handle and the steering. If the intention is to move the trolley, is the handle firm and easy to grip? How easy is it to manoeuvre the trolley?

- What is the height of the trolley compared with its width? Narrow trolleys tip over more easily.

- Drinks trolleys are not really compatible with small children and pets. Unless the bottom shelf has a rim, your dog's wagging tail will knock the bottles off.

- If the trolley is to be used for serving food, does it have a heat-resistant serving surface? It would be practical to have the whole or part of the top shelf of the trolley covered with ceramic or stainless steel mats.

- Is the space between the shelves big enough for everything you want to keep on the trolley (bottles standing upright in the living room or spray bottles and curling tongs in the bathroom)?

- What is the trolley's maximum load capacity? What does it weigh when empty? Some models become difficult to manoeuvre when loaded.

- The tread on the wheels of older trolleys may be worn. Check whether it is possible to replace them.

Desks

Choosing a desk is hardly rocket science, but there are a number of pitfalls worth avoiding, especially if you will be using the desk on a daily basis. What size and model will best suit your needs will depend mainly on . . .

1. how much room is necessary for the tasks you'll be dealing with and for all the things you need to have at hand to do the job.
2. how much space you need to set aside in the room that will house your desk.

Size of the work surface

The size of the surface area needed will depend on the size of your digital equipment plus all the necessary bits and pieces (paper, notebooks, office equipment, etc.) you need while working at the desk. The usual recommendation for the size of the desk is that it should be at least 60 centimetres deep and at least 75 centimetres wide.

Distance from the computer

The recommended viewing distance from your computer or screen depends on the size of the equipment and the recommendations made by the manufacturer, but, as a general rule, reckon on at least 50–80 centimetres (roughly an arm's length) between your eyes and the screen. The upper edge of the computer screen should be on a level with your eyes, allowing your viewing angle to be downwards without any need to bend your neck.

If you need to work for long periods at a portable computer, it's worth investing in a laptop stand and a wireless keyboard so that you can raise the screen above table level and thus avoid having to bend your neck with the concomitant risk of straining it. Raising the screen to about 15–20 centimetres above the level of the table is usually about right, always depending on the size of the screen. Don't forget that you will also need space for an external keyboard as well

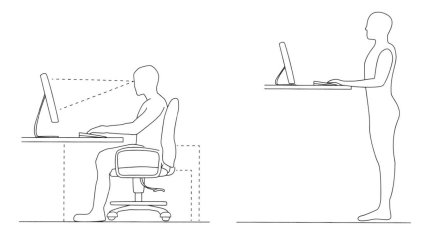

Depending on the size of screen you are using, try to position the screen so that the upper edge lines up with your eyebrows or very slightly lower: the aim is to avoid having to bend your neck at an unnatural angle. And remember to angle the computer screen or the lighting next to it so as to avoid any annoying reflections.

as space for a wireless mouse to the right of the computer (if you're right-handed) or to the left (if you're left-handed).

Height of the desk

The recommended height for a desk is around 72–75 centimetres, depending on the height of your chair and the length of your legs. This is so that you can place the soles of your feet flat on the floor while having your lower arms at a comfortable angle (*c.* 90 degrees) to the surface of the desk, keyboard and mouse. This will avoid strains.

For ergonomic reasons, you should vary your working position over the course of the day. A simple way of doing that is to have a height-adjustable desk that can be raised and lowered so that you are able to alternate your working position between sitting and standing. Since desks of this design frequently need access to an electrical socket in order to function, it's worth checking out the length of the cable and the proximity of a socket or junction box. There are also manual systems for raising and lowering the height of the desk. Make sure you choose a desk with a relatively simple system otherwise you'll find that you never bother to vary your working position. And it's a good idea to choose a desk with a display that clearly shows the height it is set at – this will avoid you having to work it out by trial and error every time.

Older desks

Older desks may be charming to look at but they are not always ideal for present-day needs. They aren't always the right height (72–75 centimetres) and may not have sufficient clear space from the floor (at least 63 centimetres) to allow you to sit comfortably.

The space for your legs under antique desks often has a broad stack of drawers or a cupboard on each side. Another common style of antique desks had profiled legs and drawers suspended below the working surface.

And these older desks weren't designed to go with the style of modern office chairs. Moreover, we can be sure that these desks weren't designed for us to sit and work at for eight hours a day while using all our modern technical devices.

- Older desks often have a fairly broad apron and drawers under the worktop. This can restrict the available space for your legs and thighs and make it more difficult to vary your sitting position over the course of the day.

- Older desks are often quite dainty and narrow. Remember how far from the computer screen you should be: the narrower the desk, the greater the risk of sitting too close to the screen, which can lead to you twisting your neck at an awkward angle.

- Drawers tend to stick and jam as they get older, and metal handles rattle when you type on the keyboard unless the desk is completely stable.

- Big, grand director's desks often have substantial side pieces, which leave very little turning space for modern office chairs.

TIP!

Desk pads are not only good for protecting the surface of the desk from marks and stains, they can also reduce the noise of typing on the hard surface and also minimize light being reflected if the surface of the desk is white. Will you be working in a dark room with poor access to light? In that case, avoid choosing a dark desk as it will absorb even more light and lead to unnecessary strain on your eyes. Taking good care of your eyes is at least as important as good ergonomics.

Bedside tables

Bedside tables, bed tables, bedside cupboards, pot cupboards, nightstands: many names for essentially the same function. Most of us want some kind of table to put things on alongside the bed – watches, jewellery, alarm clocks, books and a small bedside light. What follows are some points to think about when you are out looking for bedside tables.

Bedside table with shelf

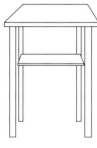

Advantage: Makes a neat impression. Easy to tidy both top and shelf.

Disadvantage: Little room to keep things and nowhere to put things away privately. Nowhere to conceal the cables for digital radios, alarm clocks, lamps or mobile chargers behind the table.

Bedside table with drawer

Advantage: A drawer to put away things you don't want left on public view. The drawer gives you the chance to choose a beautiful fitting that adds the finishing touch to the bedroom.

Disadvantage: The drawers in bedside tables are often not big enough to have space for all the things you might want to store, such as books, newspapers and so on.

Bedside table with a cupboard (pot cupboard)

Advantage: Has enough space for taller objects and bigger books. Plenty of room to keep things private.

Disadvantage: There needs to be sufficient space for the door to open. When used with a single bed, the cupboard can only go on one side of the bed since single beds are usually placed along a wall: in this situation, it's important to ensure that the door handle is closest to the bed – or that it's possible to re-hang the door. If the cupboard stands on low legs, vacuuming can be difficult.

Bedside cabinet

Advantage: Separate storage, both open and concealed.

Disadvantage: The size of the drawers defines their use. The bottom drawer may be difficult to reach if you are in bed.

Pedestal cabinet

Advantage: Concealed storage. Needs less space in front of it.

Disadvantage: Easily gets in a muddle. The doors or sliding door can easily catch on papers or books, especially when the compartments start filling up. The round shape means that it leaves dead areas in the corners that can't be used for shelving. For the same reason, there is less usable space on the top of the pedestal.

Stool

Advantage: Can be used as bedside table or as an extra seat. Light and airy solution in smaller rooms.

Disadvantage: Can be wobbly and unsteady. Is it the correct height for a table? No concealed storage. Small surface area.

Solid stool/table

Advantage: Can be used in many rooms and can follow you through the phases of life.

Disadvantage: No concealed storage. Is it the right height? Visually heavy.

Wall-mounted bedside shelving

Advantage: The height is completely up to you. No need to worry about allowing space for fixed legs, either from the point of view of positioning or of tidying and vacuuming.

Disadvantage: Once fixed, screws stay put – or make holes you have to live with.

Bedside tables for continental beds

Since continental (divan) beds are higher than frame bedsteads, bedside tables need to be taller so as to be the same height as the mattress. The risk otherwise is that the tables will look disproportionately small in relation to the bed.

Wall-mounted shelves are easier to adjust to the necessary height than tables that stand on the floor. Remember, however, not to mount them until you have made up the whole bed, including pillows, covers and overlay, otherwise you may end up fixing the shelves at the wrong level. And don't put them too close to the head of the bed – if you do, they may prevent the overlay lying smoothly over the bed.

A continental bed and its bedhead will usually be the absolutely dominant feature in the room and will need to be balanced by bedside tables that can hold their own in terms of proportion if all-round harmony is to be achieved. Bedside tables with thin legs and/or tables that can be seen through are likely to simply disappear in this context.

The space necessary for doors to open by the bed

If you have a bedside cabinet with doors, make sure you position it so that the door handles/knobs are closest to the bed, otherwise, when you are lying in bed, the cabinet door will prevent you seeing into the open cabinet. If you have a double bed, of course, the problem can probably be solved by moving the cabinets from one side of the bed to the other; if you're buying a cabinet to go with a single bed, however, it's worth checking that it has a door that can be re-hung to open the other way.

Height

The best height for your bedside table will depend on the height of your bed. There are advantages and disadvantages to having tables that are higher or lower than the mattress.

Tables lower than the mattress

Advantage: Within easy reach, which means you can see the alarm clock in the night without having to stick your head up ostrich-like or stretch far to turn the alarm off in the morning.

Disadvantage: Within easy reach – also when you don't mean to! A lower bedside table entails the risk that the bedcovers, a pillow or your arm may knock over anything on the table during the night.

Tables higher than the mattress

Advantage: If the continental bed has a high bedhead, a higher table will provide more visual balance.

Disadvantage: There's a risk that any sharp corners or edges on the table will disturb you if you happen to roll into them during the night.

TIP!

One member of the Trendenser Facebook group warned everyone who used their mobile phones as alarm clocks about a well-known bedside table made of metal. It took me a while to understand why, but the point is that when the alarm goes off it makes the whole table vibrate like a soundbox. She said it felt like waking up to a drum orchestra. Sounds like a tip worth passing on!

Storage

Storage of one sort or another covers a broad range of furniture and exists in most of the rooms in our homes. It covers everything from wardrobes and bookshelves to chests of drawers and display cabinets. What they all have in common is that the internal space is at least as important as external appearance. Not all of the finer details may be obvious to the eye, but how well these pieces are designed and constructed, and how well they function, can have a major impact on your daily life. What we shall do in this chapter is to look into some important differences in terms of quality and concept, while keeping an eye open for ways to avoid bad buys.

If you are an interior designer, you don't dare admit to finding storage pretty tedious. If you did, you'd be shooting yourself in the foot, since storage is by far the most common problem area for your customers.

At the same time, however, if it had been a nice, easy, fun area, it would hardly have been problematic for quite so many people, would it? I'm certainly not the only person who finds it troublesome, and has become allergic to those hearty storage experts who preach how simple and cool the whole business is. For my own part, I find it quite the opposite.

Storage, to me, is the interior designer's equivalent to wholegrain bread: everyone knows how important it is, but it's difficult to work up any enthusiasm for something so dry and duty-bound. You know that it's going to demand that you clean up and sort things out. You also know that it takes time and that you're unlikely to have the stamina to see the job through to the end. And that's perhaps why so many people continue to hope for a magic formula or quick fix that will provide the maximum result for the minimum effort.

Which is why I want to state right at the start what you can expect from this chapter. To a great extent it won't deal with how you store things, but what you will store them in. My aim is to help you plan your purchase of chests of drawers, wardrobes, bookcases and display cabinets so that you end up with what you actually need and avoid unnecessary mistakes. When it comes to things like organizing, sorting and folding your clothes, however, there are other people better qualified than me to help you.

DID YOU KNOW?

The Danish designer Hans Wegner, perhaps best known for the five hundred or so chairs he designed in the course of his career, was also interested in storage. In 1936 he studied at Kaare Klint's Cabinetmaker Day School in Copenhagen and measured everything from shirts and ties to rolled-up sports socks in order to calculate the optimal size for cupboards and shelves.

Wardrobes

The Swedish word *garderob* is said to be derived from the old French words *garde*, which means 'to keep', and *rob*, which means 'clothes/clothing'. So, when combined, it means 'a place to keep clothes'. The English 'wardrobe' is formed along the same linguistic lines, but since they needed a word for this phenomenon long before we did (as early as the Middle Ages), their starting point was the Germanic word *wardon*, which means 'to keep a watchful eye on', 'guard', 'protect'. In French *wardon* became *warder*, then the French added a 'g' instead of a 'w' so that became *garder* meaning 'keep' or 'care for'.

In the old days, a wardrobe was a transportable piece of furniture, a chest – often made of cedarwood to protect the precious contents from moths, mice and rats. These days a wardrobe may be freestanding or built-in, and it will have doors, hinged at the sides or sliding or folding, or it will be curtained. In recent years it has become more and more common to devote whole rooms to storing clothes – so-called 'walk-in closets', frequently abbreviated to WIC in property agents' advertising. But, even with the best will in the world, they could hardly be categorized as furniture, so this book will stick to wardrobe solutions that, to invent similarly anglified terms, might be called 'look-ins' or possibly 'lean-in closets'.

The mathematics of storage

How many wardrobes are needed per household, or which particular model is best suited to each person, is an individual matter. Not only does each of us own a different quantity of clothes, we often have different ways of hanging, folding or even rolling (!) our clothes. To work out how much space you need individually, we can start with a rough estimate. This is where most people go wrong when doing their wardrobe planning. We tend to focus on how many wardrobe units we can fit in, but we aren't so keen on working out how many cubic metres of clothes we own. We measure the space we have for wardrobes down to the nearest millimetre, but we don't have the first idea about the amount of space our possessions will take up. One ploy to get a quick overview of how much storage space you need in a wardrobe is to list and quantify the need for hanging space and for shelf space. How many metres of hanging space and how much shelving do you actually need?

Hanging storage

In other words, all the clothes you want to hang on the rail. These are often of different lengths, so list them according to length and organize them according to size.

Short items, such as blouses, shirts, jackets and short coats.

Medium length, such as trousers folded over a hanger, suits and midi-skirts.

Long items, such as dresses, trousers, maxi-skirts, capes and coats.

When counting the number of hanging clothes you have, don't simply work from the measurements – the material the clothes are made of can determine whether it's best to hang them on the rail or to fold them. Knitted garments can lose their shape if hung up, whereas other materials are better hanging loose since they are liable to crease if folded and stored in piles.

Calculate how much rail you need

- Blouses and shirts need about 2.5 centimetres per item.

- Skirts and trousers folded over a hanger need between 2.5 and 5 centimetres per item.

- Dresses, jackets and overcoats need about 5 centimetres per item.

- Suits and outer clothing usually need 5–10 centimetres per item.

- Down jackets, furs and ski clothes often need as much as 10–25 centimetres per item.

WORTH THINKING ABOUT!

When hanging clothes in a wardrobe, you can optimize storage by having two hanging rails so that no space is wasted. You can also attach a notched half-rail to the sidewall of the wardrobe so that half the hanging space remains for longer items and the other half gives you extra space for twice as many shorter items.

To avoid taking the wrong measurement when estimating the hanging length of shirts, remember that the sleeves rather than the body are the longest parts.

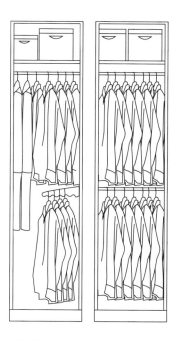

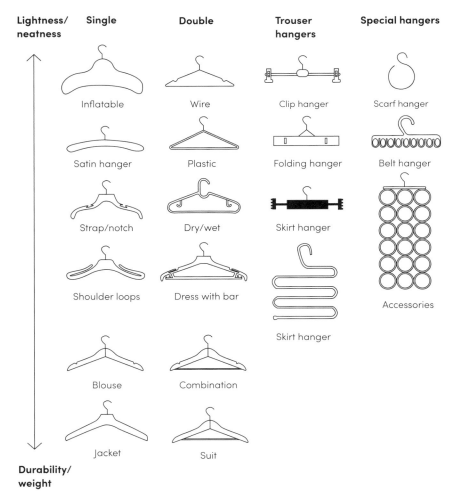

Lightness/ neatness

Single
- Inflatable
- Satin hanger
- Strap/notch
- Shoulder loops
- Blouse
- Jacket

Double
- Wire
- Plastic
- Dry/wet
- Dress with bar
- Combination
- Suit

Trouser hangers
- Clip hanger
- Folding hanger
- Skirt hanger
- Skirt hanger

Special hangers
- Scarf hanger
- Belt hanger
- Accessories

Durability/ weight

Hangers

Different hangers take up different amounts of space. Now, you may well think that that is irrelevant to you, since you have already bought twenty hangers of the same colour and shape from the store. You have a whole new world to discover. I definitely used to belong to the school of thought that considered it more important to have all the hangers the same than that they had particular functions. Then I discovered the alternatives that exist. The right hanger both takes better care of your clothes and makes storage easier in the wardrobe. And, no less importantly, your favourite clothes will last longer.

Storing flat

This works well for clothes that can be folded or stacked and stored on fixed shelves or in drawers and wire trays. We can divide these clothes into three groups:

Thick clothes
Such as knitted jumpers, cardigans and jeans.

Thin clothes
Such as T-shirts, vests and underclothes.

Accessories
Such as ties, belts, scarves and the like.

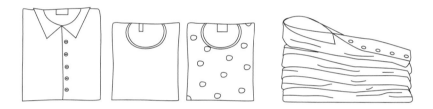

In order to allow enough space, shelves for clothing should never be smaller than 35 x 55 centimetres. The distance between the shelves should be at least 30 centimetres, but don't over-use it: tall piles of clothing tend to tip over and become disorganized. Drawers and wire trays that can be pulled out make it easier to get at clothes and see what's there compared with fixed shelves, especially if your wardrobe is more than 35 centimetres deep.

Estimating your space needs in cubic metres:

· How many folded items do you need space for?

· How tall can the stacks of clothing be without tipping over?

· How many stacks will each shelf accommodate?

· Given the space between the shelves, how tall can the stacks of clothing be?

Estimating the weight and loading strength

What do your clothes weigh and how strong are your shelves and hanging rails?

- A standard-length rail in a wardrobe 50 centimetres wide will take a load of 18 kilos.
- An MDF shelf measuring 58 x 50 centimetres will take a load of 12–20 kilos.
- Will that affect how much you can hang or store flat given your rail, shelf or drawer?

Bedding and the like

Many people store bedding, hand towels and bath towels in their wardrobes or linen cupboards. How much space will be necessary for these items depends, of course, on their size (single bedsheets or double bed?) and on their measurements (how big are your hand and bath towels?): it will also depend on how carefully you iron and fold things. The best way of estimating the necessary space is to measure the items after folding them. Sleeping in freshly ironed sheets is a joy, but – importantly – they also take up less room in the linen cupboard. And did you know that ironed sheets have a lower dust content and stay clean longer?

WORTH THINKING ABOUT!

In the 1950s, the Furnishing Institute estimated that there would be sufficient space for a family's linen store of bedding on four shelves measuring 30 x 95 centimetres. These days we probably own way more sets of bed linen and bath and hand towels, BUT is that a case of need or of desire?

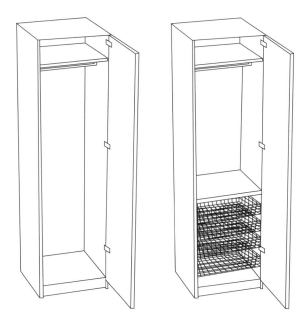

Freestanding wardrobes

Freestanding cupboards and wardrobes come in many different sizes, but they are usually based on the standard measurements of clothes hangers, allowing for the width of the clothes and for the hanger to swing. As a general rule, a wardrobe door shouldn't be wider than 60 centimetres: if it is, it will overload the hinges and there is a risk that the weight will cause the door to sag.

Advantages of freestanding wardrobes

- Freestanding wardrobes are relatively easy to move, should you or a future owner of your house want to change the room around.

- The advantage of side-hung doors is that you can have both open at once without them blocking each other. This allows you to see everything and to reach several compartments in the wardrobe at the same time. Better than sliding doors that slide to one side and consequently block full access.

- With side-hung doors you can hang your clothes up on the door while choosing what to wear, or you can attach hooks on the inside surface of the door for belts, ties and other accessories.
- Freestanding wardrobes are often a cheaper alternative compared with built-in wardrobes or sliding-door solutions,
- Most large home improvement warehouses and furniture chains have wardrobes in stock so it's usually easy to get one and much quicker than a made-to-measure wardrobe, partly because of the time needed to produce it and partly because you'll probably need a joiner to install it.

Disadvantages of freestanding wardrobes

- The size of the modules in freestanding wardrobes is usually fixed.
- To avoid the risk of tipping over, the drawers and trays in free-standing wardrobes can't always be pulled out to their full extent. If the wardrobe is deep, this can make it difficult to reach things.
- Freestanding wardrobes can often cause dead surfaces in a room – above the wardrobe, for instance. It's possible to add an extra module or to place baskets up there, but that rarely results in the sort of coherent, tailor-made impression you get from a built-in solution.
- Wardrobes with side-hung doors can't be positioned in places where the doors are at risk of banging into other doors or into other fittings and fixtures such as electrical sockets, windowsills or mouldings. Wardrobes with sliding doors offer you more freedom in such places.

BE CAREFUL!

Don't assemble your freestanding wardrobe flat on the floor, straight from its flatpack. The point here is that when you come to raising it there will be a risk of scraping paint off the ceiling. If there is insufficient space to swing it up, you should assemble it upright.

Advice when buying freestanding wardrobes

- Check that the doors show no sign of warping, especially in the case of cheaper versions. Are they stable? Are they likely to sag after a while?

- Check the thickness and the stability of the carcass and the shelving. What is their maximum weight capacity?

- Check the finish of the edges and joints. MDF and laminated doors come in a range of qualities. Check for remnants of glue and for any unevenness.

- Are the pre-drilled holes in the sides small and discreet or do they look as if someone has blasted them with a shotgun? The pre-drilled holes from some suppliers are no more than 3 millimetres in diameter: how easy is it to move the pegs if you want to adjust the space between the shelves?

- Are the doors and drawers soft-closing as a standard, or does that come as an extra?

A STANDARD MEASURE FOR UNITS

It's no accident that 60 centimetres is the usual measurement for units in Scandinavia. It is used for everything from the width of kitchen units to working out the number of people you can seat at a table or on a sofa. 6M (60 centimetres) for kitchen units was made the standard in the 1950s in order to make serial production more efficient. Behind the move lay ten years or more of investigatory work by SAR (Svenska Arkitekters Riksförbund = Swedish Architects' National Association), Svenska Slöjdföreningen = Swedish Craft Association (now known as Svensk Form = Swedish Design), HFI (Hemmets forskninginstitut = Household Research Institute) and Byggstandardiseringen = Building Standardization. Even the public housing for the Million Programme (see page 292) was designed so that wall-length was divisible by 60 centimetres. You may remember that 60 centimetres corresponds approximately to the elbow-to-elbow width of an adult.

Source: Uuve Snidare, Kök i Sverige (2004)

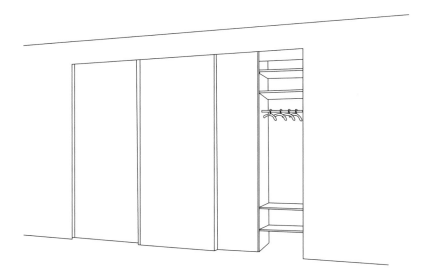

Sliding-door wardrobes

Sliding doors can be made to measure to fit exactly into the space you have available. It is usually recommended that the depth of the wardrobe should not be less than 68.5 centimetres, so that there is sufficient space for the overlapping, sliding doors. And if you make a sliding-door wardrobe too shallow, there's a risk that the sleeves of items hanging in it get caught and dragged along as you open and close the doors. If you do reduce the depth, it's better to use hanging rods rather than a rail for your clothes. The width of the sliding doors can be made to fit the horizontal space available, but bear in mind that the bigger the doors, the heavier they will be to slide. The usual recommendation is that door width should not exceed 120 centimetres.

Floor tracks

There are two basic sorts of floor track to choose between: surface-fitting or countersunk. The surface-fitting type is somewhat simpler in construction and, using heavy-duty, double-sided tape, it is easier to install. The track sits on the surface in the same way as a railway track and the doors slide along on rollers. In the countersunk type, the roller runs in a furrow in the floor, which gives the set-up a good deal more stability.

For the top of the door, both types of sliding door use a similar solution, but since the weight of the door mainly rests on the floor tracks, they are what determine the stability. The different alternatives may, superficially, look identical, but the difference lies in the feel – this can best be compared with the feel you get when closing the door of an exclusive, top-of-the-range car as opposed to a cheap model. The function is, of course, the same, but the feel is quite different.

Sliding doors

The doors on a sliding-door wardrobe come in a variety of materials. The simplest and cheapest are made of chipboard sheets. These are often quite light, which means that there is not much weight in the door – good or bad, depending on which you prefer yourself. Solid wood is heavier, keeps its shape better and has a more exclusive feel to it, but the price can shoot up, particularly if you need many large doors. You can save yourself some money by going for a sliding door with a wooden frame and the body made of melamine-faced board, but in that case you'll get a slightly plasticky look. Toughened glass is the heaviest of all the possibilities and can be good if you want mirror doors on part or all of the wardrobe – in this case, you will usually select an aluminium profile. Mirrors are popular in hallways or in darker, less spacious areas where you want to introduce a sense of space and reflected light from daylight or room lighting.

TIP!

Anything you use daily – underclothes and socks, for instance – should be placed right out at the sides of the wardrobe where the sliding-door handles are, so that you can get at them easily without having to slide several doors. The usual recommendation is that clothes rails should be put in the middle, because it's usually quite easy to reach for a hanging garment inside without having to open the whole door.

Soft closure

Soft closure is a detail that frequently gets forgotten. It's an extra that many first-time buyers of sliding-door wardrobes often set aside for reasons of cost, but they soon come to recognize its importance. The heavier the doors, the more important the soft-closure function: the mechanism is fitted on top of the door and acts as a brake on the closing of the door. This cuts down the noise and protects both the wall and your fingertips from damage. Heavier doors usually need more powerful mechanisms, so you should ask your supplier which model is most suited to your needs.

Made-to-measure solutions

If your back wall is not straight, you can install the track so that the door looks straight, even though the structure behind it will, of necessity, be less than straight. You can also have doors made to allow for a sloping ceiling, so that the whole wall is still available for storage.

If you are having a fitted wardrobe installed, always measure things at several different points. In older houses you will often find a difference of several centimetres from wall to wall when measured at the top, as opposed to the measurement wall to wall at floor level. New houses, too, may settle and, consequently, it's always worth checking the measurements at a minimum of three points.

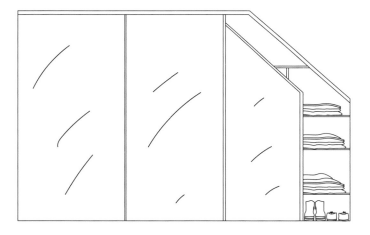

Choice of colour

These days, it's possible to order doors in whichever Natural Colour System (NCS) colour you want, so that your wardrobe doors are a perfect match for the room. Remember, however, that the gloss level on sliding doors is usually around 35 and, if you choose an NCS code with a more matt finish for the walls, exactly the same colour on the doors will look different depending on how they reflect the light. You will find more about NCS, colour codes and gloss levels in the section on colours in *The Interior Design Handbook*.

Advantages of sliding-door wardrobes

- The big advantage of sliding doors as opposed to hinged doors is that they don't need extra room to open. Freestanding wardrobes need sufficient space for the doors to open and for you to have standing room when they are open. Sliding doors are to be preferred if space is tight.
- Sliding doors often allow you to use more of the room for storage, both horizontal and vertical, than if you have standard freestanding systems.
- If you have a sloping ceiling, the corner of the sliding door can be adapted to allow the full length of the wall to be utilized for storage.
- Bespoke storage solutions create a coherent and visually harmonious impression and may add value to your home.

Disadvantages of sliding-door wardrobes

- Taken together, the doors and the tracks for sliding-door systems take up more space than the hinged door on freestanding wardrobes. You will need to allow an extra 5–10 centimetres to the depth.
- Sliding doors move to the side when you open them, which means that at least one section of the wardrobe will be blocked off when you are accessing another. This can cause upset if several members of the family are sharing the wardrobe and want to get dressed at the same time in the morning.

- If your sliding-door wardrobe has an even number of doors you will be able to access half the wardrobe at a time. It becomes more problematical if there is only space for three doors: it is sometimes possible to buy a 3-track door, which then allows access to two-thirds of the wardrobe at once. This solution, however, does demand more depth so as to enable the tracks to run parallel.

- A common error when building a sliding-door system is to fail to match up the positioning of drawers and wire trays with the width of the sliding doors, thus making it awkward to get at drawers and to open them. When a drawer is open, it locks the whole sliding system, making it impossible to move the doors to reach a different part of the wardrobe simultaneously.

- Sliding doors may be noisier than hinged doors. In a house we used to live in, we had a poor quality system that made a noise like thunder as you slid the doors open. That's not ideal if you are trying to creep out quietly and go to work without waking the family, or if you happen to be the first to wake early at the weekend. If the noise is that disruptive, my advice is that you spend a few pounds more on a quality wardrobe rather than buy a standard model from a low-price warehouse.

Advice when buying a sliding-door wardrobe

- What's the handle like? Is it easy to get hold of? Is it non-slip? If you are concerned about your nails, it's worth checking the likelihood of slipping and breaking long nails when you're in a rush in the morning.

- How easy is it to clean the doors? Remember that you'll be handling the doors several times a day and even if there are handles, you are bound to leave finger marks on the doors, so choose a type that is easy to wipe clean.

- Are the doors top-hung or do they rest on the track? Does the floor track have to be screwed firmly into the wooden or tiled floor, or is it possible to attach it with special tape? In the latter case, you will avoid damaging the floor, which is a bonus for any future owner who might want to change the position of the wardrobe.

- Are countersunk floor tracks available? If you are absolutely certain about the position and know you won't be wanting to move the sliding-door wardrobe, they may be a good alternative as they make cleaning easier. With countersunk tracks there is no beading and moulding around them and that makes for easy access to clean the sliding tracks with the vacuum cleaner.

- For top-hung doors the ceiling needs to be strong enough to take their weight. Think twice before choosing this alternative as, in my personal experience, people who've chosen it run into problems more often than not.

- Will the doors hold their shape? A common problem with cheaper sliding doors is that they can become warped over time.

- Catching your fingers in a sliding door is painful. I would recommend soft closure as an option as it helps prevents this and also minimizes noise and thuds.

- How long has your supplier existed and how likely are they to survive into the future? Will you still be able to accessorize and add to your wardrobe in ten years' time, or are you buying from a chain that frequently changes its standards and series?

- Do the wire baskets slide easily in their tracks or do they stick so that you have to push and pull hard to move them? If so, there's a risk of weakening the construction. Do they stay in their proper place when moved, or do they easily jump out when the basket is full of clothes?

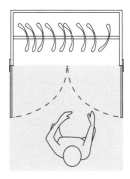
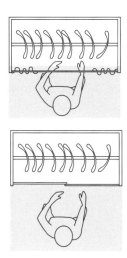

Curtains

A cloth curtain instead of sliding doors or side-hinged doors is another way of concealing the contents of your wardrobe. You don't have to worry about room to open the doors or the movement of the sliding doors, but you still have optimum storage space and slightly less need for standing room in front of the wardrobe.

Wardrobe handles

Handshake, hug or kiss . . . in the world of wardrobes we could replace that with handle, knob or strap.

Irrespective of whether it's freestanding or built in, buying new fittings for your wardrobe may offer an easy way to update an older model – or an effective way of ruining a brand new one – visually and more importantly functionally. My best advice? Don't just consider the appearance of the fittings, but think about what shape your fingers will need to be to grip the handles.

Does anyone in the family have big hands? Or small hands? Are your doors and drawers light or heavy? Even a newly constructed wardrobe systems may have doors of differing weights or various imprecisions in construction that affect how easy they are to open. And drawers tend to be more difficult to slide when they are full than when they are empty. So you need to think ahead to future use, not to how you feel just now.

Most of us can't get a good grip on a dainty little button with just one finger and thumb, nor can we pull out a heavy drawer with a single finger in a tiny leather loop. Fittings of that kind are best reserved for cupboards and drawers you don't need to access too often, or ones that slide so smoothly that little-finger strength is all that's necessary. Cup-shaped handles or handles mounted vertically are much friendlier when dealing with heavy cupboards and drawers. And handles with the standard measurement of 128 millimetres will be simpler to update if you want to change things in the future, rather than picking a special handle with an odd measurement that means you'll have to fill the holes and repaint the drawer or door if you change the handle.

Have you decided to have sliding doors? If they have an aluminium rim, the door is opened by using the rim itself as handle. If, however, you've decided on a flat door, you'll have the choice of a flush handle recessed into the door. The same ergonomic principles apply here as for knobs and handles: always check they are easy for the whole family to use. If you happen to favour long, well-manicured nails, check the feel of the handle yourself and don't just rely on a family member who bites their nails. It will give you a more realistic sense of how things will function in your ordinary everyday setting.

To sum up: think in terms of the physical language of the various handles rather than simply their style and appearance and that will make it easier to choose what is best for you and avoid bad buys and all the upset they cause. And don't go buying non-standard sizes if you know you are likely to want to change things or if your home is likely to have new owners in a couple of years.

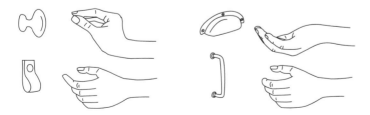

Learn to recognize the physical language of the handles. The shape your hand needs to take when using them is as important as the shape of the various handles and knobs.

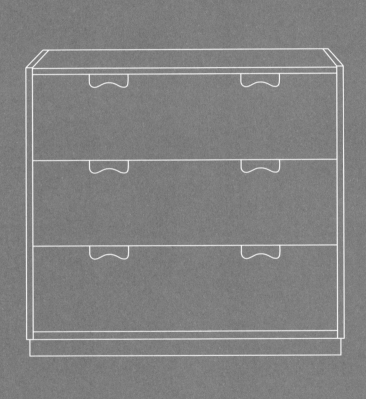

Chests of drawers

Chests of drawers are obliging pieces of furniture in that they can store a host of things on a small floor area. How well they function, however, and how well they stand up to the ravages of time, depends largely on the quality of the materials and workmanship. Those two areas have undergone a lot of rationalization in recent years and there is now a vast range between the more basic models and chests of drawers of real quality workmanship. How do you go about assessing the quality of a chest of drawers? My first piece of advice is to pull out the drawers and take a look at what is not visible at first sight.

Anatomy of a chest of drawers

A common mistake made by first-time buyers is to judge a chest of drawers by its bodywork – that is, by the shape and material of its outside and top surface. What a chest of drawers looks like is, of course, not unimportant, but how well it will serve you in your everyday life will usually be determined by how it is constructed on the inside.

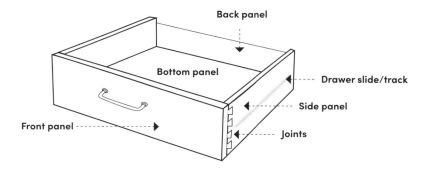

Front panel or drawer front

The front part of the drawer is usually known as the front panel. It is often the thickest part of the drawer so that any fittings and knobs can be attached there and also to make it more pleasant to open. Having the weight at the front rather than the back makes the drawer easier to open. A chest of drawers may have sophisticated fronts of various kinds and this can give you clues as to the quality and crafts-manship of the piece. In *Stora snickarboken* (The Big Book of Carpentry) the three most common types are called:

A. Inset front (complicated)
B. Rebated front (simpler)
C. Overlay front (simpler)

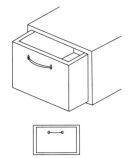

Inset

There is little room for error with the inset drawer front. It demands a well-constructed carcass of good-quality wood in order to avoid any sagging, uneven opening and drag in the construction of the drawer. This is the only type of drawer that can have dovetailed corners. You can read more about different sorts of joints in the section on materials. The gaps around the drawer front must be identical in width and as even and straight as possible.

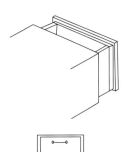

Rebated

Seen from the front, a rebated drawer is visually similar to a inset drawer front. At a quick glance they may look the same, but since this is a simpler version of an overlay front – which is less demanding in terms of precision – a manufacturer can get away with some imperfection in the construction. Not until you open the drawer, however, will you become aware of that.

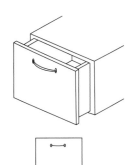

Overlay

The overlay drawer front is the simplest variety. The front of the drawer overlaps the sides completely and thus minimizes any chance of manufacturing imperfections being visible. It is impossible to dovetail a drawer of this type.

Bottom panel

The bottom panels of the drawers in chests of drawers can be of various quality. Since a bottom panel of solid wood is liable to shrink and to swell, a more complicated drawer construction is then needed to take account of expansion, which is why bottom panels are usually made of sheet material such as plywood or Masonite (see p. 252). A bottom panel of 6-millimetre plywood is the perfect quality for an average-sized drawer.

Older bottom panels of the type that are glued or nailed to the bottom of the drawer are problematical in that they may buckle and develop cracks as a result of their construction not allowing for changes in the wood.

Back panel

As a consequence of mass production, the back and front sides of furniture have become more and more different. Money is simply not spent on what cannot be seen and, consequently, many chests of drawers use thinner ply and poorer quality wood at the back. The same thing applies to drawers, so always pull them out and examine them before you buy. Ideally speaking, the back panel of a drawer should be slightly lower than the front in order to allow air to circulate within the chest of drawers.

Drawer slides

Drawers usually slide in and out on slides in grooves or on extendable metal slides mounted either on the side of the drawer or under it. Remember to examine them for quality. The drawers will run more easily if the slide is made of harder wood (beech, for instance). Read more in the section on, 'overtravel arms' on page 163.

During the 1950s, NK-bo launched a design of drawer with a guiding bottom panel. It is still called the NK-drawer. In the instructional manual used at Carl Malmsten's Capellagården these drawers are called Half French when the bottom is made of solid wood and NK when the bottom is plywood. NK-drawers are suitable for deeper units since the bottoms keep their shape. You can read more about NK-bo in the timeline in Chapter 8.

CHESTS OF DRAWERS TERMINOLOGY

Tallboy or seven-day chest of drawers

A tall chest of drawers with seven drawers is usually known in English as a tallboy or high boy, whereas its more common everyday name in Swedish seems to be seven-day chest of drawers. The name 'boy' comes from the French word 'bois', meaning 'wood', with the pronunciation anglicized to 'boy'. It often looks as if it is two chests with one placed on top of the other and, traditionally, the lower part tends to be slightly larger.

2 over 3

A chest of drawers with wide drawers in the lower part and one or two rows of smaller drawers at the top. This makes it possible to store both bulky and smaller articles in a functional way. There are a number of variations, but 2 over 3 explains the principle.

3 + 3

A wider chest of drawers with two parallel sections of three drawers each with a one-piece top surface.

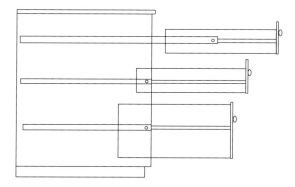

How far can the drawers be pulled out? Extension slides with an overtravel arm always have a stop, whereas it is not possible to stop drawers on wooden slides in the same way: these are usually stopped by a piece at the back, which means that part of the drawer will always remain within the body of the chest.

How far will a drawer pull out?

A point that's easy to miss, especially when buying a chest of drawers on the internet, is to see how far the drawers can be pulled out. If they are deep, drawers that only pull out to three-quarters are limiting in that you have to grope around to get at things that are far back. Full pull-out means that the whole drawer can be slid forward, whereas drawers with extendable overtravel arms can be pulled forward so that they stand clear of the body of the chest. When drawers are pulled out, they may alter the point of balance of the chest of drawers, so how does it feel with the drawers pulled forward? Is it still stable, or does it wobble and become unsteady, with a risk of tipping forward? Do the metal parts rattle and squeal? Is the drawer stop a soft-closure type or does it stop suddenly?

Space and grazing your knuckles

If you've ever had to rescue something that's slipped down between the drawers, you'll know what it feels like to bark your knuckles when trying to reach whatever it is that's disappeared into the innards of the chest of drawers. Should this happen, are the drawers easy to take out, or are you left with no choice but force your hand in and try to get hold of the offending article?

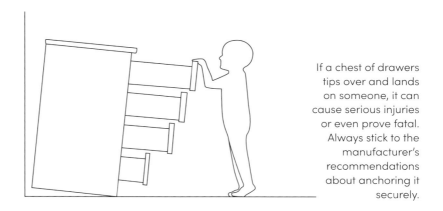

If a chest of drawers tips over and lands on someone, it can cause serious injuries or even prove fatal. Always stick to the manufacturer's recommendations about anchoring it securely.

Secure anchorage and the risk of tipping

It's impossible to over-emphasize the importance of anchoring chests of drawers to the wall. Always! The principle of levers shows that it doesn't take very much to pull a chest of drawers off balance.

By pulling out one or more drawers in a chest, you alter the point of balance, thus increasing the risk of the chest tipping over and causing serious harm to adults or children. So it's important to anchor chests of drawers to the wall using special brackets. (And make sure you stick to whatever special instructions are given for your particular chest.) Remember that different walls take different fixings – choose those that are most suitable to the circumstances, so that the chest is anchored as securely as it needs to be from the point of view of safety. The handles on chests and low pieces of furniture are tempting to small children who are learning to walk as they provide something easy to catch hold of and pull themselves up on. But even the body weight of a child can affect the point of balance and potentially create a death trap.

The type of furniture constructed of lightweight materials with thin and even lighter back panels is at greater risk of tipping forward when the drawers are full, but even solid wood chests of drawers should be anchored. You should also think about the surface the piece is standing on: a chest of drawers is more likely to become unstable and unbalanced if it is standing on an uneven floor.

Measuring your space

A common mistake is to estimate the space needed for an item of furniture when it is not being used and thus forgetting to measure the space needed for a human body using the dresser and opening the drawers. For instance, when you open the top drawer you actually need a different amount of space than when you open the bottom drawer.

It is also important to check that drawers can be fully opened without hitting fixed items like windowsills and wall sockets.

Have you left enough room? Don't just measure the chest as a static object: check the height and position of the drawers when they are pulled out and the position of your own body when using the lower drawers.

What is the chest of drawers standing on?

Do the drawers stick or can you see that the spaces between the drawers and the surrounding carcass of the chest varies? That may not necessarily have anything to do with the construction of the chest. If it's not standing on a flat surface, a chest may get lopsided with time. Check that all the screws are properly tightened and so on before you consider lodging complaints about things that don't seem to be working as they should.

Tips when buying a chest of drawers

- Do the drawers line up when you look at them from the side? The drawers in lower quality chests can sometimes be uneven when they are closed.

- Check whether the drawers glide freely or whether they catch when you pull them out. Remember that this might well change when the drawers are full rather than empty – if they jam or feel stiff in the shop, take it as a warning sign. And remember to check the opening of all the drawers, not just one of them. That's particularly important when buying an older wooden chest of drawers as even well-designed pieces may warp and go out of shape over time as a result of humidity and dryness.

- Does the drawer open with just one hand or do you need to pull evenly with two hands to prevent it opening lopsidedly?

- Will the drawer pull out fully or does part of the drawer remain in the carcass of the chest? That will determine how easy it is to get at things in the drawer and affect what you decide to store in it. Depending on your individual needs, that may or may not be important, but it's worth checking anyway rather than being caught out later.

- Do the drawers have a stop mechanism or can you pull them right out of the chest? Older chests in particular frequently lack a stop mechanism and that, in combination with sticky drawers that take a hefty tug to open, can lead to you ending up standing there with the whole drawer in your arms!

- How much noise do the drawers make when you close them? Some chests of drawers have soft-closure mechanisms whereas others slam shut, causing the whole chest to rattle. You can't see that in an illustration, but it's worth checking, especially if you are buying a chest you know you'll be opening and closing many times a day.

- Soft closure also minimizes the risk of getting your fingers pinched.

- Check whether there are dust panels between the drawers. They protect anything you are storing in the drawer from getting rubbed or caught by the drawer above.

- What does the interior of the drawer look like? This is particularly important if you are buying an older piece of furniture as the wood can scratch and damage clothing and anything else you keep in the drawer.

- The top surface needs to be much more resistant to wear than the moving parts and may be susceptible to damage from sharp objects placed on it. Or to damp stains left by bowls and vases.

- How thick are the front panels of the drawers? This might affect your choice of handles, should you want to change them in the future.

DID YOU KNOW?

Manufacturers of quality furniture take great care when choosing woods or veneers in order to ensure that the front panels on all the rows of drawers match each other. It is an enormously time-consuming task for the cabinetmakers, but the end result is something very special. The cost involved in doing this is not always taken into consideration when comparisons are being made between mass-produced furniture and authentic, craftsman-made furniture.

Bookshelves

There was a time when bookshelves were a given in Swedish homes, but the march of digitalization has meant that printed books have been pushed aside by other priorities when it comes to shelving. This section would, perhaps, better be titled Shelving Systems without beating about the bush, but so as to avoid the risk of confusion with other more anonymous storage solutions, I've decided to retain the word bookshelves. What follows will provide you with some important considerations to have in mind when approaching the purchase of bookshelves, or shelves mounted on brackets or, indeed, shelving in general.

Load capacity

When considering any unit intended to carry heavy objects, load capacity will inevitably be one of the decisive factors. How much weight will a shelf support without sagging or, worse still, ripping itself off the wall? It's estimated that the eye will notice a shelf sagging by as little as 8 millimetres, but what the eye perceives is just one aspect of why load capacity is so important – the safety aspect should, of course, be a much higher priority. You don't want your books and other heavy possessions crashing to the floor, breaking themselves and destroying anything they meet on the way.

The load that a shelf will bear depends partly on the material the shelf is made of and partly on how it is attached. By using more secure ways of attaching the shelves to end panels rather than just hanging them on simple plugs or metal pins, a much greater load capacity can be achieved. The whole set-up follows the general principle that 'the more craftsmanship there is, the more pleasing it is to the eye'.

Generally speaking, shelves that are shallower and thicker will support more weight than those that are deeper and thinner. A shelf made of laminated chipboard is less strong than solid wood, but different types of wood also vary in strength. Pine, for instance, is weaker than ash and oak.

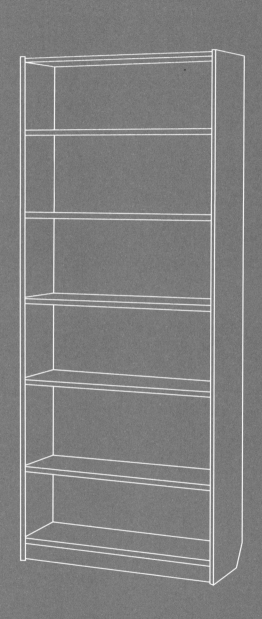

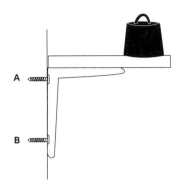

Shelves on brackets

Brackets are the usual way of mounting a freestanding shelf with no end panels. To provide proper support, the upper leg of the bracket should be two-thirds of the depth of the shelf. The deeper the shelf and the heavier the items you want to place on it, the longer the lower leg of the bracket on the wall should be. A bracket's weakest point is the upper attachment at point (a) and you can cut down the leverage effect by increasing the distance to the lower attachment at point (b).

Supporting bar

By using a horizontal supporting bar to spread the weight over a bigger area, the load capacity of a shelf unit will be increased. This brilliant innovation was used in HSB kitchens as early as the 1920s and had something of a renaissance in the 1990s when the Swedish company Norrgavel, building on the HSB principle, launched its bracketed shelf system with a supporting spar.

Systems with rails

There are many shelving systems on the market and, at first glance, they may look similar, but there are marked differences when it comes to quality and strength. Low-price suppliers are frequently criticized for their models being more time-consuming to attach. My advice to you is that you choose a shelving system that has been around a long time and is likely to remain in the future: that makes it possible for you to expand your system by adding further parts as and when you need them.

A storage system with rails attached to the wall can be combined with shelves on brackets, but also with wire baskets, clothes rails and other accessories.

Shelf depth and estimating the necessary space

How much space you need to reckon on for books (always assuming you still have books) will depend on the kind of books – hardbacks, paperbacks and so on – you want to keep on different shelves. There can be great variation in the external measurement and size of books depending on their height, width and extent. If the shelving is fixed and impossible to adjust, it would make sense to measure up the books you have at home to check on how many shelf metres of literature you actually need to have room for. The following are some guidelines to bear in mind. Don't forget that you need to allow a couple of centimetres between the top edge of the book and the shelf above so that you don't bang your knuckles every time you go to take out a book.

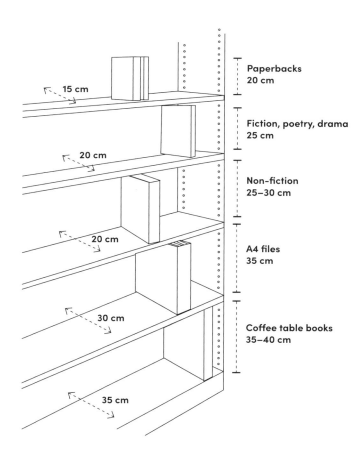

15 cm

20 cm

20 cm

30 cm

35 cm

Paperbacks
20 cm

Fiction, poetry, drama
25 cm

Non-fiction
25–30 cm

A4 files
35 cm

Coffee table books
35–40 cm

Size and width

How tall the bookcase or shelving system you should go for is a matter of taste, but it's also a matter of available space and any relevant human considerations. It is also essential to remember any wall fixtures, such as ventilation grilles, window ledges and wall sockets. The following are a few key measurements to keep in mind:

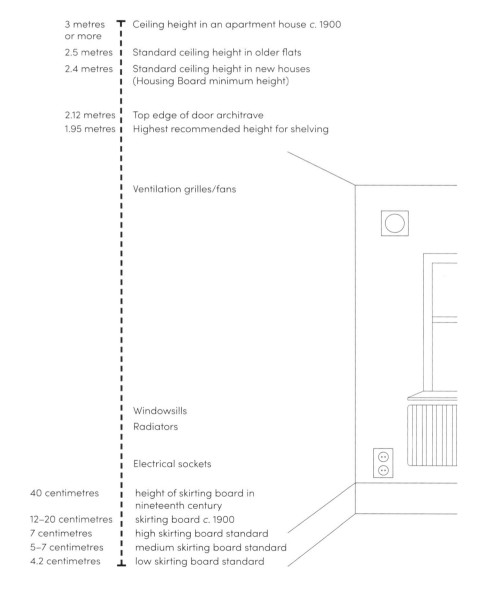

3 metres or more	Ceiling height in an apartment house *c.* 1900
2.5 metres	Standard ceiling height in older flats
2.4 metres	Standard ceiling height in new houses (Housing Board minimum height)
2.12 metres	Top edge of door architrave
1.95 metres	Highest recommended height for shelving
	Ventilation grilles/fans
	Windowsills
	Radiators
	Electrical sockets
40 centimetres	height of skirting board in nineteenth century
12–20 centimetres	skirting board *c.* 1900
7 centimetres	high skirting board standard
5–7 centimetres	medium skirting board standard
4.2 centimetres	low skirting board standard

Height of legs

In order to clean under a bookcase, you need to have space to reach in with a vacuum cleaner or mop. The appearance of cleaning equipment has changed along with technology, but for many years the recommendations for the amount of free space under cupboards has been 20 centimetres for cupboards that are 50 centimetres deep and a minimum of 15 centimetres for cupboards 35 centimetres deep. Don't forget that you will need free space in front of the bookcase, space both for you and the vacuum cleaner to move in and so that you can open cupboards, drawers and lids without knocking into other furniture.

Built-in bookcases

Many people think that constructing a built-in bookcase is a simple matter: all too often, however, the apparently simplest tasks turn out to be the most difficult.

Getting the right proportions for a bookcase is not just about its carrying capacity, but also about achieving a harmonious rhythm and balance in terms of its positioning. You don't want a bespoke piece of furniture to look as if it's been added as an afterthought, you want it to fit in as a natural and seamless element of the architecture of the house. And since it may, in its turn, change the proportions of the room, it could lead to extra work with fixtures and fittings such

DID YOU KNOW?

When the Furniture Institute was active, it recommended that the shelving in bookcases and cupboards should be moveable every other centimetre in order to make for more flexible storage. That idea is still current, which is why many bookcases provide so many holes at the side. If these perforations annoy you, you can buy special plugs – usually plastic – to cover them and to hide them as far as possible.

as ceiling roses and lighting. These are details that are obvious to professional craftsmen but easily overlooked by the inexperienced.

Many people choose to have closable cupboards as the lower sections of bookcases in order to avoid getting fluff balls among the books. If you do this, it is important to achieve an appropriate balance between the upper and lower parts of the bookcase so as to avoid an overheavy, clumsy appearance. Skewed proportions can easily create the feeling that the whole room is toppling over. These are the kinds of things an experienced joiner takes account of, whereas they may not occur to the first-timer – something that only becomes obvious in the finished job.

These days, it's popular to build the TV and entertainments system into a shelving unit. If you do so, I would recommend that you check the size of the technical equipment to ensure there is sufficient space for air to circulate and for the heat generated to exit via, for instance, a louvre above and below.

You should also leave a small margin around all the equipment and avoid constructing any parts of the shelving unit too close around your current TV screen – this is for the simple reason that you may want to change the TV in the future. The longevity of the technical equipment is likely to be shorter than that of the bookcase.

Remember, too, that good cables are expensive, so allow enough space for them not to be twisted in tight kinks against the back of the unit.

TIP!

Is there a wall you are considering turning into a bookcase? Use masking tape to help you with the planning. Mark out with tape the size and shape of the bookcase you are thinking of and test out different spacings between the shelves and other built-in elements to make it easier for you to visualize the final result.

A SWEDISH SHELVING CLASSIC

STRING SHELVING® has been a feature of ordinary Swedish homes since the 1950s, thanks to Bonnier, the publishing company. In 1949 Bonnier, together with the Swedish Crafts Association, announced a competition calling for Swedish designers to come up with a bookcase that fulfilled a number of specific demands: functional, smart, simple to pack down and timeless in design.

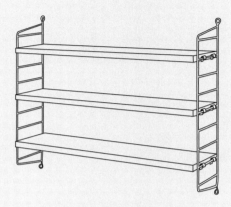

NISSE AND KAJSA STRINNING, a husband and wife team who got together while studying architecture at the Royal Institute of Technology in Stockholm, sent in their entry and emerged the winners. At first, their shelving system was called BFB shelving (Bonniers Folk Library Bookcase), but it soon changed its name to String®, inspired by the couple's surname and the name of their family farm – Strinningen in Härnösand. It marked the start of the brand and the development of the String® shelving system, which has enriched homes in Sweden and worldwide ever since.

NISSE GOT THE IDEA OF COATED WIRE PANELS from a spot-welded wire dish-rack he'd produced as an apprentice piece while at the Institute. It's said that the flash of inspiration that led to having wall-mounted side panels instead of built-in shelves came to him in a flash while musing on the toilet. Kajsa further developed the shape and is the designer behind the softly rounded details.

In 1962 the String® concept was patented and, at a stroke, thirty-two plagiarizing manufacturers had to stop production.

IN 2005 NISSE STRINNING designed a bookcase specifically for paperbacks. It has shelves 15 centimetres deep and is called String Pocket. Nowadays, the String system has expanded and there are many different units of many colours and materials, all of which may be combined in endless ways.

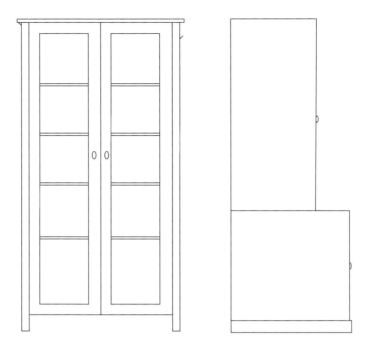

Display cabinets

Display cabinets get their Swedish name *vitrinskåp* from the Latin *vitrum* = glass/pane of glass. It's the glass element that distinguishes this type of cabinet from other cupboards with doors or hatches. The glass sections might be made up of mirrors in some parts of the front, or all of it, and the sides will be covered or glazed. The glass can be clear or frosted, smoked or etched.

For reasons of safety, it's important that you check that the glass is toughened. You'll find more about toughened glass in the section on materials. If the panes in normally priced furniture are made of ribbed glass, it is unlikely to be toughened glass, since the manufacture of toughened glass of that structure is inordinately expensive. If you have children or pets in your household, I cannot over-emphasize the importance of safety above style.

The advantage of display cabinets rather than closed cupboards is that they give the room an airier feel, while allowing you a good view of what you are keeping in them and simultaneously protecting the contents from dust and particles. That, in turn, makes cleaning easier. And having glass doors in front of motley groups of books and other bits and pieces tends to calm the visual impressions and create a more coherent feel.

Shelving, depth and spacing

A display cabinet used for storing china doesn't really need to be any deeper than the dishes you want to keep in it, though a little extra room is always good to have. Weight and load limitations usually stop you having two rows of dishes on a shelf, which means that there will be a great deal of empty and unused space if the shelving is too deep. Some display cabinets and bookcases have different depths of shelf, starting with narrow shelves at the top and down to eye level, while the shelves from waist level down are twice as deep. The optimum spacing between shelves depends on what you intend to keep on them. Here are a few points to think about, particularly in the case of shelves that are not adjustable.

- Too much vertical distance between shelves leaves far too much space that is unusable.
- Too small a distance can make it hard to reach things without knocking into the shelf above and either grazing your knuckles or breaking the stem of a wine glass. Make sure that you measure the glasses you own and ensure there is some space between them and the shelf above, as well as seeing that they have enough room not to brush against each other and consequently get chipped, damaged or broken.
- If you are planning on storing stacks of china in the cupboard, check the maximum weight load of the shelf. Modern manufacturers usually include this in the product description.
- Unless the door frames of display cabinets are solid and stable, they have a tendency to shudder after you open or close the door or when someone clumps heavily past.

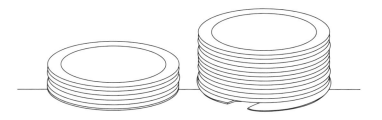

Remember not to stack plates too high. There's a limit to the amount of weight chinaware will take and you don't want the bottom plates to crack.

Cupboard smell

Older display cabinets have had a long life and may smell accordingly. That is not always immediately apparent when you're bidding for a handsome cabinet at an auction sale. Champagne glasses and wine glasses may pick up the smell and that may affect the taste of the drink.

Sick glass

Always make sure that you dry your glasses thoroughly before you put them away in the cupboard, otherwise older glass, in particular, might show signs of what's known as glass disease. Sick glass is a chemical reaction that can arise if the glasses haven't been thoroughly dried after washing and are then placed bottom up so that condensation can form within them. They develop a milky white haze that is impossible to get rid of.

Glasses may differ in height and width. Carefully measure and match what you have to the cupboard/shelf, so that you get the space for everything you need.

Advice on the purchase of display cabinets

- If the producer has skimped on the back panel and made it of a lighter material, the display cabinet is likely to be slightly front-heavy when both doors are open and the cabinet is empty.

- Check that the hinges are firm and there is no risk of them sagging. As the doors often weigh quite a lot, after a while they may start hanging off-centre and showing a gap unless the manufacturer has used really strong fittings. Even on good quality furniture, it may be necessary to tighten the screws holding the hinges after a while.

- Display cabinet doors with very thin frames tend to be rather flimsy and they shudder as you close them. Test them by opening and closing the doors a number of times to see how they behave and what they sound like. If they are very wobbly, small furniture cups may minimize the vibrations to some extent.

- Is the door closure strong enough? A common complaint about cheaper display cabinets is that the magnet gets weak and the doors begin to show a gap or even drift open after a while.

TIP!

Before the introduction of standardization for the dimensions of cabinet and module frames in the middle of the twentieth century, the usual way of testing the size of a storage cabinet before purchase was simply to see if it could hold all the chinaware you possessed. That idea still holds good, though nowadays the quantity of china is likely to vary more than the depth of the cabinet. There can be no doubt that dishes have substantially increased in size during recent decades and there is much variation in the sizes of bowls, basins and jugs.

Sideboards

Sideboard is actually an English word that has now become so much the accepted term in Swenglish that it is used by customers, suppliers and retailers alike.

The sideboard, as a category of furniture, includes a wide variety of low storage and side cabinets with or without covered cupboard doors or drawers. There are numerous different types to choose from, and what is likely to determine your choice – apart from the size of your room and the space you have available in relation to the rest of your furniture – is the size of what you intend to keep in it. Sideboards and buffet tables can vary a good deal in breadth, but they can also vary in depth, so there is a risk you might choose one so shallow and neat that it won't swallow all your china and your bowls – or that vase that won't fit into the kitchen cupboard either. So, before you decide, always measure up everything you are intending to keep in the cabinet, not just the surface area of where you'll put things. If you choose a model with folding doors, less space is needed around it when you are reaching for the contents, and sliding doors take up no room at all. If the sideboard has adjustable feet, you can easily make allowances for uneven floors.

There are also some module-based systems that allow you – the customer – to combine different units to create a finished piece that matches your particular needs. And in that case you can also choose the colour and whether you want to stand the finished piece on a pedestal, on a variety of legs, or have it mounted on the wall to give a lighter feel (and easier cleaning!).

A VITAL PIECE OF FURNITURE!

If we go back in history, right back to the fifteenth century, the buffet table or credenza was reputed to be the place where the servants tasted the food to check for poison before serving it. The name derives from the Italian word *credenza*, meaning 'trust' or 'confidence'.

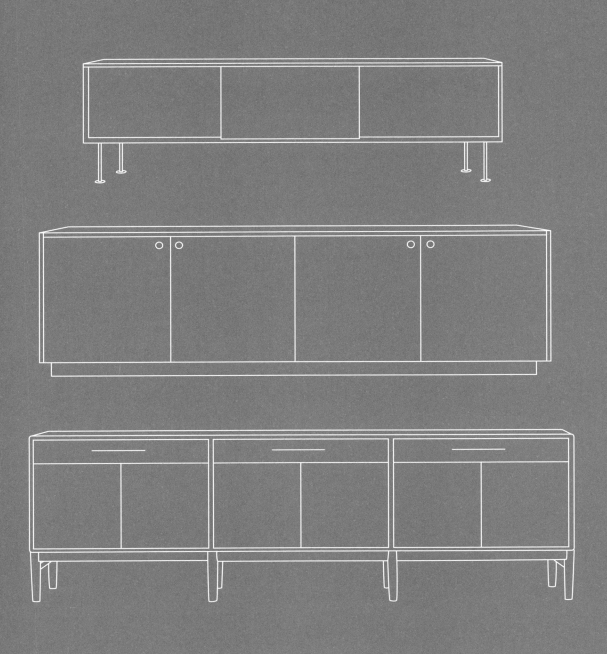

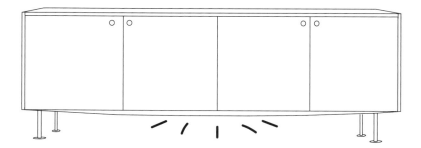

A long sideboard needs supporting legs at mid-point to lessen the risk of sagging when you have filled it with your things. The middle leg can be hidden away at the back, so that it doesn't spoil the appearance from the front.

Checking for problems

If you have a particularly wide sideboard it is likely to need one or more extra legs at midpoint to prevent the frame sagging under the load.

If you decide that the place for your buffet table is close to the dining area, it's thought best for it to be some 10 centimetres higher than the dining table, as it can then be more easily used for serving. Moreover, that also creates a better balance in terms of layout. There also needs to be enough free space left in front of the buffet table for its doors to open, otherwise those sitting at the table will have to stand up whenever they want to fetch something from the cupboard.

When buying your sideboard or buffet table online, always check how many compartments the inside of the cabinet is divided into: the fewer the internal divisions, the more space there will be for larger items.

> **TIP!**
>
> Some businesses specialize in selling doors, cover panels and worktops for IKEA cabinet frames in order to allow you to add a personal touch to your sideboard. As a rule of thumb, the fewer modules you join together, the more stable the thing will be. If you want a sideboard 120 centimetres wide, then you should start with a 120-centimetre cabinet frame rather than two 60-centimetre modules.

Media cabinets

The role of electronics in our homes has grown enormously. The freestanding fat TV (often on wheels) quickly became thin and flat and began to be wall-mounted rather than standing on a table or cabinet. In addition to which, all the space we needed until recently to house video players, DVD players and TV games, can now be used for other things because all of that has moved online.

There are still many of us, however, who stick to the tradition of having a media cabinet in the living room. Media benches should have holes in the back panel, partly so that cables can easily be slipped through and partly to allow the air to circulate given that the equipment creates heat. When you measure the units you intend to keep in the media cabinet, don't forget to include the space needed for the attached cables and to ensure that the shelf is sufficiently deep to house them. The sliding doors on some media cabinets may have inside parts that can jam if they catch on protruding volume controls and regulators. A lot of people have ended up taking off the back panels of their media cabinets in order to have room for home cinemas and technological kit – mainly to make increased space for the cables rather than have them all pressed against the back panel. For similar reasons, and so that you're not stuck with fixed spaces, it's useful if the shelves are adjustable up and down and can also be taken right out of the cabinet.

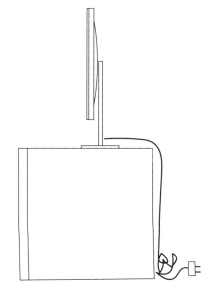

Since various types of media equipment generate heat when in use, it is sensible to ensure that the space it's kept in has ventilation holes so that hot air is not trapped, thus risking damage to the electronics. And if you are putting the equipment in a cabinet, check that the remote control works through the doors.

If you are going to place a TV on top of the cabinet, there are two further things worth checking: the first is the load-bearing capacity of the top surface; the second is the height of the TV screen in relation to the seating in front of it. By no means all manufacturers of media cabinets have given any thought to the full range of TV sets, so, in order to avoid accidents or top panels that sag and make the doors or hatches difficult to open, it's worth double-checking this before you order. The height of the TV is important as it should fit in with the height of the seating used when viewing. It's difficult to give any exact advice about this as it depends to some extent on the angle of the back of your sofa and armchairs, and on whether you and your family prefer to sit or to recline when watching films. It may seem banal to mention it, but it's frequently the case that one partner chooses the technology and the other the furniture, and the two of them don't talk to one another about it until they realize that the chosen combination is silly. Either that or the test-viewing is done in an upright position, which is hardly the way anyone ever watches TV. If that's how you do things, the problems will come later!

'The primary factor is all about proportions.'

Arne Jacobsen

When buying a shoe rack, think of the biggest pair of shoes the family has. Men's boots will take up more room than women's high heels not just because the soles of women's shoes are thinner but also because the heels add to height rather than length.

Hall furniture and coat racks

It doesn't matter whether it's a coat rack, hat shelf, coat stand or just hangers, the furniture that greets you when you come home or greets your visitors when they arrive and want to take off their outdoor coats and shoes in the hall should offer a welcoming smile rather than be the cause of scowls and irritation. Anyway, to judge from the thousands of product reviews I've read while writing this book, these seemingly simple bits of furniture nevertheless appear to be difficult to get right. What follows are some tips and advice about things to look out for and check before buying when you are hunting for nice but functional hall furniture.

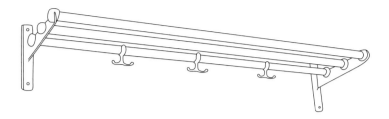

Load capacity

Hat and cap racks have a heavy job – literally. They have to support light summer clothes and thick outer garments, heavy winter jackets and substantial coats. A common complaint about hat shelves is that they collapse: that, of course, is at least partly the fault of the screws and wall plugs used to put them up but, surprisingly often, results from the construction and materials the shelves are made of. The principle of levers is what you have to remember when visually assessing any item with the task of supporting a vertical loading. If the distance between the upper wall fixing and the lower wall fixing is too short, the leverage effect will be great when you pile all the family outdoor jackets and helmets on the unit. The weight of the shelf itself must also be taken into account, especially if you know that your walls are weak, in which case it is not wise to choose a shelf that feels heavy even before you load it with clothes.

- If the rack or hat stand is made of wood, you should check for any knots, cracks or other faults that could potentially weaken the structure.
- If there are welded parts, check that the joints have been properly soldered, and also check the positioning of the screw holes and any other pre-drilled apertures that might result in weak points under load.
- Hat racks with metal rails tend to sound scratchier and noisier when you use wire coat hangers than racks with a wooden dowel rail. If you happen to be one of those people whose teeth are set on edge by small metallic screeches, this might be worth thinking about.

Attachment

The fact that the hat and coat rack in question does not have pre-drilled holes of the right size to take the type of screw necessary to mount it sufficiently firmly might seem a trivial one-off problem. On a daily basis, however, it can become a nuisance, leading to wobbly hat racks or, worse still, coat racks that fall off and break things. And holes that are much too small may end up causing cracks in the construction and possibly weakening it.

In the kind of situation where the fixing system cannot actually be seen when you are standing in front of the shelf, getting the shelf in the right position demands precision to the nearest millimetre. If the walls in your hall are of the awkward sort that make it impossible to get a screw into an exact position (or if you have expensive wallpaper), my advice would be to choose a coat or hat rack that can be screwed in from directly in front. That lessens the risk of making scratch marks or damaging the wall.

Fixed dimensions or flexibility?

All halls present challenges. Light switches, meter cupboards, inspection hatches and radiators can make furnishing difficult, so make sure you choose a coat rack flexible enough to be adjusted to the space you have and to the clothes you are likely to hang on it. Something as simple as choosing a hat or coat rack with rails that can be cut or sawn makes it easier for you to make worthwhile adjustments.

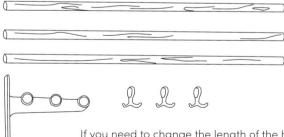

If you need to change the length of the hat and coat rack, you should choose one with steel or aluminium supports and wooden rods as wood is the easiest material to cut with an ordinary saw.

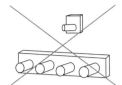

Size and angle of the hooks and knobs

Designing a coat rack might sound a trivial business, but the fact of the matter is that getting the size and angle of the hooks and knobs right demands precision unless you want your coats to get damaged, fall off or be difficult if not impossible to hang up. There is a reason for the knobs to be angled upwards: those that point straight out need a small stop attached, which is why they frequently have a bigger end piece.

If the hooks are too big or of the wrong size so that you can only hang your coat by the material or by the hood, it can easily get damaged, especially if it's a heavy coat or if you've left heavy things like keys or mobile phones in the pockets.

Dimensions

Something that only becomes obvious when your winter coats emerge is that hanging space in the hall is not always of the right dimensions to hold thick outdoor clothing. To avoid getting it wrong, you shouldn't just measure the width of the coat hanger but the width of the coat hanger (*c.* 45 centimetres) + 5 centimetres on each side for the shoulder width of the garment + 5 centimetres air space on the wall side. Other-

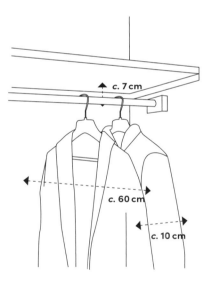

wise there will be a risk of one shoulder of the garment rubbing against the wall and suffering unnecessary wear or of the coat hanger swinging and making marks on the wall when you are taking the garment down. Also ensure that there is at least 7 centimetres space between the rail and the shelf immediately above so that you are able to lift the hanger without scratching the shelf. As every coat also needs about 10 centimetres hanging space, don't skimp on the length of the rail, especially if there are many of you in the family.

Check, too, that the wooden rails hold the hooks on the hangers firmly. If the rails are too thin, the hangers will tend to rock, whereas if the rails are too thick, it may be awkward to hook the hanger on when in a hurry.

Hat stands

Freestanding hat stands are sometimes known as hall trees or coat trees. To be considered good quality, the design and construction of coat trees has to be ingenious, with a low and carefully calculated centre of gravity able to deal with heavy coats hung up unevenly. When you hang coats and jackets on it, the extra load will alter the tree's centre of gravity, but as long as the loading remains within a vertical line that reaches the floor inside the tree's footprint (within the diameter of the leg stand), the coat tree will usually remain stable.

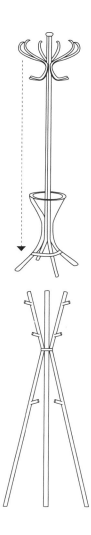

My parents had a very fine metal coat tree in their hall. We jokingly referred to it as the guillotine since it threatened to chop off the heads of any guests unaware of which hooks you could hang garments on and which could not be used. A coat tree laden with heavy winter coats can cause a lot of damage if it tips over, particularly if there are children or pets in the house.

Check the shape of the arms and the hooks. Can you and your guests hang up your coats without problems? Do they stay in place or is there a risk of them sliding off when the tree fills up with more coats? Is it easy to unhook your coats? The arms of my parents' tree had small stops at the end and, while these certainly prevented coats from sliding off, they also meant you had to stand there fumbling to take the coat off the hook without breaking its loop. Impatient to get away to training during my teenage years, I often tore things down, ripping the lining of the coat as a result.

The shape of the hooks on the coat tree, along with their positioning in relation to each other, can give you some idea of how many garments the tree can take and whether it's likely to be user-friendly.

Beds

Did you sleep well last night? Regardless of how you answer that question, how you feel about the quality of last night's sleep will influence your day. The quality of our sleep depends on many different factors, but few people would disagree with the fact that what we are sleeping on is really important. If we get a poor or mediocre night's sleep because of an uncomfortable bed, it will affect every aspect of our lives. But it's nice to know it's a problem that is relatively easy to deal with: with the help of the right mattress, and the support and comfort designed specifically for your body type.

Choosing a bed

Beds are a bit like running shoes: just because your neighbour is completely enamoured with a particular brand, it doesn't mean that they are guaranteed to suit you. Your shoe size may perhaps be different, but so may your stride, your height, weight and need to support the arch of your foot. And styles of sleeping can differ likewise, depending on your height, weight, physical shape and proportions.

So, what is important when you consider your present bed or decide on a new one? After all, buying a bed is a significant investment and my best advice to you is to get personal help from knowledgeable shop assistants. Some retailers go so far as to offer free advice sessions with a resident chiropractor. Even though this section can offer you some guidance on the important points to bear in mind as you set about sifting through the huge range of beds on offer, it cannot replace the invaluable help of an experienced individual who works in this area on a daily basis and wants to help you get a better night's sleep. What this chapter can do, however, is help clear your mind in advance of such a meeting, so that you are better informed and have given some thought to your sleeping habits and needs and can consequently get the most out of a consultation.

TIP!

Don't forget the pillow! Your choice of pillow can improve or spoil your night's sleep regardless of which bed you choose. Just as with the mattress, you should choose a pillow that suits your particular style of sleeping. The pillow is a key element in finding a good sleeping position.

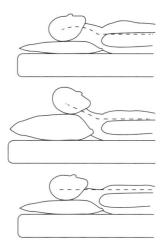

Swedish bed sizes

Bassinet = 45 x 70 centimetres

Cot = 60 x 120 centimetres

Toddler = 70 x 160 centimetres

Small single = 80 x 200/210 centimetres

Single (English twin bed) = 90 x 200/210 centimetres

Wider single = 105 x 200/210 centimetres

Wider single = 120 x 200/210 centimetres

Wider single (English double bed) = 140 x 200/210 centimetres

Small double (Queen size) = 160 x 200/210 centimetres

Standard double (King size) = 180 x 200/210 centimetres

Family bed = 210–360 x 200/210 centimetres

Bed sizes were standardized in Sweden in the 1950s in order to rationalize everything from bedclothes to bed frames. The size of the bedroom and the individual or individuals who'll be sleeping in it are, of course, the deciding factor when it comes to the size of the bed. Listed above are the most common bed dimensions.

Note that dimensions differ from one part of the world to another. For instance, a king-size bed in the USA is usually 193 x 203 centimetres compared with the king-size in Europe, which is 180 x 200. A standard Swedish double bed is called a California king bed in the USA, which is useful to know if you are buying bedclothes from an American source or are booking a hotel room abroad.

An average man has an elbow-to-elbow breadth of 97 centimetres when lying on his back with his arms held at a 90° angle, but we all sleep in different ways: on our tummies, on our sides, outstretched or curled up, so the choice of bed size usually involves everything from body size and sleeping position to the proportions of the room.

The standard length of bed is 200 centimetres, but if you or your partner are more than 190 centimetres, a bed size of 210 centimetres is recommended to allow you to sleep comfortably and to be able to put your arms around the pillow or stretch your legs without your feet sticking out of the end. A fun fact: when you lie on your tummy with your ankles outstretched, your feet take up considerably more room than when you lie on your back with your toes pointing up.

Height above the floor

In order to reach under the bed with the head of a vacuum cleaner and make for easier cleaning, there should be 17–23 centimetres clearance between bed and floor. The less space there is under the bed, the more you have to angle the vacuum cleaner down, which means you will need more room around the bed. (This depends, of course, on the type of vacuum cleaner you have, but it's an everyday issue that's easy to forget when you are focusing on the comfort of the bed and choosing between the aesthetic appeal of different possibilities.) For it to be reasonably easy to make the bed, the mattress height should not be too low – the usual recommendation is for a height around 55 centimetres. And it shouldn't be too high for you to sit on the edge of the bed to get dressed in the morning: you don't want it to be difficult to reach your feet and put your socks on, especially when you're a bit older and a little stiff. In the latter case, the usually recommended seat height for chairs (*c.* 45 centimetres) is preferable and that cuts out quite a few significantly higher continental beds.

Firmness

A good bed offers pressure relief and provides your body with ergonomic support. How firm your bed needs to be will depend on your weight, your physical shape and your sleeping position (i.e. the position you usually lie in when you sleep).

You should NOT be lying on top of the bed – that means it is too firm.

You should NOT be sinking into the bed – that means it is too soft.

You should be lying in the bed – that means it is pressure-relieving and just right.

Guidelines for body weight

Simply going on body weight when deciding on the firmness of the mattress is risky, as your weight on the scales doesn't offer any guidance as to how the weight is distributed around your body and where the relief should come when you are lying down. Many manufacturers and retailers do, however, take that as their starting point when selecting which beds you should try out. That's absolutely fine in a shop where you can actually test things out, but not so smart when you are ordering a bed online without having tried it first. The usual recommendation for anyone who weighs more than 115 kilos is to choose a firm or extra-firm mattress (preferably with a bed frame) as continental beds and softer versions can feel more unstable.

Pressure relief based on physical shape

It is also important to consider your physical shape when buying a bed. Two people of identical weight may need pressure relief in different places. If you know you are carrying most weight around the hips or on the upper body, a bed with targeted zones or a memory foam model might be an individualized answer. Avoid buying a bed when you are pregnant as what feels comfortable at that time probably won't do so once you have given birth.

Choice based on sleeping position

When choosing how firm your bed should be, last but not least, your usual sleeping position is a decisive factor. The same firmness will seem less comfortable depending on whether you sleep on your back, on your side, or on your front.

Do you sleep on your front? Choose a firm mattress that gives support and doesn't sag.

Do you sleep on your back? Choose a medium or firm mattress.

Do you sleep on your side? Also choose a medium or firm mattress.

From an ergonomic point of view, sleeping on your front is not considered ideal. There is, actually, a logic to this: after all, there are few occasions when you would feel comfortable with your head turned so far to the side that your chin almost touches your shoulder. And for eight hours! For most people it would be an unthinkable position in the workplace or even for a short time in the cinema.

If you sleep on your front and feel that it is causing problems for your neck and shoulders, you could try to get used to sleeping on your side instead. That is usually the easiest change to make, unless you can adapt to sleeping on your back straightaway. In this case you will need a bed that is not too hard at the hips and shoulders to help you get used to sleeping on your side – in what's known as the recovery position.

Worth thinking about?

Are our preferred sleeping positions – back, front or side – inborn or are they habits we just acquire, adjusting them to best adapt to our physical shape or to what we are lying on? I haven't managed to find any studies that answer that question with any certainty. Are our sleeping positions inborn or do we adjust them to best adapt to physical shape or to what we are lying on?

The distinction between firmness and softness

Don't confuse the hardness or support the bed gives you with the soft comfort of the surface. The support from the mattress your body needs in order to relieve pressure in the right places is not the same thing as you feeling that the top layer on which you are sleeping is either hard or soft. On the topmost layer closest to your body, most beds are pleasantly soft, but a lower layer that is too soft isn't good for the back and, after a while, you'll feel as if you've been sleeping in a hammock. So desirable firmness and surface softness are two different things.

The turning over test

Have you heard of the turning over test? If you can't turn over in bed easily and have to struggle, it probably means that your bed is too soft for you. If you wake up with a numb arm or shoulder (as long as there's no medical reason for it), it probably means your bed is too hard for you.

Future developments

Having to decide between hard beds and soft beds may not be such a major decision in the future as it is now, as new technology might offer the possibility of adjustable mattresses that suit the level of support to the current shape of the sleeping individual. Given that the body changes during pregnancy, for instance, or when you put on or lose weight, that would be a good development.

What's hiding inside a bed?

What is the actual difference between a cheaper bed and a more expensive one? It's difficult to tell with the naked eye since the innards of the bed are concealed by the mattress cover, but, in general, we can say that the more higher and better spring systems a bed has the more luxurious it is thought to be. The quality of these things depends on the materials they are made of, how many turns each coil has and how responsive it is to external pressure both in terms of weight and shape. The two main types are as follows:

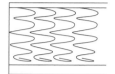

Bonnell spring

Bonnell sprung is the simplest type of springing. This type is the norm in cheaper beds, whereas in more expensive beds they usually sit at the bottom next to the wooden stretchers of the bed frame, to act as shock absorbers. Bonnell springing consists of spiral-shaped metal springs that are linked together and, since they are linked metal to metal, they sometimes make squeaking noises. From the point of view of durability, Bonnell springs perform better, relatively speaking, than many other more complicated spring systems since they are made of 100 per cent steel: currently, when it's time to dispose of the mattress, that makes it easier to separate for recycling, unlike spring systems that include other materials.

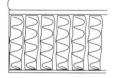

Pocket springs

Pocket sprung, as the name suggests, means that the springs are enclosed in bags or pockets that sit alongside each other. This means that each spring can move individually without affecting or becoming entangled with neighbouring springs. The bags are thin and breathable, which means that air can ventilate the bed. A normal double bed will have *c.* 1000 pocket springs and, if the bed has two layers of springs, there will be many more than that. In slightly cheaper pocket sprung beds the pouches are glued or welded together, whereas in more exclusive beds they are sewn. The fabric, gram weight and durability of the bags enclosing the coils also differs between the various price brackets and this may affect both the life expectancy of the bed and its environmental impact. The fabric that many bags are made of feels like cloth, but since natural fibres can't be bonded, it's often a type of non-woven fabric (PP fabric, polypropylene) or of polyurethane. If you want to be an environmentally conscious consumer, you might ask the retailer or producer of the bed you are thinking of buying what the bags in the bed are actually made from and which glue was used in the process.

Zone systems

Over and above the two main types, Bonnell and pocket, bed springs are divided into a whole series of different zones with a variety of names – progressive pocket sprung, chess-patterned sprung and active zones. The idea is that the bed becomes more flexible by adapting different parts of it to provide the variations in support needed based on body weight and physical shape. The shoulders and the hips, in particular, and sometimes the bust, are the parts that frequently differ most from the needs of the rest of the body.

The zoning technique means that the springs are distributed differently across different zones to provide varying levels of support from the foot end up to the head end. The most common types are 3 zone, 5 zone or 7 zone. This comfort and ergonomic benefit is available in sprung mattresses, divan bases, continental beds and adjustable beds.

The number of turns in a coil spring

How many turns do the coil springs have? Some producers have turned the choice of bed into a competitive sport by proclaiming the number of turns as if they were talking about the horsepower of a motor car: 'the more, the better'.

- 4.5–5 turns is standard in many of the beds at major stores.
- 6 turns is more usual in the specialist bed trade and in slightly pricier beds.
- 8 turns is uncommon but is available in the higher price range.

Mattresses are often advertised and rated according to the number of coil springs and the number of turns per spring. However, some of the suppliers I have talked to take the view that this is more of a marketing gimmick than a guarantee of comfort. Springs do suffer some degree of fatigue over time and it seems logical that the odd extra turn increases their durability, but there is no unanimity on the link between comfort and the number of turns per spring. The fact is that many of the premium Swedish manufacturers, who market their beds on customers' experience of comfort, do not put the same focus on the number of turns per spring, since there are many other factors that come into play to determine whether a bed is experienced as being comfortable or not.

And to take a different view – one that takes material resources into account – the more turns a spring has, the more steel is needed to produce it. If you want to be a conscious consumer, you ought perhaps be asking where the balance between maximum comfort, durability and consumption of material resources lies.

Padding

A sprung mattress is usually padded with various kinds of materials, both over and between the sprung layers. Alternatively, however, the mattress may have no metal springs at all and consist of plastic or wood fibre foams or other types of natural materials. The following are some of the sorts of padding commonly used.

Latex

It is important to make a distinction between natural latex (a product of rubber trees) and synthetic latex (a chemically produced product). The natural material is produced from the milky sap of the rubber tree (*Hevea brasiliensis*). It has a high degree of air permeability, which is good for those who get hot at night. It is also softer than polyurethane. Its ventilating properties contribute to a healthy and allergy friendly sleeping environment. Even though the content description may state that the latex in the bed is 100 per cent natural, that is not always the case, so you should always ask about the mix in the particular model you are looking at.

Cold foam

High resilience polyurethane has better elasticity than ordinary polyurethane (plastic foam). Cold foam and polyurethane are completely allergy neutral. Cold foam, as distinct from polyurethane, has a bigger and more irregular cell structure, which means that its elasticity is superior to pure polyurethane.

Foam rubber/polyurethane

Plastic foam is a collective term for several different types of cellular plastic, particularly polyurethane (polyurethane plastic foam). Polyurethane has good mechanical resistance and has elasticity. Products made of polyurethane tend to be very resistant to wetness and to sweat. On the other hand, it has low tear strength and is sensitive to sunlight. The material is also less good at following the movement of the springs than, for instance, latex.

Memory foam

A viscose-elastic material with a cellular structure of 100 per cent flexible polyurethane that absorbs pressure. It was launched with the brand name TEMPUR 1991®. Since then, many suppliers have attempted to create similar products commonly referred to as memory foam, but – just like the recipe for a world-renowned soft drink – there is only one original recipe. When you lie down, the heat of your body softens the material and makes it adapt to every curve and to support those parts of your body that need it most. It provides individualized pressure relief for your body. Memory foam must always be placed on a ventilated base, such as springs, slats or a base on legs or wheels, so that air can circulate freely underneath and prevent any build-up of moisture. The material is heat-sensitive and, consequently, you shouldn't use a mattress topper but simply lay the sheets directly on the mattress. For reasons of hygiene, however, the use of a mattress protector is recommended. And for reasons of heat, you should also avoid electric blankets or hot water bottles. NOTE! Do not leave babies, small children or the elderly unattended on memory foam mattresses or pillows unless they are capable of turning over or moving of their own accord.

Horsehair

Horsehair consists of long, coarse strands of hair from the mane and tails of horses or from the tails of ruminants. It is a hygroscopic material. Each strand functions as a miniature airway: a hollow tube that channels moisture away and allows fresh air to enter. It is so efficient that if you submerge horsehair in water and then shake it a little, it will dry almost instantly.

Wool

The wool that is used in beds usually comes from sheep: it is an elastic fibre with a structure that traps a large volume of air between the fibres. This is what gives wool its heat-insulating properties, as well as its flexibility, elasticity and resilience. Wool can absorb up to 30 per cent of its own weight in water without feeling wet. The two symbols below denote wool.

 Woolmark (new wool). Indicates that the wool content is new, clean and fulfils certain standards of quality and purity. A 5 per cent mixture of other materials is permitted for decorative and technical purposes.

 Wool Blend (fibre mixture). Indicates that the wool content contains at least 60 per cent pure, new wool. The fibre mixture will be stated alongside the mark.

Recycled wool, also known as 'shoddy', is frequently mixed with new fibres.

Natural fibres

There are also mattresses that are wholly or partly filled with various kinds of natural fibres such as sisal, vegetable fibres and coconut fibre. Coconut fibre combined with natural rubber produces rubber-ized coir, which is a material that will support the body, but is also springy, elastic and comfortable.

A good conscience is the best pillow?

Not only mattresses but pillows, too, can be filled with materials that, unlike polyurethane and foam, are not petroleum-based. You can find pillows that are filled with natural rubber, natural latex, camel hair, cotton, lamb's wool or millet husks, to name just a few alternatives. They are certainly worth thinking about if you are keen on using natural materials.

A bucket of sweat per person per night?

Has it ever occurred to you that your body doesn't only breathe through the mouth? Everyone has about six million pores that respire and remove poisons from the body day and night. We are said to sweat up to one and a half litres a night. If we are to stay dry and comfortable through eight hours of sleep, it is really important that air can circulate around us. A piece of clothing made of some synthetic material can quickly feel sticky and sweaty against the skin on a hot summer's day, compared with a cotton or linen, which have a natural ability to wick away the moisture. The materials in your bed and in the bedclothes you choose work in the same way. That is definitely worth thinking about when choosing mattresses and pillows, bedsheets and pyjamas. And also washable mattress protectors to go between the mattress and the sheet make for easy hygiene.

Never make a damp bed

Natural materials are biodegradable, which means that, with use, they can return to nature, to the earth. And since they are natural, they may be attacked by mould and insects. So remember to allow the bed to dry properly before you make it, rather than shut the moisture in. Mites, too, flourish in places that are warm and damp.

Mattresses

Bed platforms

With older beds and more basic models, you start with the platform. What is the mattress going to lie on? Wooden platforms are most common, but older beds may have zigzag springs, also called Nozag springs, steel straps or various kinds of perforated sheets of wood or metal strips.

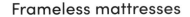

Frameless mattresses

The simplest type of bed is a frameless mattress placed straight on the base. This is usually made of foam or latex material (rubber), but may also consist of pocket springs and memory foam. There are also mattresses made of natural materials, in which the harder core consists of, for instance, rye, hemp, horsehair or coconut fibre with a softer filling of natural rubber, cotton and/or wool. It's important to remember that even organic materials may contain residual elements of pesticides and the like, so you should check carefully that the mattress you are buying, whatever sort it may be, has been allergy-tested and eco-labelled.

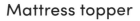

Mattress topper

Regardless of the type of bed you choose, it's usual to lay a topper over it. Toppers are normally 3–5 centimetres thick with a core of foam or latex material (rubber) and a thin covering of fibre material. The cover is often quilted/stitched on, but there are also detachable types that are machine-washable. If the bed is used every night, the usual recommendation is for the topper to be replaced every five years or so. If you turn the topper regularly and air it, it will last longer and you will lessen the risk of it settling.

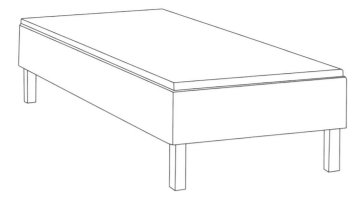

Box-spring beds

This type of bed has the mattress and the spring base in one, which means that legs can be fitted directly to the bed or it can be placed on a bed frame. There are different sorts of springing and they offer differing levels of pressure relief. These beds are usually lighter and neater, which makes them easier to move, and they also take up less space in the room which, if your bedroom is small and narrow, gives the room an airier feel. Slatted bases increase the durability and comfort of spring or foam or latex mattresses by absorbing and distributing your weight on the bed.

When beds are tested in the laboratory, the levels of support and firmness of the bed are not the only things tested: the risk of settling – that is, changes in firmness both over time and as a result of harsh treatment (such as small children using the bed as a trampoline) – is a measure of quality. Cast a critical eye over the tests the manufacturers refer to: were they carried out independently or were they chosen and performed by the manufacturers themselves?

TIP!

Japanese-inspired futon beds (*shikibuton*), with a mattress laid on a low wooden structure, are seen more and more often in Scandinavian interior design magazines. The base of the futon may be as little as 20 centimetres above the floor. Cool! But does it work in terms of the proportions of your room and the way you live?

Continental beds

This type of bed consists of three layers: the base, a spring mattress and the top pad. This means that continental beds are higher than most standard beds and consequently occupy more space in the room. As long as the size and proportions of the room are suitable, they can seem impressive and exclusive. The major practical advantage is that you can choose different levels of firmness for different parts of the bed. This is perfect for those buying a double bed for two people with differing needs for comfort, or for anyone whose body needs differing levels of support and relaxation on different parts of the mattress.

In some versions of the continental bed the middle mattress has a removable top layer that makes it possible to adjust the firmness as you grow older, if your body or your needs change.

There is a widespread misconception that all continental beds are double. That is not the case – they also come as single beds with the following sizes: 80, 90, 105, 120 and 140 centimetres.

A double bed (160–210 centimetres) offering different levels of firmness on different sides of the bed so that a couple can each have individualized comfort can be achieved in two ways – with very different final results.

- Continental beds in price classes of roughly up to £1,500 usually have two 'cassettes' of springs, that are concealed under the fabric of the middle mattress. The supplier has a stock of pre-produced cassettes that can quickly be selected to suit the firmness the customer wants. So, superficially, it looks like a whole mattress, but it will nevertheless have a join between the beds (cassettes) in the double bed.

- In beds costing £1,500 and over, however, the whole mattress is often factory-made with the firmness on each side of the bed bespoke for what the customer desires. This avoids having a hard edge/join down the middle of the bed that many people find annoying. This is, without any doubt, the biggest difference between the continental beds: you will get a double bed without a join, but one that still provides the correct level of firmness for both people, and it comes in a form that can be taken up the stairs or got into the lift. Contrary to what many people think, it is easier to move these large continental beds than spring beds, since the large mattress is foldable and bendable. The option of having individual levels of firmness is also available in some spring beds, but their format makes them much more difficult to handle.

TIP!

If you are a couple buying a double bed together, test it by both lying on it at the same time and check how it moves when one of you turns over or sits up to get out of bed. Some beds are more affected by movement than others and, if one of you is a light sleeper, this may be a problem.

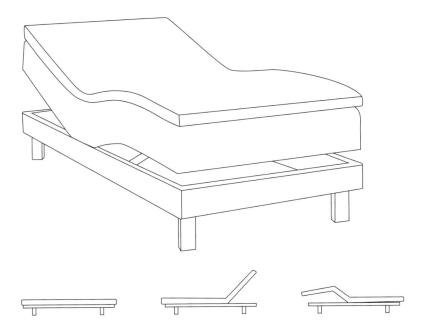

Adjustable beds

Adjustable beds can vary the angles of parts of the mattress using a manual control or an electric motor to enable you to lie, half-lie or sit up in your bed more ergonomically. They are good for people with medical conditions such as sciatica, backache, snoring or breathing difficulties, and, given that the height of the head and foot ends of the bed can be adjusted, also for people who have difficulty getting out of bed.

Adjustable beds are also popular with people who like to sit up and read or watch TV in the bedroom, since you can vary your position easily and comfortably. But be aware of the possible danger of pets or small children getting squashed. It is vital to choose a serious supplier and a model that is tested and approved by Möbelfakta and has the international standards EN and ISO.

Water beds

In Sweden, the great period of water bed popularity was during the 1980s and 1990s, and they are still around today. The first versions only had one chamber containing all the water, which resulted in troublesome glugging noises and major waves if anyone turned over. Current water beds have a rather more refined construction with, for instance, wave-reducing layers. It's also possible to find a water bed with reinforced lumbar support. The mattress protectors that enclose water beds have developed a great deal, and these days it is possible to get hold of varieties that are free from phthalates, toxins and heavy metals.

Since water takes the shape of your body, there are no pressure points in a water bed and durability over time tends to be really good since, unlike other materials, water does not lose its buoyancy. To achieve the maximum comfort level, it's important to have the right quantity of water in the bed. To keep the water fresh and to counteract the growth of algae and microorganisms and calcification, you will need to add anti-algal agents. It is now possible to get biological agents that can prevent the development of bacteria without damaging nature.

We usually make a distinction between the two different types of water bed:

Hard-sided bed This model has the water-filled mattress enclosed in a hard frame of wood – hence the name.

Soft-sided bed This model is shaped to fit into an existing bed frame and the water-filled mattress is held in place with the help of soft foam edges.

An advantage of water beds is that the comfort can be increased by warming up the water. A disadvantage is that the heating element takes a constant flow of electricity, which means that running costs are higher than with an 'ordinary' bed. And the temperature of the water only has to fall a degree or so below that of your body for the mattress to feel cold and uncomfortable.

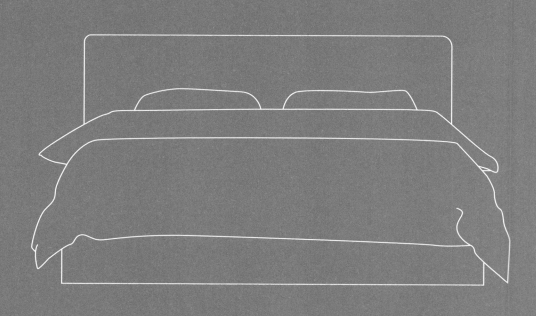

Headboards

Why do we actually bother with headboards or bedsteads? Well, aesthetically speaking, they help make the bedroom feel cosier, and from a practical point of view, they help protect the wall from stains, marks and dents. And they protect you from the wall: if you are sleeping in a room with plastered walls, you can easily knock your arm against the wall quite painfully. In older houses, headboards and bedsteads can provide a degree of insulation against cold outside walls, and in new-build houses with many hard surfaces and annoying acoustics, they can help dampen the noise.

Wall-mounted or bed-mounted?
Fixed or Freestanding?

A headboard can be fixed to the wall or to the bed and the legs of the bed. Alternatively, it can lean against the wall and the bed can be pushed against to hold it in place. The advantage of the wall-mounted version is that it usually provides a more stable backrest – on the other hand, the pressure of the person sitting in the bed and leaning back can push the bed away and cause gaps between the headboard and the mattress. The advantage with the bed-mounted version or the freestanding type is that they give you greater flexibility if you want to change furniture around or to get at things when cleaning, without needing to dismantle the headboard. The disadvantage is that they can be unstable and squeaky.

Headboard legs are an excellent accessory for freestanding headboards. They raise the bottom edge of the headboard off the floor and allow it to be lined up with the base of the bed; they also raise the headboard above the level of the skirting, which means it is no longer constantly rocking against the wall because of the thickness of the skirting. And the extra height of the headboard also means that it is visible behind a high bed and a stack of pillows. Better suppliers often include the legs in with the purchase of the headboard, or they can be bought separately.

Do you often sit up in your bed?

Just because you choose your bed from the point of view of sleeping comfort and sleep patterns doesn't mean that you shouldn't also choose a bed that suits the way you use it in daytime as well as at night. Many people like to sit up and read in bed, others like to lean back on the headboard while watching TV or surfing on tablets and mobiles. If, however, you only use the bed for sleeping and nothing else, then you have a lot more freedom when it comes to the choice of material, surface and shape of your headboard. In this latter case, it is probably less important if the headboard has cavities and spaces, is made of more fragile material or has decorative elements that wouldn't tolerate being used as a backrest.

The height of your back and the height of the mattress

Two important factors to keep in mind when choosing a headboard are the height of the bed and mattress from the floor and the height of your back when sitting up on the mattress. A headboard that is too low won't be visible, nor will it provide you with the back support you need when sitting up in bed. Given that continental beds are a good deal higher than spring beds, they will usually call for a much higher headboard if it is to be visible at the head of the bed, particularly if it is fixed to the bed or standing on the floor. When it comes to deciding on height, a wall-mounted version will, of course, give you a good deal more freedom of choice. But don't forget to take the size and proportion of the room into account.

TIP!

Have the headboard a little wider than the width of the bed. The duvet, pillows and coverlet often overhang slightly at the sides, so remember to take that into account, otherwise the headboard might look too small.

Shapes and lines

Depending on the style and shape you prefer, there is a wide range of headboards to choose from. Here are a number of the most common varieties and their names:

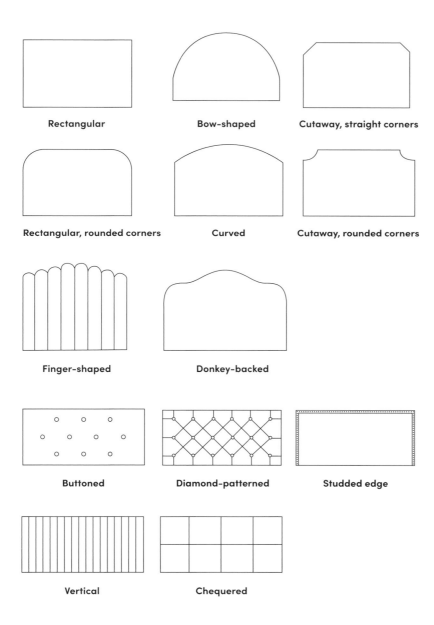

Rectangular

Bow-shaped

Cutaway, straight corners

Rectangular, rounded corners

Curved

Cutaway, rounded corners

Finger-shaped

Donkey-backed

Buttoned

Diamond-patterned

Studded edge

Vertical

Chequered

Covered headboards

How covering on a padded headboard is fixed and dressed affects the comfort as well as the appearance. It depends on how you intend using the headboard as well as what you prefer in terms of taste.

Smooth covers

The simplest kind of padded headboards have a removable cover that is easy to take off and wash, or to change if you want a different colour. If you choose a linen cover, you'll find that the fabric is very forgiving when it comes to creasing and any stains are less prominent.

Buttons and tufting

The simplest type of padding is held in place with buttons on the surface of the padding.

The bottom of deep-stitched tufting is attached to the headboard, creating high relief patterns. This provides an irregular surface that can be more or less comfortable depending on how hard the padding material is and how many buttons have been used to do the tufting.

Studded edge

Furniture nails and metal tacks (that resemble rivets when hammered in) are often nailed around the outer edge of the headboard.

Hard headboards

As alternatives to the popular padded headboards, I would like to put a word in for headboards made of wood, steel and iron. These hard and durable materials are easier to keep clean and dust free (as well as being immune to mites). What's more, they don't break easily and tend to have a higher second-hand value.

Beds at different levels

In some rooms and at some stages of life, we need different kinds of beds to those we've dealt with so far. For growing children, for instance, or for occasional overnight guests. Here are a few points to bear in mind when you are looking for ideas.

Bunk beds and loft beds

A bunk bed consists of two (sometimes more) single beds, one above the other. A good rule of thumb for this kind of bed is that it should be possible to sit on the lower section without banging your head on the upper bed. Similarly, it's also important to check how close the upper bed comes to the ceiling in the room where you are placing it.

DID YOU KNOW?

According to EU safety recommendations, children under six years old should not sleep on the upper bunk, nor on a high bed of the type known as a loft bed.

Even if the supplier assembled the bed correctly, it may be that, once you've bought it, you locate it in a space where the sleeper in the upper bunk ends up with bruises all over their head from banging it on the ceiling when sitting up in the night.

If the bunk bed has a ladder, the ladder should be moveable to any position along the long sides of the bunk. This gives you plenty of flexibility should you want to move the furniture around or should you move to a new house with a different layout. Be aware that some manufacturers don't paint the whole bunk bed in the same colour. In some cases, the so-called C-sides – that is, the back and the parts covered by the mattress – are left unpainted. They are coldly calculating that these parts aren't visible to the eye when you look at the bed, but, of course, when you are lying in it, or if you have it wholly or partially freestanding in the room, these parts may well be visible.

Family beds

This is effectively a bunk bed in which the lower bed is wider and has room for two people. They are popular in children's rooms where an adult may want to lie alongside the child to read stories, to settle the child down, or just to sleep with the child. They are also common in summerhouses, mountain huts and country places, where you want to accommodate more people in a small space. Just as with ordinary bunk beds, it is important to choose a bed that allows you to sit up without banging your head on the upper bunk. To avoid accidents, check the construction in the same way as you would for bunk beds and loft beds.

BUNK BEDS: IMPORTANT POINTS TO CHECK

- The base of the bed should tolerate normal wear and tear.

- The base of the upper bunk should not have loose slats that might slide out of place, with the consequent risk of the sleeper getting stuck, pushing through the base or even falling through. This is why the stretchers in the base of beds should be firmly attached to a strap that links them together into a firm base.

- Are the safety rails high enough and are they the right distance apart to prevent children getting jammed or slipping between the rails and ending up hanging there? What kind of static loading and pressure can the safety rails tolerate? Are they stable? Also check that the mattress you are intending to use in the top bunk is not so deep that it negates the effect of the safety rails.

- How firmly is the upper bunk attached to the lower? This will affect the stability of the whole structure. It is important that the upper bunk cannot be pushed upwards and out of position, with the associated risk of it collapsing altogether.

- Check that the ladder between the bunks is on the long side of the beds – the Consumer Council recommends this as the safer position. Also, that the distance between the rungs is appropriate and that the rungs are not slippery, particularly if the bunks are to be in children's rooms.

- A bunk bed that has corner posts that stick up may possibly be dangerous, in that clothes can catch on them and cause falls or even the risk of strangulation.

- Are there any parts of the bed or any folding mechanisms in which fingers might be caught and pinched?

Source: Consumer Council, Marketing of Bunk Beds

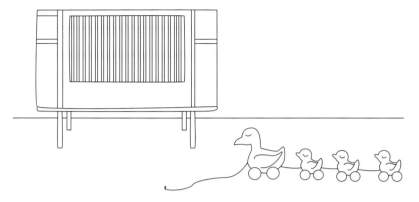

Children's beds

Cots

Small children vary a lot in how they sleep, but a cot is usually a good choice during the child's first two years. There are a number of points to bear in mind when choosing a cot.

Before you fall in love with the idea of a particular model or get hung up on splendid visions of what it will all look like, I want to emphasize the importance of thinking what is best for the child. Nothing can be more important than for you and your child to sleep well and safely through the night. It's easy to get carried away by images of what you want the child's room to look like, particularly if it's your first pregnancy, but I can promise you that as soon as the child is born you will find yourself prioritizing other things and thinking of factors that hadn't occurred to you before. So, first and foremost, think of safety.

The width and positioning of the bars

Children's beds are constructed with a minimum measurement between the bars for a very good reason, which is to protect the child's head and body: given the opportunity, children will try to squeeze through the bars. The 2022 standard in Sweden is that the maximum distance between vertical bars should be 65 millimetres, but you will need to read up on the rules that are current where you live at the time of reading.

Height of bed

The sides of a cot must not be so low that a child is able to climb out of the bed. When I was a young mother, many people quoted an apocryphal story of a child who climbed out of their cot and ended up with life-changing injuries. That may be an old wives' tale, but you won't want to take the risk. In 2022, the usual recommendation is that the height of the sides should be 60 centimetres, with at least 50 centimetres between the top of the mattress and the top of the bars. But do check carefully what the recommendations are where you live and always follow the official guidelines as to child safety.

Variable height mattresses

Many cots have mattresses that are adjustable in terms of height. It's useful to be able to raise the mattress to make it easy to reach a small child during early months, before the child has learned to stand or walk. But as soon as you see the child starting to hold on and pull itself upright, it's vital to adjust the mattress lower so it can't fall out. Check how many levels the mattress can be adjusted to so that you can raise or lower it as you need. It's also important that the bottom of the cot is tight (no holes bigger than 25 millimetres) so that little feet can't go through. The base should be stable and firm, with no squeaks and rattles.

Cots on wheels

Cots on wheels allow you a good deal more flexibility and mobility. While you are pregnant you still won't know how much your child will need to be close to you, but some children find it very difficult to go to sleep if they are in another room. In this situation, a cot on wheels provides parents with much more freedom of movement, especially during the day when the cot can be wheeled through to other parts of the house. Check that the wheels are lockable and that the locks can be worked with a simple movement of your foot. As a parent, you'll often have your hands full, so being able to lock and unlock the wheels with your foot is useful. To get the best use out of a mobile cot, it's important that it is the right size to pass easily through the inside doors and passages of the house. Bear in mind that you may have put furniture such as sideboards and so on in the passageways, thus making them narrower, so – before making your mind up – it would at least be worth double-checking the passages and spaces between the rooms you are most likely to want to move the cot through.

Common complaints about cots

- The bed is too low, thus making it difficult to reach the child and pick it up.
- The whole construction feels flimsy. The cot rocks and sways when the child catches hold of the bars and shakes them.
- The cot and its bars are too smooth and straight, making it difficult to get the wrap-around cot bumper cover to stay in place and not slide down.
- Setting the cot up is difficult and time-consuming. This is particularly the case with travel cots.
- The bed rattles – this is particularly so with cots that have protective plastic parts on the bars.

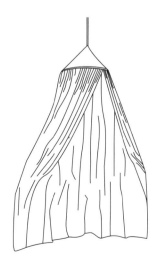

WARNING!

Having a cot canopy hanging over the cot has become extremely popular and the internet is full of tempting pictures. But there is actually an age limit on many of them – for a good reason. Think of the risk of the child being smothered if your little treasure gets hold of the fabric. It's all too easy for a child to get tangled in a fallen canopy while asleep. Just because everyone else has them doesn't mean they are safe.

SAFETY TIPS FOR COTS

If you are buying a second-hand cot, it's important to check that the space between the bars is between 45 and 65 millimetres, the reason being to prevent small children pushing their way through the bars feet first, getting jammed by the chest, sticking fast and being unable to breathe. And beds designed for children should not have protruding parts that a child's clothing could catch on and get hooked, once again leading to the risk of strangulation.

- Check once again that the bed is at least 50 centimetres deep, i.e. that the distance between the top of the mattress and the top of the bars is sufficient to prevent any possibility of the child climbing over.

- Does the mattress you are intending to use fit tight to the sides of the cot? It's important that there should not be any gap into which a child could push their head.

- Are you buying an old cot that has been repainted? Always ask which paint has been used. While investigating the world around them, children chew and bite on everything and the last thing you want is to find that the flakes of paint in their mouths contain substances that may be dangerous. My youngest son must have been a beaver in an earlier life with the consequence that many pieces of furniture in our house carry signs of his teething process. It's not possible to protect children from everything, but the paint on the cot in which they spend most of their time is perhaps the simplest thing to be sure of.

- Once the child is over 85 centimetres or has developed sufficient motor skills, the usual recommendation is that you remove one of the long sides of the cot or buy a new bed.

- Think about the toys and other items the child has in the cot – things that can be climbed up on. I have some experience of this, having nourished at my breast a little escape artist, a real Houdini.

Source: Hello Consumer

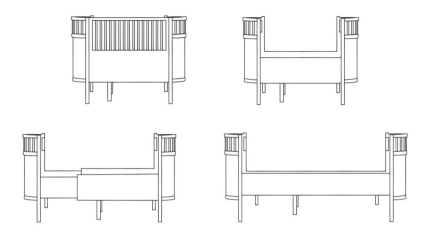

Extendable beds

Thinking ahead long-term about children's beds, it might be a good idea to choose an extendable bed, which, thanks to pull-out units and extensions, can grow along with the child. These usually cost a little more, but that will pay off since they last the child for longer and, given that there is a substantial demand for them, they'll also have a higher second-hand value. The mattress is frequently a cost driver that gets forgotten when comparing the prices of extendable beds. The child will, of course, need different mattresses as it gets older and grows bigger, so you should check how the manufacturer has approached that issue. Is it possible to lengthen the mattress by adding insets, or will the whole mattress have to be replaced at intervals? What will the various alternatives cost?

 TIP!

If you happen to have a 'beaver child', think carefully when choosing an extendable bed. The finish and the overall quality need to be of a higher standard, since the same bed will accompany the child from the time it is teething to when it is losing its milk teeth.

Sofa beds

Regardless of whether you need a sofa that can function as an extra bed or a bed that can also be turned into a sofa, the sofa bed will inevitably be a compromise. You are getting two functions for the price of one, but rarely the same level of comfort for both. So, it's important to be clear about where the priority lies – sleeping or sitting?

Is the sofa bed going to be used as an extra bed for elderly guests? If the sofa bed is turned into a bed that stands out into the room with the pillows in the sitting position of the sofa, it's easy for two adults to get into bed from opposite sides without having to climb over the other's sleeping place. Choose a sofa bed of normal bed height, or higher.

Be aware that the wear and tear on sofa beds often shows in other places and other ways than on ordinary sofas, which increases the need to have an easy way to freshen up the covers.

There are several styles of sofa bed.

- English sofa beds: the sleeper lies the length of the sofa.
- English sleeper sofas: sleeper lies at right angles to the back edge of the sofa.
- Pull-out or truckle beds.
- Futons.
- Chaises longues/day beds.
- Armchair beds.

Common complaints about beds

- The colour of the mattresses/bedheads does not accord with the photograph in the advert. This usually occurs with light colours (grey, beige, white and green).
- On delivery, the bed smells bad or has a strong smell of chemicals.
- The top mattress curls up at the edges, in spite of the large sheet and efforts to bend them in the other direction.
- The mattress slides on the slatted wooden base. Can be cured using the anti-slip grips designed for rugs.
- The actual measurements do not match the measurements in the product description. Check the supplier's tolerances: a bed is rarely exact to the millimetre and different producers differ in their margins of acceptability.

Materials

The materials that are used in the manufacture of the furniture we buy and use has an importance that goes well beyond the purely visual. A handsome chair can be unpleasant to sit on if the material doesn't appeal to our bodies as much as to our eyes. An optimally functional piece of furniture can seem ill-considered if it doesn't also have some element of sensuality in the choice of material and craftmanship. And if the producer has skimped on raw materials, any benefits of the actual design can easily be ruined. In this section of the book we shall take a closer look at the materials and the qualities to be found in furniture and interior design.

Wood

There are thousands of species of tree in the world and timber characteristics vary not only from species to species, but can also vary between one tree and another of the same species. There can even be a range of different qualities in one and the same tree, depending on the conditions in which the tree grew and which parts of the trunk the timber has been taken from. In spite of that, we frequently tend to lump wood together as one concept, rather as if we were to say 'this meal is meat', with no mention of whether it is beef, pork or chicken.

Something about different qualities

When it comes to food, most of us have acquired some basic knowledge that enables us to distinguish good quality from bad. But, hand on heart now, can you tell a good piece of wood from a bad for a particular job in the same way as you can tell good meat from bad. When you were at school, how often were you shown a cuts chart for timber? It was a moment of revelation to me when I was shown that a tree-trunk has its equivalent of beef tenderloin and its less good parts that are better suited to hash. When dividing up a tree-trunk it is important, just as it is with meat, to pay attention to the muscles – in tree terminology, the grain, the twigs, the rings and moisture content. There is a wide range of better and worse quality even within what we collectively refer to as 'solid wood'. What were the conditions in which the tree grew? What nourished it? Has it been subjected to abnormal conditions? How was it felled, dried, sawn, worked and prepared? Which parts of the trunk have been selected? Only half joking, we might say that chipboard is the interior design equivalent of minced meat. There are times when it can be the most appropriate choice of material for a particular task, whereas at other times it's a way of coming up with a cheaper alternative. In the following section I shall explain some basic facts about materials that may help you come to better informed decisions about furniture and interior design.

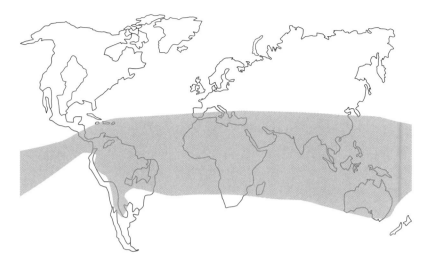

Give some thought to where the wood in your furniture comes from. Just as with food, the raw materials in your furnishings may come from near at hand or from far away, depending partly on where you live, but partly, too, on the location of the factories and carpentry workshops that refined the various raw materials. Tropical woods, derived from rainforests, grow exclusively in the southern parts of the globe.

Wood that grew nearby or wood from far away?

Anyone making an informed and conscious choice will usually want to choose raw materials produced nearby in order to avoid lengthy transport distances. But, surprisingly often, the same individual who is careful to buy locally produced food will long for furniture made from exotic and slow-growing varieties of wood that grow on the other side of the globe. This is worth giving some thought to if you find yourself craving a specific type of wood that doesn't grow near where you live or near the factory that manufactures the furniture. And it's worth remembering that certain exotic woods – even though they may be renewable and are cultivated in certified woodlands – may take several centuries to grow to maturity.

A hygroscopic material

Wood is a living material that moves. Obviously, that doesn't mean that your furniture is going to get up and walk out of the door one day, but that wood is a hygroscopic material – one that absorbs moisture from the air – that is constantly swelling and shrinking in an effort to stay in balance with the environment in which it finds itself – in other words, with the relative humidity of the air and the temperature in the room. This means, for instance, that an indoor wooden floor changes a little according to the time of year: in summer, when the humidity of the air is higher, it will swell, whereas in winter when the air is drier, it will shrink. So, when the floor is being laid, it's important to allow space for this movement, otherwise the floor will bulge when it swells. As every skilled and experienced carpenter knows, the same thing holds true for the wood used in furniture – those less knowledgeable, however, don't know the right way to deal with this.

Where we place the furniture in our houses can also make a significant difference to the wood they are made of. The material will behave slightly differently, for instance, if we place it very close to a radiator compared with in a conservatory that isn't heated all year round, or in a damp bathroom.

The following types of damage can be caused to a wooden piece of furniture that is subjected to major changes in the indoor climate:

- cracks
- bulges
- shrinkage
- veneer blisters
- veneer loosening and lifting
- veneer cracks
- cracks in the colour
- creaking
- colour changes
- skewing

Source: SNIRI

231

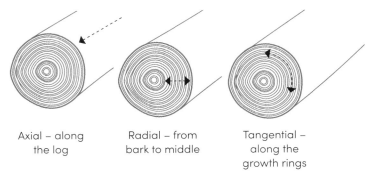

Axial – along
the log

Radial – from
bark to middle

Tangential –
along the
growth rings

The way in which the parts of the log have been sawn in relation to the annual growth rings will affect both the pattern and the stability of form.

The importance of selecting the right wood

Wood swells and shrinks according to the humidity of the air. It swells when the air is damper and shrinks when it is drier. The material is affected to a different extent depending on the various directions of the wood: axial, radial and tangential. Wood swells and shrinks almost twice as much in a tangential direction (that is, following the direction of the growth rings) as it does in a radial direction (that is, from the bark to the core). And virtually no change at all occurs in the axial direction.

How the parts of the log are sawn relative to the annual growth rings affects the technical quality of the wood and pattern (the texture). Also, thicker cuts tend to move more when they swell and shrink than thinner cuts. It's important to know and take account of these factors in order to minimize movement in the finished piece of furniture.

How the timber is cut relative to the annual growth rings affects both the pattern and the shape changes.

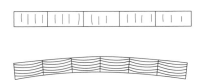

Table top constructed from timber with upright growth rings in the end grain is more likely stable.

Table top constructed from timber with horizontal growth rings in the end grain is usually less stable.

Timber that has upright growth rings holds its shape best given variations of humidity. You can virtually exclude the chances of cracks forming in a table top of this sort.

On the other hand, a board with horizontal growth rings in the end grain of the timber is less stable in terms of shape and the risk of damage to the board increases.

It's important to pay attention to all these things when selecting which cuts should be used for which purposes in manufacturing furniture. If they aren't taken account of during production, the risks of cracking and damage become greater. This is something that separates skilled furniture makers from those less careful.

There is another aspect, too. The strength of wood varies in different directions: it is considerably stronger following the direction of the fibres along the trunk than it is across the fibres at right angles. And varieties of wood with short fibres are more liable to breakage than wood with long fibres.

Getting round the problems

To prevent warping in larger table tops of solid wood, a strut fitted beneath the table top is needed to hold it flat. The apron at the short ends of the table is also usually utilized for this purpose.

If tangentially cut wood is being used, you should lay all the boards of the table top so that the core sides are facing up (as opposed to alternating the boards): in this way the surface of the table will be even and it is easier to pull flat with the help of the screws through the apron.

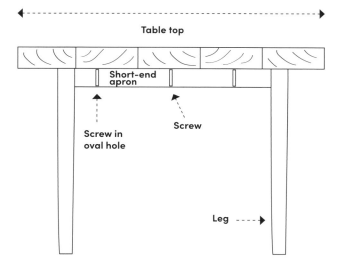

Fast or slow

Slow: good timber has grown slowly. The annual growth rings are consequently narrow and close together. This kind of wood is less liable to swelling and shrinkage.

Fast: timber that has grown quickly usually has fewer knots and the growth rings are more widely spaced. This means that the wood moves more and is more easily damaged with changes in humidity.

Knots are the birthmarks of branches

We can trace the growth of branches in a tree from the dark marks in the timber. Trees growing close together have fewer branches. Cultivated birch, for instance, often has fewer knots because it is possible, in cultivation, to control the environment in which the tree grows in order to produce the timber we want. In the case of pine, the pattern of knots varies from one part of the trunk to another. The lower part of the trunk is relatively knot-free in the outer parts; in the middle part of the trunk, the lower branches are generally thickest and, consequently, that's where the biggest knots in the trunk are found; in a growing tree, the branches become more and more sparse nearer the top of the trunk. Knots can both weaken and spoil the appearance of furniture, rather depending on where they are and what kind of appearance you prefer.

Aesthetics and economy

Some people think that knots spoil the appearance of wood whereas others think that wood is lifeless without them. Wood without any knots at all is hard to find, but it is possible to buy it – at a price – from more exclusive selection.

The sawing method is also important from an aesthetic perspective since it affects the surface pattern of the wood. You can choose to saw it in different ways in order to bring out and highlight the visual characteristics of the variety of wood. After being sawn and dried, the wood is sorted into various classes depending on its quality and price. Obviously, a piece of furniture made from the very best raw materials will be more expensive than one made from cheaper materials and with a higher tolerance of irregularities.

Summary of varieties of wood commonly used for furniture and interior design

Conifers

The coniferous trees most commonly used in the Scandinavian furniture and interior design industry are pine and spruce. Both are collective terms for many species of tree. Conifers often have relatively obvious annual growth rings but not a high density of fibres, which makes the material softer, lighter and more elastic. This means that point loading makes permanent pressure marks on coniferous wood and it does not tolerate wear and tear as well as harder deciduous woods. Pine heartwood – the innermost and hardest part of pine logs – contains great quantities of resins, which make it resistant to damp and to decay. Pine is characterized by oval knots and by its brown heartwood, whereas spruce usually has small pearl knots between the whorls of branches.

Deciduous trees

There are many differences between deciduous trees and coniferous trees, but first and foremost is the fact that deciduous trees have leaves instead of needles. In most cases, deciduous trees have shorter fibres than coniferous trees. The deciduous trees commonly used in the furniture and interior design industries are acacia, alder, ash, aspen, beech, birch, maple and oak. Generally speaking, deciduous trees have less obvious growth rings since they don't show the same colour difference between spring wood and summer wood as conifers. The wood is fibre-dense and durable.

Deciduous trees may be divided into ring-porous types (with large vessels concentrated in the spring and early summer wood) and diffuse-porous types (where the larger vessels are more evenly distributed). Oak and ash, for instance, are ring-porous trees and birch and beech are diffuse-porous trees.

SPECIES	COLOUR	GRAIN
Alder Alder is the only deciduous tree that has cones. There are two varieties of alder in Sweden: common alder and grey alder.	New-sawn alder is yellow, but the colour changes to red-brown.	Growth rings are faint. There are sometimes brown streaks between the growth rings: these are caused by insect infestation.
Ash Often the last Swedish deciduous tree to come into leaf in spring and among the first to lose its leaves.	The wood is a light greyish-yellow with tones of red. Light brown heartwood. Darkens with the age of the tree and may become really dark on old trees – so-called 'olive ash'.	Straighter grain with very few knots. Glossy surface. The spring wood is rough and the autumn wood has fine pores, which leads to a marked colour difference and exciting patterning on tangential cuts.
Aspen A fast-growing tree that needs plenty of light. After birch, the most common deciduous tree in Sweden.	Pale yellowish-white, shading over to grey. Aspen retains its light colour better than most other woods. Turns grey outdoors.	Almost invisible growth rings and very weak veins.
Beech Beech trees create dense and leafy foliage that forms a roof-like canopy to the forest, the result of which is that there is rarely any ground vegetation in a beech wood.	Light yellow or red-grey. After steam treatment takes on a more reddish shade and is called red beech. Older trees often have a zone of darker wood, called redheart. Utilized properly, it can give the wood a decorative appearance.	Weak, but dotted with obvious medullary rays.
Birch The most common deciduous tree in Sweden, where there are three varieties of birch: dwarf birch, silver birch and downy birch. Masur birch is not a particular variety, but an inherited defect in the silver birch which leads to the tree producing knots. This affects the growth rings, causing uneven and wavy patterns which are often used to make high-end furniture.	Pale yellow to honey yellow.	Flame-like, wavy patterns. Weak markings.

PROPERTIES	USES	MISCELLANEOUS
Soft, stable, straight-fibred. Very resistant to rot (in oxygen-deficient environments).	Easy to work. Often used in carpentry, wooden sculptures and model-making. Also used for veneers. The wood of grey alder is softer and less durable and is usually used as fuel.	Often used for clogs. On felling, the sap is blood-coloured.
Hard, tough, durable. Flexible and difficult to split. Should be pre-drilled for nails and screws. Should not be used outdoors.	Furniture, both solid and as veneer. Frequently used for the seats of chairs and for drawers, floors, table tops, doors, shelves and banisters.	Used for tool handles and sporting equipment. Used to be common for bandy and hockey sticks and billiard cues before composite materials came in.
Light, soft, easy to split, but difficult to get a smooth surface. When unplaned it is fuzzy – it needs very sharp tools to avoid it lifting. It rots if subjected to constant damp, but, on the other hand, it lasts a long time if dried out thoroughly.	Matchsticks, coreboard and cross veneer. Also common as sauna panelling as it does not ooze resin.	Half a cubic metre of aspen wood will produce a million matches.
Heavy but simple to split and to work.	Very suitable for parquet, and for furniture and wooden items subject to heavy wear. Since the lignin can be softened by steam, beech is frequently used for café chairs and other steam-bent furniture.	Used for ice-cream lollies. Beech is also used to produce potash (for use in manufacture of soap and glass).
Elastic and tough. Its flexibility means that narrow dimensions can be used and the material still be durable. Surface easy to work.	Furniture, often glued-laminated seating and furniture for public environments. Spoons and butter knives (since birch is both odourless and taste-free).	May be used for skis. Some birches form burls (rounded knotty growths) which have become popular to carve into bowls and drinking vessels.

SPECIES	COLOUR	GRAIN
Cherry Also includes wood from plum trees.	Reddish. Takes on a cognac tone after lengthy exposure to daylight. American cherry wood is darker than European.	Distinct growth rings
Elm A common tree in parks and avenues as it doesn't have low branches. Rarely found in Swedish forests.	Outer wood is a light yellowish-grey. Heartwood is reddish-grey to dark chocolate-brown.	Varying markings. Distinct growth rings. Sometimes greenish veins. The strong contrast between spring wood and summer wood can provide an interesting appearance on tangential surfaces.
Lime Lime is the perfect wood for carving. Often used in school handicrafts.	Light, sometimes almost white to greyish white.	When untreated, the grain is very weak. When the surface is treated with linseed oil, the grain shows up more.
Maple Durable, and consequently commonly used for flooring sports halls and bowling alleys.	White to yellowish-white.	Thin, sharp growth rings. Wood with wavy patterns occurs (flame maple), as does wood with undeveloped knots (bird's-eye maple).
[Mahogany] Not a tree but a prized variety of timber from within the mahogany family *Meliaceae*. *Swietenia mahagoni* or macrophylla, for instance, is called West Indian mahogany since it grows on the Caribbean islands. South American *Swietenia macrophylla* is also known as Honduras mahogany, Atlantic mahogany or big-leafed mahogany.	Dark red. Mahogany fades in the sun and consequently has to be treated to retain its colour.	Often weakly marked.

PROPERTIES	USES	MISCELLANEOUS
Often grows straight and is easy to work. Fairly flexible and elastic. Cherry wood with irregular fibre is difficult to split. A lot of movement with changes in moisture.	Suitable for veneers. Used in finer handicraft and furniture work and for fitted joinery.	Used for musical instruments. The wood darkens when in contact with alkaline substances. Sometimes known as Swedish teak.
Hard, durable and relatively tough, with coarse fibres. Relatively quick-drying.	Furniture, tool handles, ladders, floors, thresholds, mill wheels and boat building. Can also be used in various kinds of visible supporting structures since its strength is good. Should be pre-drilled to avoid risk of splitting.	Used to provide the best flour for bark bread (not bitter). The smell of untreated, sawn elmwood can be unpleasant. Elm root has similar marbled patterns to masur birch. (See under birch)
Not suitable where subject to mechanical stresses or where there is moisture.	Wood carving, wooden statues, fine carpentry, turning. Also panels, household articles, Venetian blinds, etc.	Makes good charcoal for sketching. When Carl Linnaeus, the botanist and taxonomist who developed the scientific system of naming – e.g. *Homo sapiens*, became a nobleman, he changed his surname to von Linné. The names Linnaeus and Linné were derived from a lime tree with three trunks that grew at the family farmstead in Stegaryd in Småland.
Hard, dense, homogenous, very durable and hard to split.	High-end furniture, parquet flooring, stairs, panels, doors, handles for tools and the teeth of wooden rakes.	Also used for gun butts. The North American sugar maple has a high concentration of sugar in its sap and is tapped for the production of maple syrup.
Firm and hard. Good resistance to damp and rot. Good resistance to termites.	High-end furniture and interior design. Frequently found in boats and sailing equipment.	The trade in many kinds of mahogany is regulated by CITES, a voluntary agreement dealing with the trade in threatened animals and plants.

SPECIES	COLOUR	GRAIN
Oak One of the commonest varieties of wood in Scandinavia. In the past, all oaks belonged to the Crown since they were used in shipbuilding for the Swedish Navy.	Yellow-grey or red-grey (American oak). With time it takes on a more amber tone. Oak for furniture making is divided into two types: white oak and red oak. Red oak usually grows in America.	Very marked veins in a darker colour. The surface veining and colour nuances vary. The surface of the wood takes on different structures depending on how the plank is sawn from the log.
Pine In the right conditions, pine can grow up to a height of 30 metres, with a straight stem like a mast and with the crown high up.	Pale yellowish-white (sapwood) or reddish-yellow/brown (heartwood). Bear in mind that pine darkens with age. If you want it to retain its lightness, treat it with lye.	Clearly marked in darker tones.
Spruce The most common tree in Sweden, but not when it comes to the furniture industry.	Pale yellowish-white. When dried, the sapwood and the heartwood are the same colour. It sweats resin so accumulations of resin are more common in spruces than in other conifers. When spruce is stained, the colour is stronger since the pigment does not get absorbed where the wood is already saturated with resin.	Grey or greyish brown veins. Usually has 'pearl knots' (small, dry knots between the annual growth rings).
Teak Collective name for three different trees. Mainly grows in tropical regions and is sometimes referred to as a rainforest wood. The EU Timber Regulation regulates the harvesting of teak and how it is traced back to the plantations in which it is cultivated.	Newly sawn teak is olive green, but when dried it has a dark, reddish-brown colour. To some extent, the colour of the wood depends on the particular variety and where the teak was grown. Teak from Java is slightly lighter, whereas Burma teak is darker.	Generally speaking, teak is knot-free.
Walnut The timber derived from trees that produce walnuts.	Dark brown (chocolate brown to a dark reddish-brown). Unlike many other woods, walnut becomes paler with time, taking on a more golden-brown shade.	Irregular dark streaks that can vary between slightly patterned and strongly patterned. It is important to bear in mind the big variations in patterning when ordering furniture, especially if you are sensitive to differences between drawer fronts, cupboard fronts, table tops and the like.

PROPERTIES	USES	MISCELLANEOUS
A hard, dense and strong wood. Oaks contain tannic acid and will darken a great deal if treated with lye. In contact with metals, especially iron, oak will discolour: you need to use stainless steel nails and screws to avoid this problem.	Shipbuilding, housebuilding (castles and half-timbered buildings).	The bark of oak is used for tanning leather. The oak is the provincial flower of Blekinge. Swedish oaks tend to be twisted – a consequence of growing wild rather than being cultivated. Thus, the oak used in furniture making is usually imported, most of it originating in Central Europe.
A soft and moisture-resistant wood. The surface can be treated with linseed oil, but mature pine has a high resin content which means that the oil cannot easily penetrate the wood. Is easily scratched.	Housebuilding (walls, roof, doors, windows, panelling, floors), furniture, woodwork, wooden boards, baskets, boatbuilding, telephone poles.	Acetic acid, turpentine, wood alcohol, tar, resin and glue can all be produced from pine. The Douglas fir is a North American variety that is almost without knots (it's also known as the Douglas spruce or Oregon pine).
Long-fibred and soft. Little shrinkage. Difficult to impregnate.	Construction and building timber (glued wooden beams, chipboard and fibreboard), flagpoles, masts and stakes. Also used for looms.	Spruce that has grown slowly and straight on the northern slopes of the Alps is used to make the very best stringed instruments. Vanillin aroma (not to be confused with real vanilla) can be produced from rotted spruce. The roots of spruce are often used in handicrafts – basket-making, for instance.
Hard, heavy, elastic and oily. Very resistant to moisture and attacks. Difficult to glue.	Furniture and outdoor furniture. Develops an attractive greyish-silver patina if left untreated outdoors. To retain the colour and lustre of the wood outdoors, it has to be treated with oil.	Once a teak tree is over three years old, it starts to develop fire-resistant properties that provide natural protection. Takes between 100 and 200 years to grow to a diameter of 75 centimetres. When cultivated in more favourable conditions, it may grow more quickly.
Medium hard. Easy to carve and turn. Very flexible when steamed.	Furniture, doors and mouldings. Expensive and consequently more common as veneer than as solid wood in order to make it more affordable.	American walnut is darker and has a more even colouring than European. There is a walnut from Peru that has a dark brown to black nuance.

Veneer

Veneers are very thin sheets of wood, used among other things as surface covering for cheaper wood, MDF, plywood, chipboard and various kinds of backing materials. Veneers come in a number of thicknesses, most commonly:

- 0.8 millimetres
- 0.6 millimetres
- 1.5 millimetres

In general, it is accepted that the term 'veneer' is no longer appropriate when the thickness of the wood exceeds 3–4 millimetres.

In order to produce veneers, the log is first heated and then sawn, rotary cut, sliced or planed into thin sheets. Sawn veneers are often thicker, whereas those that are sliced or rotary cut are thinner. Thereafter, depending on how the veneer is positioned and glued, different patterns and shapes can be formed. The top level is called the surface veneer and the invisible level that is used to prevent movement is called the cross veneer. A veneered board should always be veneered on both sides in order to minimize the risk of the board warping – the same amount of moisture (glue) should be applied to both sides of the board. In the case of a door, the same type of surface veneer is applied to both faces, since both faces are visible. On the undersides of table tops, however, which are not visible to the eye, some manufacturers choose to use a simpler veneer in order to cut costs.

WORTH THINKING ABOUT!

Light veneers darken with time, whereas dark veneers grow lighter. How quickly this occurs will depend on how much exposure to light the veneers are subjected to.

Since the cost of veneered furniture can be kept down if only the outer layer consists of wood, whereas the baseboard can be of other materials, veneer has gained a bad reputation for being a cheap alternative. But the fact is that veneered sheets can be a more stable solution than solid wood. Large surfaces, things like table tops and solid wood doors, may warp or deform if exposed to very major changes in humidity, temperature, or strong light in conservatories or summer houses, for instance, which are left unheated for large parts of the year. On the other hand, veneered sheets can emit formaldehyde into the indoor air: the more glue there is in the sheets, the greater the risk of emissions.

Veneers are also used in the production of glue-laminated and moulded furniture. They are useful when the aim is to produce furniture with more complex shapes, since veneers offer greater possibilities for forming curves, which permits the creation of objects not possible in solid wood. Glue-lamination also makes it possible to achieve springy and bouncy qualities that solid wood simply can't compete with.

Veneers are also used in intarsia, a decorative technique in which pieces of wood are inlayed to create geometric patterns or figurative pictures. (In marquetry veneers are glued to the surface to create patterns.)

The appearance of veneers

What veneer looks like will depend not only on the variety of wood, but also on how the veneer was cut or rotary cut from the log and the direction in which this was done in relation to the growth rings.

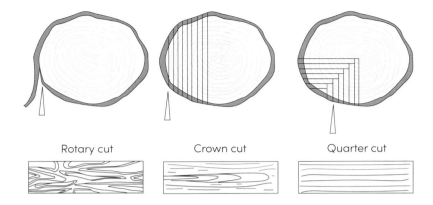

Rotary cut   Crown cut   Quarter cut

Rotary peeling

By using a plane blade on a rotating log, the wood is planed off in layers like a Swiss roll, producing an 'endless' sheet of veneer. This technique produces a flamelike pattern with strong contrasts, since the growth rings are widened and extended. Rotary peeling is usually used for the manufacture of plywood or for cross veneer (which is not seen). The method produces wide slices of veneer, with fewer joins and less wastage, all of which make the material relatively cheap.

Crown cut

The log is split down the middle lengthways and sliced from the outside in. This produces an elliptical ring-shaped pattern (also called pyramid or cathedral shaped) in which the rays have thin contours.

Quarter cut

The log is divided into four quarters before being sliced, which means that the cut is radial and the veneer will have straighter lines.

Examples of veneering

The appearance of the surface is largely dependent on how the pieces of veneer are laid out and glued. An analysis of the veneering gives an indication of the producer's level of ambition and the craftsmanship of the product.

Book matching

This is the traditional method of veneering. The veneers are taken in sequence from the log and laid mirror-image with each other, thus producing a symmetrical pattern of graining. However, this produces a repetitive pattern that some people are bothered by – and, since the sheets are mirrored, light falling on the surface is reflected differently.

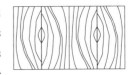

Random matching

Veneers of the same variety of wood but not necessarily from the same log are laid to resemble the appearance of joined planks. In this way, knotholes and markings are dispersed and do not line up to form undesired patterning.

Mismatching

Veneers from one and the same log are mixed on purpose in order to give a random effect while simultaneously retaining an overall consistent grain and colour.

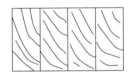

Slip matching

Veneers are taken in order from the same log and jointed together without turning alternate veneers over as in book matching. This produces a recurrent pattern that gradually varies across the panel. This method works best when the veneer has a straight and even grain. The lustre of the surface is enhanced because it reflects the light particularly well. This is the recommended method if the veneer is to be stained.

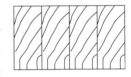

Reverse slip matching

The veneer is taken successively in order from the log. Every other veneer is turned 180° so that the pattern varies.

Pattern-laid veneer

Diagonal laying can create interesting patterns in different directions.

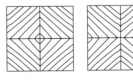

Studying the joints of the furniture

Studying the joints and corners of a piece of furniture may be likened to checking the seams of a garment. This precision work tells you a good deal about the skill and ambition of the producer.

Dowel wood joint

Glued, but can also be done with a screw and no glue. The mass producer's best friend. With the help of the dowelling, the parts are fitted together by the customer.

Butt joint

The pieces are glued together. Since the glue is absorbed into the end cut, this is not particularly strong and should be reinforced with a screw or peg.

Tongue and groove

Gives a bigger surface for glue and control across the joint. Often used in drawers.

Mortice and tenon joint

Creates a strong joint and a stable frame. The neck of the tenon acts as a stop and prevents the joint twisting. Can be single or double.

Finger joint

Often used to lengthen a piece of wood. Has a very large glue surface and makes an extremely strong joint.

Mitre joint

The pieces of wood join at 45 degrees, between the end wood and the fibres running lengthwise. Demands precision. Can be glued, but splines are often added for reinforcement and this gives a strong and neat corner. At best, the wood can look as if it continues around the corner untouched. No end wood visible.

Dovetail joint

A quality craftsman's joint with high strength and pleasing appearance. Used in the construction of first-class cabinets and carcasses.

Treating the surface

Wooden surfaces can be treated in various ways to enhance their appearance and character and to provide protection. What follows is a very short description of some of the most common methods.

Untreated

Wood that remains unpainted or is not sealed by oils or other surface treatments is more sensitive and has a shorter lifespan.

Oil

Oil is absorbed into the wood and enhances its characteristic grain. On each occasion furniture is treated with oil, the wood is fed and its resistance to liquids is increased. Oil also offers good protection against scratches and marks. Since an oiled surface has already been treated with fats, fat stains are less likely on such a surface. Spring wood has coarse pores and autumn wood has fine pores: this makes for a distinct change of colour and very interesting patterning in tangential cuts. Oiled wood does, however, need a little more care than other surface treatments. The surface needs to be fed regularly, particularly at the start, but the reward for all that trouble over time is a very durable, warm and living finish. After oiling a piece of furniture it will usually be dry within a couple of days, but the hardening process will continue for many weeks, so you should avoid laying textiles on a recently oiled surface.

COMPRESSION WOOD

Compression wood, also known as reaction wood, is the result of trees being subjected to abnormal stresses – the weight of masses of heavy snow, for instance, or growing on a slope, or the force of strong, prevailing winds. This can lead to the growth of compression wood, which is darker and harder than the normal wood of a growing tree. When sawn as timber, these parts are more easily damaged and liable to warp when it dries out.

Pigmented oil

If you want to change the appearance of the wood, you can always choose a pigmented oil such as white oil or brown oil. They have the same open-to-diffusion characteristics as oil, along with the ability to lighten or darken the wood. They can make the upkeep a little more awkward in that you can't work one spot at a time; you have to treat the whole piece evenly, otherwise you will end up with streaks. The surface will be somewhat glossier compared with soaped wood.

Hard wax oil

Brings out the wood's natural characteristics and gives it a water and dirt-repellent surface. Hard wax oil protects the wood against water and spillage, but is less tolerant of strong solvents and cleaners. Hard wax oil comes in different levels of gloss and can also be combined with pigment to strengthen or change the appearance of the wood. Should be applied in several layers in order to achieve a more resistant surface.

Soap

To soap wood, you use natural soap flakes. It's a common treatment for ash, oak and beech woods in order to achieve a lighter feel (white soaping). Soaped furniture often becomes a little lighter/whiter and has a colder tone. Needs regular care to retain its lightness.

Lye

Lye is commonly used on pine in order to minimize the tendency of pine to go yellow.

Staining

A technique for colouring wood while still allowing the natural grain and patterns to be visible. Staining evens out the nuances in the wood, but usually needs an additional surface treatment (oil or lacquer, for instance) to prevent it rubbing off. As a surface treatment, this does not demand great upkeep and it can easily be freshened up with furniture polish.

Clear lacquer

Clear lacquer is a transparent surface treatment. Lacquered wood has a sealed surface (lacquer layer) which closes off the pores and forms a hard membrane over the surface of the wood. This provides stronger protection than many other surface treatments for wood. The disadvantage is that any marks and chips that do arise may be more difficult to repair on a lacquered surface than on a diffusion-open surface, where they can be sanded locally and repaired.

Matt lacquer

Matt lacquer has the same characteristics as clear lacquer or coloured lacquer, but has a more matt surface. Because of its silky-matt finish, it can feel almost like an oiled surface.

Painting

Wood that has been painted loses its natural grain and patterning. Both water-based and oil-based paints are available. Bear in mind that even water-based paints contribute to microplastics in the environment. Anyone who wants to avoid dangerous solvents completely is usually recommended to go for furniture painted with linseed oil paint or egg oil tempera.

TIP!

Are you buying painted furniture? Ask the furniture store or the manufacturer whether the glues used in manufacture are solvent free or whether they contain formaldehyde that can be released into the indoor air. Also ask what kind of paint has been used and whether it contains plasticizers, preservatives and solvents? As far as is possible, paints that contain volatile organic compounds should be avoided as they emit gases into the indoor air.

Egg oil tempera

This is an environmentally sound paint made from natural ingredients (egg being one of them, as the name implies). It gives a completely matt surface that, with time, develops a surface patina similar to that of an eggshell. It reflects the ambient light beautifully and feels a little different depending on where the furniture stands. It has a long drying time (up to ten weeks) since the hardening process does not rely on evaporation but on oxidisation together with the underlying wood. As a consequence of this, furniture painted with egg oil tempera has a longer delivery time. The surface can be slightly sensitive to knocks when new but, over time, it develops an almost indestructible surface.

Egg oil tempera is perishable and must be kept in the fridge.

DID YOU KNOW?

All wood must be dried (seasoned) before any further treatment. Professional furniture makers will only use wood that is dried to a moisture content of 6–8 per cent. Depending on how the drying process is carried out, it takes various lengths of time. If the drying process is speeded up too quickly, the wood can develop cracks that are invisible on the surface, but will shorten the life of the item.

Composites

Modern technology has given us new materials, particularly combinations of materials – composites – which have become commonplace in furniture and interior design. There are different kinds of plastics that are also available in sheet form and these can make products cheaper and simpler to produce, as well as stronger and more resistant. Sheets based on wood materials are, however, nothing new. Wood-based composites come in the form of sawdust, fibres, wood chips, veneers and rods held together with various adhesives such as resins and glues. The sheets have differing characteristics depending on their composition. What follows will give you a little more information about composites so that you can better follow and understand the content descriptions given on furniture.

Chipboard/particle board

These are made from the by-products of the sawmill industry (sawdust and wood chips), or from recycled materials bound together under pressure with glue. The adhesive is most often carbamide glue or urea glue. Chipboard sheets come in many different thicknesses, shapes and edgings. We can say that, as a general rule, chipboard is denser, lighter and more easily shaped than wood, but on the other hand it does not tolerate moisture well. A chipboard sheet exposed to moisture will swell and buckle. Chipboard is divided into two main groups based on its tolerance to moisture: sheets for the indoor environment (Climate class 0 or 1) is known as V20 according to the terminology of the German standard (DIN68761); sheets that are more tolerant of moisture are called V313 after the French testing method for certifying moisture resistance. Chipboard is often used as the backing material for veneers.

Some composite boards common in the furniture industry
- Masonite (sheets of steam-treated wood fibres)
- MDF (Medium Density Fibreboard)
- HDF (High Density Fibreboard)
- Melamine-faced sheets
- Plywood
- OSB sheets (Oriented Stranded Board)
- Glued laminated timber

Masonite

The name Masonite comes from the American trademark Masonite, which was invented by William H. Mason. As distinct from chipboard, no additional glue is added, and the lignin of the wood itself is used as the adhesive. In the manufacturing process, the wood pulp is expanded under high pressure from steam and is then pressure-moulded into sheets with the help of the lignin. This technique has made it possible to turn waste from the sawing process into material for the building and interior design sector.

Masonite broke through in the 1930s and was a cheap, easy-to-shape and hygienic material compared with other materials of the time. Rundvik, just outside Umeå where I grew up, had the only European factory for the manufacture of Masonite for many years. It was run by Masonit AB, under licence from Mason in the USA, until it went bankrupt in 2011, at which point the business was moved to Thailand.

MDF

MDF stands for Medium Density Fibreboard, which are sheets manufactured from wood fibres that usually come 100 per cent from coniferous trees. The material is hard and has a smooth surface, which makes it suitable for the manufacture of furniture, since it can be worked in the same way as solid wood. The higher the density of a sheet of MDF, the easier it is to mill it. MDF is manufactured to various standard sizes, suitable for the most frequently used machines, but also to suit our standard module size which, in the Swedish furniture and interior design industry, has long been 600 millimetres. HDF (High Density Fibreboard) and LDF (Low Density Fibreboard) are variants manufactured on similar lines to MDF but of higher or lower densities. HDF, for instance, is more suitable for door leaves, whereas LDF is more often used for packaging. The disadvantage of MDF is that the edge is much more porous than solid wood and is thus not suitable for screwing. Some kind of fitting is usually necessary in order to join MDF sheets, and screws that get loose can't be re-tightened.

MDF attracts moisture and should not be used outdoors or in rooms, such as kitchens and bathrooms, where it can be attacked by moisture.

Melamine-faced boards

Many materials that are just lumped together as laminates are, properly speaking, melamine-faced boards and can be divided into two groups:

- Direct laminate or low-pressure laminate

Also known as melamine. This is a plastic laminate that is glued onto MDF sheets or cardboard. Melamine is a hard material for the surface, but will not tolerate the same loading as laminates and is consequently more often used for vertical surfaces, such as doors, cabinet sides and shelves rather than table tops.

- High-pressure laminate

Also known as laminate. May look like wood or stone from a distance, but, close up, it becomes obvious both to the hand and the eye that the pattern is a result of photographic imitation. The laminate is formed by many layers of impregnated paper being compressed under high pressure at a high temperature. This creates a durable and water-resistant surface, but, if damaged, it is more difficult to repair neatly.

Plywood (cross veneers)

Plywood is actually a trademark and product name that has become so accepted that it is now used to cover the whole range of cross-veneered boards. The material consists of thin layers of wood veneers glued together with the direction of the fibres in each adjacent layer at right angles to its neighbour.

DID YOU KNOW?

It's said that material similar to plywood existed 3,000 years ago. The first plywood factory in Sweden was built at Edsbyn in 1912 and is still active.

Plywood can be made of many kinds of wood – pine, spruce and birch, for instance. Birch plywood is the most commonly used in the furniture industry. Plywood is made in many different thicknesses and qualities. The most common thicknesses used in Sweden are 4, 6, 9, 12, 15, 18 and 21 millimetres. Because of its composition, plywood is a remarkably tough and strong material in all directions – unlike ordinary wood. Plywood also has relatively little movement as a result of moisture and does not change as much as solid wood. Unlike MDF and chipboard, it is possible to re-tighten loose screws in plywood. (In a sheet of MDF, you need to move the screw and drill a new hole if you want it to hold.) On the other hand, plywood can be difficult to saw, since sawing leaves ragged edges. Among the disadvantages of the material is the fact that you have to add glue to hold the boards together and, depending on the content of the glue you use, it can add some level of emissions to the atmosphere of the house.

OSB

OSB, which stands for Oriented strand board, consists of strands and fibres of wood, anything up to several centimetres wide and up to 10 centimetres long. It is made up of several layers in which the fibres of each part are oriented in the same direction. When the layers are glued together the material is extremely robust and stable. OSB boards are also much more resistant to the corners being broken than plywood, and since it is so tough, it is mostly used in the building industry. It is also used in the carcasses of really cheap sofas and padded armchairs. Since it is made of such coarse chips, it is often cheaper than chipboard and MDF.

Blockboard

Blockboard consists of a core of strips of solid timber placed between two sheets of plywood and glued under high pressure. (The sheets may be MDF or chipboard, sometimes coated in melamine.) Blockboard weighs little, is stable in form and strong. Blockboard, just like edge-glued boards, is used in shelving, table tops and worktops because, as a result of its construction, it has a higher weight-bearing capacity than many other wooden boards.

Edge-glued-board

Edge-glued-board consists of strips of solid wood glued together lengthways to form a solid sheet. It is very commonly used for shelving, table tops and worktops.

Linoleum

Linoleum is made from linseed oil, cork dust and wood dust with the addition of resin and natural colour pigments. This mixture is then spread on burlap to create a hard-wearing, elastic material. If the lino gets small scratches or damage, they aren't usually obvious to the eye thanks to a natural oxidation process which makes the material appear to swell back. Moreover, linoleum is also UV-resistant and retains its colour even when exposed to strong sunlight. The material can be sanded and the surface can be treated, so that, given the right treatment, the surface can become as new. Linoleum is mainly used for flooring, but is also popular as the top layer on, for instance, table tops, stools and pedestal units.

Plastic

Plastic has become a general collective term for a wide group of synthetic, semi-synthetic or bio-based materials that are used in furnishing and interior design. Synthetic plastic is derived from fossil and finite resources such as crude oil and natural gas, whereas bio-based plastic (PLA) is made from plant-based oils and other biological substances. Since minute microparticles of plastic can escape into nature and into the ecosystem, the handling of the material, as well as its manufacture, has to be done responsibly. That means both by the producers and by us, the users. Up to now, it has only been possible to recycle many sorts of plastic a limited number of times before the fibres lose their elasticity. A great deal of research is, however, being done in this area. I know too little at present to say much more, but I tend, as far as I can, to avoid it unless it's absolutely necessary, for instance, to increase the durability or lifespan of a product.

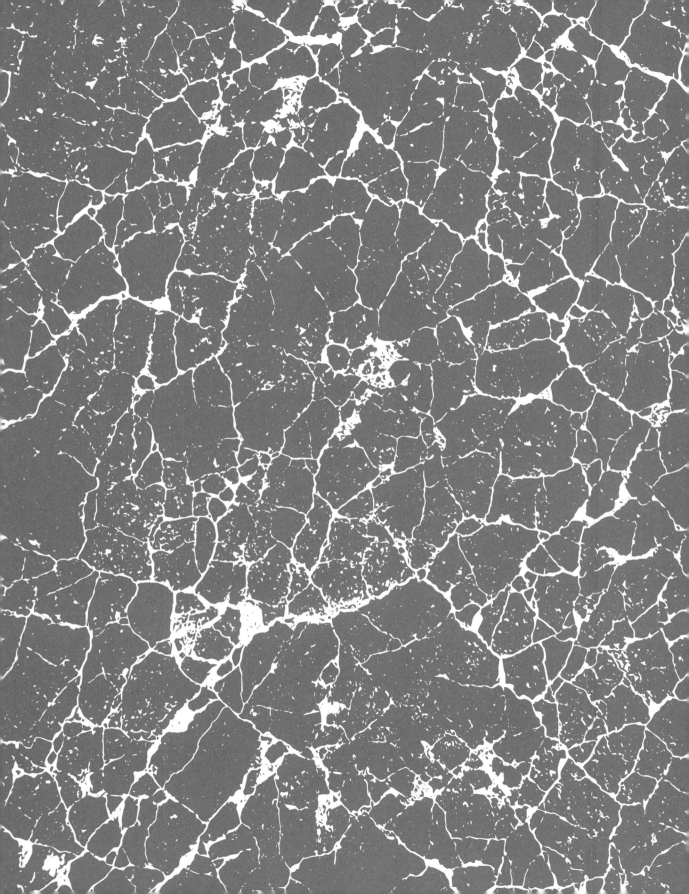

Stone

Choosing stone is exactly like choosing wood: it's not just a matter of colour and appearance, but also one of its materiality and other qualities. We often pay more attention to the differences of appearance between various types of stone, rather than what really matters – the ways in which they may be more or less suitable for use for different purposes and circumstances. Stone is a collective name for many rocks and minerals. It is a natural material and may be called natural stone. Once we have dug it from the ground, there is no way of returning it to its original state, which is why I think we should treat the material with respect. Being properly informed is essential if we are to reach well-considered decisions, so, what follows is a brief overview for those of you who want a better grasp of the common rock types used in furniture and design.

Variation is part and parcel of the concept

Buying natural stone is not the same thing as buying paint. You can, of course, take home samples to see what the stone looks like in the light you have at home, but no orders are exactly the same: one stone is never identical to another. Not even if you choose the same type of stone from the same quarry. So you can never count on the table top you are ordering being exactly the same as the one you are looking at in the shop. That means, of course, that the tops of two adjacent coffee or bedside tables will always look just a little different. Top-class suppliers will not usually tolerate great differences, whereas suppliers keen on pushing the price down often don't even bother to check before sending you the goods. Some variation is part and parcel of the concept and is also part of the charm. If you want to be absolutely certain of getting two identical slabs of stone, I would recommend you to choose composite stone or ceramic granite.

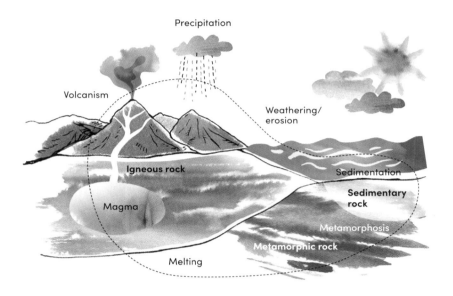

The geological cycle.

Igneous, sedimentary and metamorphic rocks

Rocks are divided into three main categories: igneous, sedimentary and metamorphic.

Igneous rocks are formed when hot magma crystallizes. This can either happen within the earth or above the surface when volcanic lava runs out and cools. To simplify somewhat, these rocks often have a 'spotted' appearance, with mineral grains of different colours. Granite and dolerite are igneous rocks. The colour is dependent on the combination of minerals that make up the rock.

Sedimentary rocks are formed by the deposition and cementing of loose sediment, which means that this type of rock often has a stratified structure. Depositions of lime slurry and shell fragments mean that it's sometimes possible to see the fossils, such as Orthoceras or trilobites. Examples of sedimentary rocks are sandstone, shale and limestone.

Metamorphic rocks are formed when igneous or sedimentary rocks are subjected to high pressure and heat far below the surface of the earth. It gives them a veined structure of the kind we see in marble. Gneiss, quartzite and marble are examples of metamorphic rocks.

The geological cycle

One rock type can become another in a cyclical process called 'the geological cycle'. The cycle includes, for example, erosion, sedimentation, compacting and cementing, metamorphosis, melting, magmatism and volcanism. Under pressure, sedimentary and igneous rocks can then change to being metamorphic rocks. If the heat is sufficiently intense, these can then melt and form magma, which then crystallizes to form a new igneous rock type.

Igneous rocks

Dolerite

Dolerite is often called black granite and is a dark, very hard, igneous rock. Sweden is a major exporter of dolerite. Moheda is the tradename for a dolerite quarried in north-east Skåne, Småland and Blekinge.

Granite

The bedrock in large parts of Sweden is granite. It has become popular across the world for surfaces as it can be cut in any direction. In commercial terms, the most common Swedish varieties are grey and red Bohus granite.

Bianco Sardo is a coarse-grained, light-grey granite from Italy. Rosa Sardo is tinged with pink and beige. Kuru Grey is light grey and fine-grained. Granite should be free of quartz veins and any hints of cracks. Granite work surfaces are hard-wearing, scratch resistant and will tolerate high temperatures.

Sedimentary rocks

Limestone

The limestone used for furniture and interior design must be compact and free from any hint of cracks. Any visible fossils must not be loose and must not reach the edge of the tile. Öland limestone is a world-famous Swedish limestone, which may be grey or reddish-brown. A planed surface gives it a slightly rough and lighter feel and when polished it becomes a little darker. Is suitable as the top surface in places where you want there to be a bit more character in the stone.

Jura limestone comes from Germany and is a warm beige or grey. The speckled surface gives it a lively appearance and natural patterning.

Azul, a Portuguese limestone, was originally quarried around Valverde (hence the name Azul Valverde), but is now resourced from several other areas, which is why not all the limestone varieties have the suffix Valverde. Azul is popular internationally as it shades from beige to grey and blue, but without too sharp a contrast between the tones.

Giza sandstone is quarried in Egypt and has a greyish brown colour with a lot of patterning in it. A nice quirky fact is that the pyramids are built of this limestone.

Sandstone

This can be composed of a combination of different minerals and consequently comes in different colours with different names. It commonly contains quartz (quartz sandstone), but can also have calcite (calcite sandstone) and limonite (iron sandstone).

In terms of quality, sandstone needs to be fine- or medium-grained and free from any signs of cracking.

Shale

Shale is formed at great depth in the oceans from very fine sediment, mainly clay, and is compressed into rock by heat and pressure. Shale is sliced by hand along its bedding planes, unlike marble and granite, for instance, that are cut into slabs mechanically using a multi-blade saw. The colour varies from a lighter grey to deep black.

Metamorphic Rocks

Marble

Marble is to be found in many places around the world and turns up in many different colours. Possibly the best-known type is Italian Carrara marble, which is typically white or blue/white/grey in tone. The markings in the marble are sharply defined, which gives the patterning a special effect.

The classic Kolmården marble has been quarried in Sweden since the 1600s and it is one of the most characteristic Swedish rocks, as well as having an international reputation. It is greenish, with a wavy patterning, and its unique pattern and coloration has made it one of the most exclusive varieties of marble. The abbreviation OX signifies that the marble comes from the Oxåker quarry in Kolmården, which is situated immediately north-east of Norrköping. Kolmården marble has different patterns, depending on how it is sawn.

Marble is one of the softer rock types and consequently sensitive to mechanical and chemical damage. Many substances can leave stains on it – red wine, coffee, tea, beetroot, pomegranate, turmeric – but it's also sensitive to acids and strong cleaning products.

Schist

Schist is a metamorphic rock which glitters beautifully since, by volume, it contains up to 50 per cent of glittering minerals, mainly micas. Scandinavian schist is known for its high quality and resilience.

Surface treatments for natural rock

Broken

This is the term for the surface of schist when the rock is split. Can only be done with certain kinds of schist.

Diamond milling

This is often the first stage of polishing. The surface is planed off with a rotating diamond tool which leaves ring-shaped marks.

Brushing

Brushing is carried out with rotating brushes that are set with diamonds. The surface gets polished, but, depending on the type of rock and earlier treatment, it is left with some undulations.

Blasted/sandblasted

Using air pressure, a special abrasive sand is blown against the rock. This produces a slightly granular surface and is best suited for quartzite and sandstone since these rocks have a grainy structure. Is mainly used to create decorations, patterns or text in the stone.

Finely ground

Produces a smooth, but not mirror-like, surface to the rock.

Polished

Produces a smooth and mirror-like surface. The lustre should still remain even after being washed with solvents.

TIP!

Polished stone is usually more resistant to water since the smooth surface allows water to run off. Polished stone, however, is more slippery than non-polished.

Planing

Planing the surface of the stone produces a rough surface with a streaky, scored texture with irregularities. A smoother, dark edge with a decorative effect is left where the plane-runs overlap. Planing can also be used to profile the edges.

Bush hammering

This is done with a hydraulic tool that chips the stone, leaving a rough surface with indentations and elevations.

Chipping

An older technique, carried out by hand with a mallet and chisel, mainly on limestone and marble. Usually used for edges and decoration.

Ageing

There is no single technique and different suppliers use various methods to achieve a worn surface with a patina of age. It can be done by planing, brushing or honing. Used mainly on limestone.

Impregnating stone

You can impregnate stone with preservative chemicals in order to protect the surface. This is particularly important, perhaps, for floors, but also for table tops, work surfaces and kitchen tops that are subjected to hard wear and tear, sometimes of a mechanical nature. Read the supplier's instructions for your particular kind of stone in order to select the right chemical for the stone and one that can be used where you want it, where foodstuffs are being prepared, for instance.

Artificial stone

Terrazzo

Terrazzo is an artificial stone produced from crushed natural stone. It is hard, durable and easy to look after. It was extremely popular in the 1950s. Terrazzo has become popular again in recent years and is now available in many different colours. Since it contains resins, terrazzo is sensitive to heat. And since there is also cement in the mixture, terrazzo weighs a little more than natural stone, which means that it makes greater demands on the construction of the furniture and carcasses, as well as on the beams supporting the floor. There is also some risk of the material cracking. On the other hand, it is often significantly cheaper than natural stone and there is a wide range to choose from.

Composite quartz

There are a number of brands of quartz composites on the market. Without going into detail on their respective characteristics, what we can say is that the common recipe is based on ground natural stone (mainly quartz, hence the name) mixed with colour pigments and adhesive before being pressed and poured as a sheet. Some of these composites are so heat-resistant that you can place hot saucepans on them – others, however, are not very heat-resistant at all. These surfaces are extremely resistant to dirt and stains.

Concrete

Concrete is not stone, it is made from sand and gravel (or crushed rock) mixed with water and cement. As a building material, it is resistant to heat, cold and damp. It lasts a long time and demands little upkeep. All this has made concrete a popular element in furniture and interior design – as the tops for side tables, sideboards and chests of drawers.

Concrete has a tendency to 'dust'. Concrete sealer provides extra protection against dust and scratches, as well as nourishing the surface. There are also different surface treatments to choose from: straw-polished or wet-polished concrete, for instance, which will give you different looks.

Leather

Leather is a collective name for the natural material derived from animal hides. Its advantages are that it's flexible, tough and it breathes. If it's been properly tanned and looked after, it lasts a long time and becomes more beautiful with the passing years. Depending on which animal the hide has come from and how it has been treated, leather has different qualities and characteristics. What follows is a quick overview of the most common types of leather, what they are most frequently used for in furniture, and why.

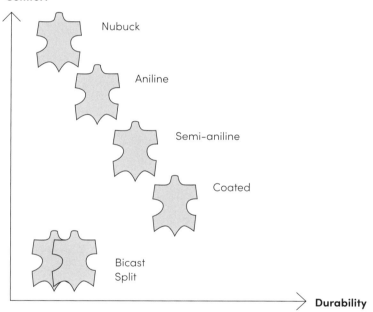

Comfort

Nubuck

Aniline

Semi-aniline

Coated

Bicast
Split

Durability

Nubuck

A quality of leather in which the hair side (the outer side from which the hair has been removed) has been smoothed lightly to bring it to a matt, almost peach-like feel. It is somewhat reminiscent of mocha, though mocha is derived from the flesh side of the hide. Nubuck is soft and fine, but delicate and susceptible to stains. It doesn't tolerate light very well.

Aniline leather

Aniline leather is a natural leather, dyed right through but without a top coat or surface lacquer. At the final stage it is given light treatment to protect against stains and spills. Aniline is produced from full grain hides (unaltered) and is characterized by its luxurious, soft surface and excellent sitting comfort in that it also retains an even temperature. Since the leather has not been altered or finished, natural marks such as insect bites and scars are part of this leather's unique and natural appearance. And given the fact that the leather has not been treated with a colour or lacquer, it continues to breathe and develops a fine patina as it ages. In order to retain this, regular care with skincare products is necessary (just as with human beings).

Aniline leather can be sensitive to stains and spillage, but nowadays there are excellent products capable of removing traces of such accidents. You should avoid oily products (grease) that don't dry. They will change the shade of the leather, making it darker and giving it a shiny surface which, in turn, make it easier for grease and dirt to stick to the surface of the leather. If you are buying leather furniture second-hand, it's a good idea to pay attention to dark patches at the head, neck and elbow positions: they can indicate that grease from the user's skin has penetrated the leather and it needs to be cleaned.

Semi-aniline leather

Semi-aniline leather is aniline leather in which the full grain (the hard side of the leather) has been surface treated with a thin layer of colour and lacquer to increase its resistance to stains and dirt. It has

DID YOU KNOW?

The elasticity of leather depends on which part of the animal's hide it is taken from. Close to the backbone, the hide is least elastic, and the elasticity increases the further away from the spine you go.

a natural structure and needs less care than aniline. Thanks to this thin finish, the leather is dirt and water-resistant, as well as tolerating light. It also makes for very comfortable seating.

Coated leather

Like aniline and semi-aniline, coated leather (also known as pigmented leather) is available in many different colours and nuances. The leather has been treated with even more colours and lacquers and is consequently both tough, dirt- and water-resistant and light-tolerant.

The treatment of the surface of the leather means that it does not breathe, but in return it is easier to dry and to look after. Nevertheless, like all natural materials, a certain amount of care is necessary to preserve the appearance and character of the leather: the right care products are vital. Avoid greasy products that simply lie on the surface and do not dry. This type of leather is available in its natural state, but it is also quite common to emboss the leather to get the desired appearance.

Split leather, bicast leather, bonded leather or PU-leather

Split leather is the lower part of the hide after the splitting process, the latter being the mechanical process of splitting the hide before tanning. The upper slice is called grain leather, the lower slice is split leather. Split leather is often used for the cheaper details and for shoes, belts, work gloves and the like.

Bicast is usually made from split leather with a film of polyurethane glued on to it, which gives it a gleaming, plastic-like surface. It has proved difficult to produce more flexible forms with bicast leather, so someone came up with the idea of using a textile weave as backing instead of split leather – this makes the texture softer and more malleable. Bicast is cheaper and needs less upkeep than real leather, but it is stiffer and less flexible. As it gets older, the outer layer often starts to flake off.

Bonded leather is produced from the waste pieces after splitting. Rather like sawdust and chips, these pieces are collected, mixed with an adhesive and pressed into sheets, which can then be stamped and coloured with whichever patterns and colours are desired.

PU-leather is a mainly artificial material similar to imitation leather; it is essentially a polyurethane surface on a textile base layer. A layer of leather fibres is sometimes coated on to the reverse side in order to achieve a product more similar to leather. The material known as vegan leather is often PU-leather manufactured from polyurethane.

NB! It is important that the care of these mixed materials uses products designed specifically for them and not for traditional leather.

Imitation leather

This is an artificial leather produced from a textile coated with PU. It is a little harder than leather and has a more plasticky smell.

Tanning

The process of taking the hide of an animal and processing it to prevent rotting and to make the leather soft and pliable. The process can be carried out in a number of different ways and has undergone considerable refinement over the years in line with increased environmental demands and sustainable production. In the past it was a fairly dirty industry, since strong chemicals and heavy metals, such as chrome, were used – these were damaging to nature and to the health of the workers in the tanning industry, and, indeed, to the end users of the product.

In the case of vegetable tanning, the conservation process is done with bark instead of chrome. The process is rather slower and more demanding and, as a consequence, the leather tends to be a little dearer than with traditional chrome tanning. It is more environmentally friendly, but it does not produce a leather with the same characteristics as chrome tanning and can't be used for all types of furniture. Chrome-tanned leather is more flexible, though on the other hand it does not always age as nicely as vegetable tanned leather.

Legislation regarding which substances are permitted in tanning and how they should be treated before being released into the environment vary from country to country. When you buy a piece of furniture that has leather parts, it's worth asking about how and where they were tanned and coloured.

Check that the leather in the piece you are buying comes from registered tanneries that follow the REACH regulation and that the producer can guarantee that there is no Chrome 6 in it. The use of Chrome 6 has been forbidden in the EU for many years, whereas it is still common in tanneries outside the EU and America, particularly in South America, India and Asia. If you want to be 100 per cent sure of buying leather that hasn't been tanned using Chrome 6, buy furniture with leather produced in Sweden or the EU, where the tannery owns the whole production process.

You should also ask whether the leather has been treated with flame-proofing or allergy-inducing anti-mould agents, since they can cause problems if you sit on the leather with parts of your body exposed – if you have bare arms and legs when wearing shorts or a T-shirt, for instance.

'It's all right if the hide shows some signs of scratches and rips, they just go to prove that the cow has had some freedom in its life.'

Börge Lindau, Blå Station

Textiles

In everyday speech, textiles are usually just called cloth – a collective term for the products of textile fibres that have been woven into a material that can be used *inter alia* for covering furniture and other aspects of interior design. To gain a better understanding of the characteristics of the different textiles, they can be grouped together on the basis of what the textile fibres come from. This is an area of rapid development, not least for environmental reasons, and when you look at the listing below, it becomes a bit easier to get some idea why.

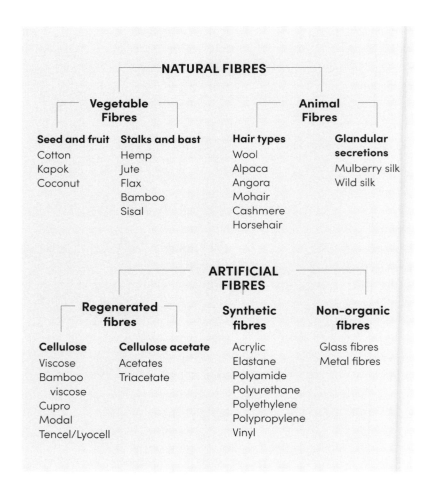

NATURAL FIBRES

Vegetable Fibres

Seed and fruit
Cotton
Kapok
Coconut

Stalks and bast
Hemp
Jute
Flax
Bamboo
Sisal

Animal Fibres

Hair types
Wool
Alpaca
Angora
Mohair
Cashmere
Horsehair

Glandular secretions
Mulberry silk
Wild silk

ARTIFICIAL FIBRES

Regenerated fibres

Cellulose
Viscose
Bamboo viscose
Cupro
Modal
Tencel/Lyocell

Cellulose acetate
Acetates
Triacetate

Synthetic fibres
Acrylic
Elastane
Polyamide
Polyurethane
Polyethylene
Polypropylene
Vinyl

Non-organic fibres
Glass fibres
Metal fibres

Natural fibres

These are derived from animals and plants and are therefore considered natural materials. Since new plants grow and new animals are born, they are renewable, but better or worse varieties exist depending on how well they are cultivated and tended.

Vegetable fibres

SEEDS AND FRUIT

The first sub-categories of vegetable fibres are those that are derived from seeds and fruit.

Cotton

Cotton comes from the cotton plant and it is the seed capsule beneath the flower that gives us the material we call cotton. There are about twenty varieties within the cotton family, but there are mainly four types that are grown commercially. The advantages of the material are, among other things, that it is strong, durable and flexible. It is washable, and it wicks away moisture and heat. Among its downsides are that it shrinks a little when washed, it is not elastic and it creases easily. Compared with other textiles, cotton is a very thirsty plant and it needs to be fed with a lot of chemicals in terms of fertilizing, as well as pesticides. Consequently, even though it is natural, it is possibly not the best thing for the environment – nor for you, depending on which substances remain in the finished product. This is why ecologically and sustainably grown cotton is to be recommended. The longer and thinner the cotton fibres are, the stronger, glossier and more pliable the threads and the fabric will be. Cotton can be woven in a number of different ways to produce fabrics such as *inter alia* flannel, percale, satin, poplin, terry cloth, corduroy and denim. They may all have different characteristics, but they all consist of the same basic material – cotton, with no admixture of synthetic fibres.

Coconut

Coconut fibre is derived from coconuts. It provides a light and porous material, used, among other uses, for padding and carpets. Both brown coconut fibre (coir) and white exist, the brown coming from ripe coconuts and the white from unripe coconuts. The coconut fibre is twisted tight in order to make it curly and supple. Softer and finer parts of the fibre from the shells of coconuts is called elancrin, a refined fibre. The brown fibres are used as padding in armchairs, sofas and mattresses and may also be woven into carpets. The white fibre is often used for making rope and brushes.

Kapok

Kapok fibres are the seed hairs from the tree *Ceiba pentandra*, which grows wild in the tropical rainforests of South and Central America, India and the western parts of Africa. Kapok contains about 80 per cent air, which makes it the world's lightest natural fibre. It is actually no less than eight times lighter than cotton. It is most commonly used as a filling for duvets, cushions and mattresses. The fibres have anti-bacterial qualities, which often makes them suitable for those who suffer from allergies.

STALKS AND BAST FIBRES

Stalk and bast fibres (from the insides of plants) are derived from plants such as flax and hemp. Exploiting them is often a more time-consuming process than that for seed fibres.

Linen

Linen is derived from flax. The cultivation of flax needs little by way of water and pesticides, which means it is naturally more sustainable than many other textile raw materials. Flax fibre has considerable ability to absorb water, but does not tolerate being washed at high temperatures. Flax fabrics crease a great deal, become softer the more they are used and develop a nice lustre. Higher quality flax feels slightly 'fuller' and nicer to the touch, whereas lower quality flax fabric feels drier and stiffer and lacks the lustre you experience from premium quality flax. Flax fabric takes on an extra sheen from being cold-mangled.

Hemp

The fibres in the bark of the stalks of hemp can be processed into textile fibres either mechanically or chemically. The plant is hardy and fast growing, even in poor soil. Similar to flax, the fibres are longer and they can be spun to different thicknesses. They make strong material. Webbing, for instance, is made from hemp.

Jute

Jute or burlap, from the fibres of *Corchorus capsularis* (white jute) or *Corchorus olitorius* (red jute), come from a bush that grows in tropical regions. Tough and durable, it is used in carpets, seats and chairs. The lignin in the fibres means that jute turns yellow and becomes brittle when exposed to light – just like newspaper in the sun.

Sisal

A strong, coarse and resistant fibre cultivated mainly in Africa. It is used in carpets, robust mats, rope, coarse fabrics and baskets.

Animal fibres

HAIR TYPES

Fibres from animals can be used in interior design in clothes, textiles, throws and carpets.

Sheep's wool

Wool from the curly fleece of sheep varies in length (staple) and thickness. Wool is clipped from live animals then cleaned, carded (combed) before it can be spun into a yarn. Wool comes in different qualities depending on the quality of the fleece on the sheep and how well it is sorted and processed. The common feature of the fibres is that they contain a great deal of air, which gives the fabric good heat-insulating qualities. Wool is resistant to creasing, but it does shrink in the wash and thus needs to be cleaned with care. You must never rub at a stain on woollen clothing or carpet as that leads to felting. The finer the quality of the wool, the greater the risk of getting bobbles.

Merino

Merino sheep originated in Spain and have been bred specifically to produce a great deal of fine-quality wool. Always look for certified merino wool, which is guaranteed to be 'mulesing-free'. That means that the sheep have not had strips of skin scalped from their rumps to get rid of the larvae of flies.

Alpaca wool

Derived from the alpaca, a member of the llama family, this wool has very long fibres, sometimes as much as 10 centimetres. That means that alpaca wool does not feel itchy and does not form bobbles to any great extent. It is also soft and glossy.

Angora wool

Angora wool comes from rabbits and has a fine fibre structure that makes it warmer and softer than many other kinds of wool. Angora wool may be clipped or it may be plucked, so make sure you buy *cruelty-free angora* even if it's a little more expensive. Rabbit wool, unlike sheep's wool, does not contain oil.

Cashmere wool

Cashmere wool is from goats that originally came from the Kashmir region of India – hence the name.

Mohair

Mohair is wool fibre from angora goats and it is one of the softest and most exclusive types of yarn on the market. It is often used in expensive throws and cushions.

Horsehair and cattle-tail hair

Horsehair from the tails of horses is strong and supple, whereas hair from the mane is soft but lacks suppleness. Hair from cattle or cows' tails is soft but with no suppleness at all. The hair is clipped from the animals when they are alive: hair taken from dead animals lacks sheen and suppleness. Horsehair is commonly used as stuffing for seating and for beds, but it's also used to make brushes. Engineered horsehair has undergone a process that makes it both curly and resilient.

SILKS

Mulberry silk

Silk is a natural protein fibre derived from the larvae of the silk moth, which lives on the leaves of the mulberry tree. To ensure a good and even quality, the larvae are bred in controlled conditions and are fed on mulberry leaves. The larvae exude a secretion and spin it into a thread which they wind around themselves into a cocoon – one single cocoon consists of a thread of silk that can be up to 3,000 metres long. Once the larva has finished spinning, the cocoon is put in boiling water to kill the pupa. Then, very carefully, the silk is unwound, before being spun into many different sorts of fabric, particularly silk. Names like twill and organza describe different methods of weaving. Silk is sensitive to high temperatures and can be difficult to wash, so it often needs chemical cleaning. Since silk is an expensive and exclusive fabric, some producers treat their silk with metallic salts to achieve the same feel but with a smaller quantity of silk; this gives the material weight, but risks making it crease more and lose resilience.

Wild silk

Tussah silk comes from a larva that feeds on oak leaves. Since wild larvae eat more irregularly than cultivated larvae, the colours may vary. The threads of wild silk are also coarser and more uneven than mulberry silk. Thai silk, which is often woven from wild silk, exemplifies the quality of this fabric, which has a natural unevenness about it.

TIP!

Always enquire as to how the surface of furniture covers and textiles has been treated. Sofa and armchair covers and carpets may have been treated with PFC/PFAS to make them water- and dirt-resistant, or treated with inflammable preparations to make it less likely they will catch fire. Read more about PFC-free and PFAS-free, perfluorinated chemicals and polyfluorinated substances, to learn more about what these things mean.

Artificial fibres

Fibres created by human-made processes are called artificial fibres. They fall into two groups: rayon or regenerated fibres, which are produced from cellulose (from trees) and synthetic fibres, which are oil-based products. Oil is a finite resource, which is why it's called a non-renewable or fossil raw material.

Regenerated fibres

These are the product of cellulose from the cell walls of plants (spruce trees included). With chemicals, they can be converted to a spinnable solution. Regenerated fibres tend to be strong when dry, but become substantially weaker when wet. A great deal of research and development is going on in this area. Viscose, viscose bamboo, cupro (vegan silk), modal, Lyocell/Tencel, cellulose acetate (lining fabric) and tri-acetate (filling material) are widely used in the furniture industry.

Synthetic fibres

Mainly derived from fossil raw materials, such as oil, synthetic fibres soften when heated and therefore cannot be ironed at high temperatures. They can also be sensitive to sunlight and should consequently be avoided in curtains. Some commonly occurring examples of synthetic fibres in furniture and interior design are acrylics, elastane (elastic and stretchy), polyamide (light-sensitive), polyurethane (non-crease), polyethylene, polypropylene and vinyl fibres.

Non-organic fibres

Carbon fibre, glass fibre, optical fibre and metallic fibre. These are mainly used for heat insulation and soundproofing, but also in curtains and decorative materials in public places. Textiles containing metals are also used to protect against the sun in curtains, for instance.

Mixtures

Textile fibres are woven using the same material or, in order to achieve different qualities, in a variety of mixtures. When fibres are mixed, they can complete and enhance each other's qualities.

Metals and alloys

Chair legs, table legs, shelf units, nails, screws and nuts are just a few examples of the various metals and alloys in furniture it is useful for us to be familiar with. What follows is a very rapid survey of the kind of thing that's good to know when buying.

Aluminium

Aluminium is a durable, light metal with considerable strength relative to its weight. It tolerates both frost and rain, which means it is commonly used in furniture that is left outdoors, permanently or temporarily. Aluminium is 100 per cent recyclable and loses none of its quality in the course of that process – and it can be recycled endlessly.

Aluminium is often considered to be a rust-free metal, but that only holds within the pH 4–9 zone. If aluminium comes into contact with a more noble metal (copper, zinc and certain types of steel, for instance), the aluminium may be broken down, which means that it cannot be combined willy-nilly in furniture or interior design work.

Steel

Steel is an alloy of iron and is manufactured to a wide range of qualities. It has high flexural strength, which means that furniture and frames with very little give in them can be made of it. It is completely recyclable, but it rusts unless the surface is treated and given a protective layer. Steel can, for instance, be galvanized or hot-zinc-sprayed to protect it from corrosion, in which case the material will need no further upkeep and its lifetime will be extended.

Stainless steel

Stainless steel is an iron alloy with a high chromium content and it is very resistant to corrosion. The material has an even finish and furniture made of stainless steel is usually very stable, even when the tubing is slim. Stainless steel loses its rust-resistant properties when exposed to high temperature, such as welding: to restore rust protection the welding points, must be surface-treated by spraying or dipping. Stainless steel is very malleable and can be bent and worked even at low temperatures. Never use wire wool or metallic sponges when cleaning the stainless steel parts of furniture as they may cause scratches and damage the surface.

Cast iron and wrought iron

Cast iron is a common material for fittings, brackets, garden furniture and cooking pots. The material is robust, but the weight is such that it's not used in large amounts, though it's often used for parts and details in furniture and design. Outdoor furniture made of cast iron is solid and remains stable in the strongest winds, but it can, however, be very heavy to move. It can withstand high temperatures and compression, but is sensitive to knocks and blows. The difference between cast iron and wrought iron is mainly that cast iron has a higher carbon content. The lower carbon content makes wrought iron softer and easier to work.

Brass

Brass is one of our oldest alloys and is a mixture of copper and zinc. The more zinc there is in the brass, the more resistant to corrosion it is. The colour can vary from whitish-yellow to reddish-brown depending on the copper content. Brass is non-magnetic. Since brass is easy to shape at low temperatures, does not rust and is sufficiently hard to be milled and punched, cast and welded, it is used for all kinds of things from mountings and door handles to lamps, candlesticks, jewellery and plumbing products. Because of its glittering yellow colour, brass used to be known as poor man's gold.

Unless it is kept polished, brass will darken with time and pick up damp stains and fingermarks, but it is relatively easy to polish it back to looking like new. Brass details and fittings are a little more demanding in that they need regular attention if they are to retain their fresh look.

Copper

The element copper is mined from the earth in the form of copper ore, a reddish-coloured substance. After a while the substance develops an oxide layer that forms a blue-green patina. Copper is a reddish gold, relatively soft metal that can be melted down any number of times and any impurities can be removed. Since copper is an extremely good conductor of electricity, it is also used in electronics.

Copper runs as a red thread throughout Swedish history. In the middle of the seventeenth century, Falu Coppermine was the biggest in Europe and the profitable mining of the ore was an important Swedish export and a major contributor to the economy of the country. Falu red, the house paint known worldwide, is a by-product of the copper mines, and red cottages with white-painted corners have become Sweden's trademark.

Tin

Tin is a silvery white metallic element which is extracted primarily from the mineral cassiterite found in granite, slate and so on. Since tin has such a low melting point, it is often used for casting. Tin does not normally oxidize with oxygen, but it can be affected by acids and alkalis. Avoid storing tin objects at temperatures below 10 degrees as this can cause tin pest – blemishing of the metal surface. Tin is a soft material that needs to be handled carefully. It is not recommended to use polishes on tin as it can easily be scratched.

Glass

Glass may be transparent, but it isn't always that obvious what it is made of and what kind of safety you are getting when you buy it. Glass is manufactured from three main raw materials: sand (silicon dioxide), soda (sodium carbonate) and lime (calcium carbonate), mixed together, heated and then cooled. The material can be given different qualities with the help of various additives which, for instance, affect the colour, weight, lustre and load strength.

An example of the breakage pattern on glass that hasn't been safety-hardened: the glass forms large, sharp shards on breaking.

An example of the breakage pattern on hardened glass: the glass disintegrates into a mass of very small granules.

An example of the breakage pattern on laminated glass: the plastic film holds the pieces of glass together, thus minimizing the risk of cuts and injuries.

Hardened safety glass (tempered glass)

Since glass is susceptible to breakage and scratches from bangs and thumps, mechanical loads, high heat and uneven stresses, it is always important to choose hardened glass when you can. When hardened glass breaks, it shatters into myriad small pellets, which have only a very small risk of causing cuts, whereas the shards and splinters of ordinary glass when it shatters can be as long and sharp as knives and lead to serious wounds. Tempered glass – hardened safety glass – is heated to *c.* 650 degrees and then cooled quickly. This leads to contraction of the outer layer of the glass and compression of the middle layer, making the glass stronger than ordinary glass.

Hardened glass will withstand heavier loading, but it may lose its strength if scratched, which is why you should be careful about placing things like rough ceramics and decorative items with uneven bases on hardened glass. Even small scratches can lead to the glass shattering with any major changes in heat or tension. You don't need do any more than google 'glass table explodes' to find newspaper articles proving that it really does happen now and then. Hardened glass is relatively cheap, but you have to state the size when ordering as it is not possible to cut it once it's been hardened.

Laminated safety glass

As well as hardening, the risk of cuts from broken glass can be minimized by a process of lamination, in which two or more sheets of glass are alternated with plastic film. That makes the glass tougher and, should the glass break, the splinters remain attached to the plastic film.

Coloured glass

By colouring molten glass during the manufacturing process, it's possible to achieve a variety of effects, such as smoked glass (popular for side tables and glass tops) or coloured glass. Different effects can be created by using different colour films when laminating safety glass.

Leaded glass

Leaded glasswork is a kind of mosaic created by coloured pieces being soldered together or held together by lead edging. You can see it, for instance, in older display cabinets and also on lamps. Lead and lead compounds are poisonous, so you should always wear gloves to avoid the lead being in contact with your skin. If a sheet of leaded glass breaks, it is important to collect up all the pieces. You must not throw them into the rubbish or into the ordinary glass recycling bin, they should be taken to a recycling centre.

Etched glass

Etched glass is created by mechanically roughening selected areas of the surface so that they become matt and cloudy (not transparent). It is to be found quite commonly as a decorative feature on inside doors and also on display cabinets.

Plexiglas

The name Plexiglas is actually misleading, partly because it's a form of plastic, not glass in the proper sense of the word, and partly because it's actually the trademark for Polymethyl methacrylate (PMMA). Plexiglas is considerably stronger than real glass and it also weighs less, which means that furnishings made partly or wholly of Plexiglas are much lighter than if they had been made of real glass. Moreover, Plexiglas is malleable and flexible and easy to colour, but, on the other hand, it is more sensitive to scratching and strong cleaning treatments.

Timeline

When my first book was translated into twenty-nine languages, many of the questions asked by journalists from abroad concerned Scandinavian aesthetics. They were asking how our houses and furniture differ from those of the rest of the world and why our design language has become such an international success.

My initial response was instinctive and I answered in more or less the same way as I'd heard many other people say before me: that our watchword is 'form should follow function'; that many designers have been inspired by a closeness to nature; that our democratic system in Sweden has undoubtedly contributed to raising the standard of the Swedish welfare state. But the more often I repeated this explanation, the more questioning I became about what I really meant. I honestly found that I couldn't give many concrete or illustrative descriptions to go with these loose assertions. So I decided to dig deeper into our design history in order to find out more.

From poverty to artistry

When we look around Swedish homes as they are today, it is difficult to imagine that at the start of the twentieth century Sweden actually had the lowest standard of housing in the whole of Europe. The population doubled during the nineteenth century as a result of, in the words of the poet Esaias Tegnér, 'peace, potatoes and the vaccine'. At the same time, however, we suffered many years of bad harvests, which led to more and more shortages. And the ever- harder competition for farmland meant that more and more Swedes began moving into the towns in search of work, which meant that by the beginning of the twentieth century there was a considerable surplus of labour.

Many people found it difficult to support themselves, and they lived in poverty, overcrowding and filth. At that time, moreover, our electoral franchise was based on income, so the only thing that could be said to have flourished among the general population was discontent. These are some of the reasons why so many people chose to take a ship across the Atlantic in the hope of finding better living conditions. Between 1860 and 1930, 1,400,000 Swedes emigrated, mainly to North America.

It may be the case, however, that those who stayed behind were the ones who made the biggest journey, because in less than 75 years Sweden actually rose from the bottom to the top. By 1975 the housing shortage had been addressed and Sweden was considered to have by far the highest standard of housing in the world.

The development from poverty to artistry that Sweden is renowned for has been driven by many political reforms, by economic stimulus packages, by state-financed housing research, by strong cooperation between different interest and trade organizations, as well as through diligent and steady work with government consumer information. What follows offers a quick survey of some of the important milestones that may be good to know for those interested in interior design.

Important milestones in the history of Swedish design

1844

Drawing School for Craftsmen

In 1844 Nils Månsson Mandelgren from Skåne founded his Sunday Drawing School for Craftsmen in the Royal Swedish Academy of Fine Arts in Stockholm. Journeymen and apprentices within the various craft trades could attend in order to learn freehand drawing and gain a wider artistic education on their days off (Sundays).

1845

Foundation of the Swedish Craft Association

The Sunday Drawing School for Craftsmen struggled to secure funding, so Nils Månsson Mandelgren started an association that could support its activity financially. It was called the Swedish Craft Association and is considered to be the oldest association of its kind in the world – these days it goes by the name Swedish Design. The government gave it the task of safeguarding the quality of handcrafted products. The Swedish Craft Association soon took over Nils Månsson Mandelgren's educational activities and 1845 marked the starting point of what is now called Konstfack (University of Arts, Crafts and Design). In other words, Sweden was an early starter both in terms of associations for design and in terms of higher education for what we now know as product design.

1846

Reform that simplified business enterprises

The Factory and Craft Act, a reform affecting business and commercial life, was introduced in Sweden. It ended the guilds and freed up the right to develop factories and manufacturing. To ensure continued cooperation, the Swedish state recommended that craftsmen should form their own associations – what were called factory and craft associations – to exploit their common interests. It was probably this duty that formed the basis of the many trades' associations and the cooperative work that has been of such value to us since in the development of Swedish housing and design.

1867– 1869

'The Year of Great Weakness'

During these years Sweden and Finland were struck by bad harvests and failed crops, leading to famine and misery. 1867 is called the Year of Great Weakness or the Lichen Year because the lack of food pushed people into baking bark bread and using lichen to make porridge. The famine led to a dramatic increase in emigration from Sweden during this and the following period.

1905

The Swedish Craft Association Journal started – it changed its name to *Form* (Design) in 1932. The magazine still appears and is considered one of the foremost as well as oldest journals covering the Scandinavian design industry.

1907
Emigration and the Own-Home Movement

An emigration commission was held at the start of the twentieth century in an attempt to put a brake on the significant level of emigration from the country. High on the popular wish-list was both the minimizing of class divisions and improved housing: these led to important political reforms and to the breakthrough and spread of the Own-Home Movement. This was an organization for self-build: Swedish towns and cities provided citizens with favourable loans that enabled them to build a low-cost type of house while the house-owners undertook to do the work and build the house with their own hands.

1912
The Housing Commission and the Housing Census

Once it had become obvious that the housing question was a real hot potato, a national Housing Commission was set up to discover the real situation with regard to Swedes and housing. As well as inspecting and examining the situation, the aim was to offer advice, contribute to cheaper methods of building, and to simplify building regulations and house loans. The first Swedish census of the population and housing was carried out in this period.

1914
Employment service between the arts and industry

The Swedish Craft Association set up its own employment agency under the leadership of Elsa Gullberg: its function was to act as an exchange between artists and industry, the aim being to raise the level of factory-produced items and to create more attractive everyday wares. The ambition was for cheap factory products to have a similarly high level of quality as expensive handmade goods, so that the working class might have access to beauty and not have to put up with rubbish or 'bad copies of bourgeois aesthetics'.

1917
The Home Exhibition at Liljevalch's

The Home Exhibition arranged at Liljevalch's Art Gallery by the Swedish Craft Association aimed to provide the working class with simple furniture and household equipment at reasonable prices but designed by well-known Swedish artists and architects. In advance of the exhibition, a competition was held in which the designers and businesses taking part were to produce items for the show. These were then shown in twenty-three furnished rooms. The exhibition was a major public success and it is where Gunnar Asplund, Uno Åhrén and Carl Malmsten achieved their breakthrough. Eight thousand visitors had been expected, but there was more than forty thousand. Critics, however, are of the opinion that the main target group, the working class, was conspicuous by its absence and, instead, the exhibition created new interior design trends for the better off.

1918

Association of Furniture Dealers

During the 1910s the trade in furniture moved away from local craftsmen to specialized furniture shops with factory-produced goods. The increasing number of furniture shops eventually led to the formation of an association of furniture dealers in order to protect the interests of its members with common price lists, the regulation of trade between factory and individual shop, courses and education along with common advertising campaigns.

1919

More Beautiful Everyday Commodities

Gregor Paulsson wrote the ground-breaking book *More Beautiful Everyday Commodities* for an exhibition at the Swedish Fair in Gothenburg. It also became the first propaganda publication of the Swedish Craft Association. Paulsson argued that artists and crafts people should cooperate with industry to raise the quality of everyday commodities.

1922

Foundation of SIS

The Swedish Industry Standardization Commission (SIS) was formed to promote standards that could scale up production and trade without losing sight of important functional and safety aspects.

1927

The very first furniture fair was held in Sweden.

1928

Prime Minister Per Albin Hansson gave his famous speech about 'folkhemmet', a home for the people, which dealt – among much else – with every citizen's right to good housing.

1930

The birth of Functionalism.

The Stockholm Exhibition was organized by the city of Stockholm and the Swedish Craft Association in order to present ideas for Swedish architecture, design and crafts. Generally recognized as being the great breakthrough for the ideals of Functionalism in Sweden. It promoted a healthier and more democratic standard of living with, for instance, a clear functional distinction between the use of rooms, i.e. separate rooms for sleeping, living, eating and cooking. The aesthetics of furnishing and interior design were to be characterized by the ideal and the will to unite form and function. Ideally, houses should feel close to nature by having large windows and allowing in plenty of daylight, compared with the dark, heavy interiors and ostentatious ideals that had been dominant for so long.

1931

The manifesto acceptera

When the Stockholm Exhibition closed, the exhibition architects – Gunnar Asplund, Walter Gahn, Sven Markelius, Eskil Sundahl, Uno Åhrén and Gregor Paulsson – retired to the Vaxholm Hotel, where they collaborated on the writing of the manifesto *acceptera* (accept). This opened the road for the formal and social innovations of functionalist architecture in the building of the Swedish welfare state. The manifesto came out in May 1931 and was clearly inspired by the German Bauhaus school.

1932

The Housing Social Policy Commission.

At the beginning of the 1930s, the Minister for Social Affairs appointed a commission on housing policy that would have a major impact on the development of Swedish housing. The commission worked from 1933 to 1947 and laid the foundations for the standardization that defined housing policy during this period.

1939

Enquiry into living habits.

As part of the housing policy commission, the Swedish Craft Association and the Swedish Architects Association had been tasked with carrying out enquiries into the way people lived. The furniture designer, interior design architect and social commentator Lena Larsson was given the job of interviewing housewives about how they used their homes and the results of her work formed the basis for the post-war housebuilding programme.

1940

Housekeeping in a crisis.

A special section of the National Board of Information was set up a year after the outbreak of war. It was called Active Housekeeping and its function was to provide advice and information on housekeeping questions to the public at large in order to ease their transition to crisis housekeeping.

1941

Population survey

A population survey was undertaken. The Delegation for Home and Family Affairs tasked an expert group with setting up a series of working studies to look into various areas of domestic work.

1942

The experts concluded that there was a great deal of work to be done in this area. They got into contact with the Housewives' Cooperative Committee and the Domestic Science Teachers' Joint Organization and proposed setting up a research institute for questions of domestic work.

1944

Foundation of the Home Research Institute (HFI)

The Home Research Institute was founded by the Housewives' Cooperative Committee, along with National Union of Housewives, the Swedish Social Democratic Women's Association, the Swedish Rural Women's Institute, the Cooperative Women's Guild and the Domestic Science Teacher's Joint Organization. The activities of the Home Research Institute were financed by the state and its purpose was to improve the efficiency of domestic and household work. The Institute carried out wide-ranging studies into the design and equipping of the kitchen and these studies later formed the basis of recommendations regarding the most suitable heights for seating, cupboards and work surfaces, and for the positioning of stoves and sinks.

The Housing Policy Commission's first report came in 1945. It made various proposals for future housing policy, among which – to prevent overcrowding – was that no household should have more than two people per room (excluding the kitchen). There was a proposed target that no more than 20 per cent of the household income should be paid in rent, and a family housing allowance and a building allowance were introduced.

NK-bo (Nordic Company Living) opened and was the first Swedish furniture shop in which interior design was displayed in inspirational surroundings. It was a specialist shop managed by NK and it gave furnishing advice as well as selling cheap and experimental furniture for the whole family. Lena Larsson, social commentator and pioneering interior designer, was the artistic director of NK-bo between 1947 and 1956 – she had earlier been a leader of the enquiry into living habits. At NK-bo she was able to use her knowledge to develop smart solutions in terms of interior design. She also paved the way for both established and new designers, such as Stig Lindberg, Bertil Vallien and Yngve Ekström. Lena Larsson, along with the furnishing architect Elias Svedberg and Erik Wort's and NK's workshops in Nyköping, was also involved in the development of Triva-furniture. The idea was picked up and further

developed by IKEA: customers should be able to collect their chair or table from the store in a flat pack and assemble it themselves at home with the help of the accompanying instructions. (IKEA was founded by Ingvar Kamprad in 1943, but during the first years it sold mainly small items. Sales of furniture were launched in 1947, but it wasn't until 1956 that the flat-pack concept took off.)

The first research into the functionality of furniture was carried out in Sweden under the leadership of Erik Berglund: it focused on bed furniture 'in order to improve Swedish bed culture'. Swedes suffered from inferior sleeping furniture and the standards the research came up with both improved and simplified the production of beds, bedclothes, duvets and pillows.

The Swedish Industry Standardization Commission adopted a standard for kitchens. It was based on detailed research produced originally by the Swedish Craft Association and the 1939 Housing Survey. It now became possible to standardize and serially manufacture kitchens and to simplify the process of kitchen fitting.

Swedish Institute for Informative Labelling (VDN) was set up with the aim of promoting the increased use of informative labelling on consumer goods.

1953

The first laboratory for testing furniture was established. The concepts of interior design architecture and interior design architects were given formal definitions in connection with the founding of the National Swedish Interior Architects Organization (now a section within Swedish Architects).

1954

God Bostad (Good Home) appears.

The Home Research Institute joined together with Active Housekeeping and was given the name Consumer Institute. The first publication of *God Bostad* by the Housing Board appeared. It stated the minimum standards for housing design and construction necessary to qualify for advantageous state housing loans. Every part of the house was covered, everything from the measurements required for room size and hygiene areas, to standards for cupboards, work surfaces in kitchens and wardrobes. *God Bostad* continued to appear in updated and revised editions until 1976.

1955

H55

The Helsingborg Exhibition 1955 (H55) was organized by the Swedish Craft Association to show modern styles of living, new building technology and new design.

1956

How do Swedes sit?

A second major functional study of furniture was carried out, focusing this time on dining tables and chairs.

It dealt with such things as the optimal height for chairs, the positioning of the table legs and so on. It was led by Erik Berglund.

After an inspirational trial period during the summer of 1957, Carl Malmsten (70 years old at the time) decided to put his pedagogical ideas into practice and started the Capellagården school of crafts. His vision was to create a school 'for hand and soul, a meeting place for young people from all over the country, imbued with a desire to unite beauty and function in their craft'.

1958

The consumer magazine *Råd och Rön* (*Advice and Results*) was launched by the National Consumer Institute.

1962

Start of Household Goods Institute.

The Household Goods Section of the Swedish Craft Association was formed on the initiative of Brita Åkerman, who had been involved in the living habits enquiries in the 1940s and been head of Active Housekeeping from 1940 to 1946. The project was financed with grants from the Consumer Board. The Household Goods Section ran courses, lectures and study circles, organized travelling exhibitions and many informational publications. They also had their own radio programme (*Good Wares for Everyday*).

1964

Swedish
Colour Institute

The foundation of the Swedish Colour Institute. Until the 1970s, the Colour Institute – along with architects, designers, psychologists, physicists, chemists and colour researchers – concentrated on scientific research into colours and their development. This formed the basis of what later developed into the NCS – the Natural Colour System – which is now both the Swedish and the international standard. (Not accepted everywhere, but in the overwhelming majority of countries.)

1965

The Million
Programme.

Parliament decided that a million modern new houses needed to be built over the next ten years to avoid a housing shortage, and that they should be reasonably priced. In order to achieve this, the building sector would need to be rationalized and industrialized. The building engineer Ernst Sundh in Avesta was one of the first to import what was known as the gantry crane, which mechanized the process of house building and tripled the speed of work. The size of the prefabricated parts used at that time determined the size of the rooms – they were often disproportionately deep. On many building sites, cranes were mounted on rails and were able to move along the row of housing plots during the building process. The distance between the houses on sites of this kind was determined by what could be reached by the same crane.

1967

Foundation
of the
Furniture
Institute.

The Furniture Institute was set up, partly financed by the state, to carry out research and development in the field of furniture and serve the interests of consumers, producers and distributors.

1967

Complaints
Board.

Sweden was one of the first countries in Europe to set up a Public Complaints Board, which gave consumers and businesses the mechanism for solving disputes about complaints impartially and without recourse to courts of law.

1971

Consumer
Ombudsman
and
Consumer
Congress.

The Consumer Ombudsman was instituted and the law against misleading advertising came into force on 1 January 1971.

During this year the Cooperative Movement arranged a Consumer Congress, at which Olof Palme made a speech calling for more consumer influence. It was preceded by study sessions, with 12,775 participants taking part in 1,334 study circles. These discussions resulted in over 5,000 motions being put to the congress. Among the ideas put forward was that of 'unbranded' goods, what later became 'Blåvitt', that later covered everything from food to household equipment to furniture.

1972

Furniture
Facts.

The Furniture Institute launched the concept Furniture Facts as a reference and labelling system for the Swedish furniture sector.

1973
Consumer
Agency.

The National Institute for Consumer Questions was amalgamated with the Consumer Council and the Institute for Informative Labelling to form a new institution called the Consumer Agency.

1976
Swedish
Design and
Cooperative
Movement
basic furniture.

The Swedish Craft Association changed its name to Swedish Design. It focused more and more on production and consumption, based on the recognition that existing resources are finite. The Cooperative Movement and Swedish Design collaborated in developing a range of durable, simple 'Bluewhite' furniture designed by Swedish designers. To mark the launch of the new basic furniture range, the designers Kersti Sandin and Lars Bülow presented it at an exhibition at the KF-House, the Coop headquarters. Two years later they designed the Bas armchair, which was the winning entry in the Coop competition for the second stage of ideas for the development of the basic furniture range, along with a sofa, three tables and a kitchen chair.

1978

The Scandinavian Colour Institute AB (now NCS Colour AB) was set up. This was owned by the then trade and employers organization for the painting and decorating business, the Master Painters National Association.

1979

NCS – Natural Colour System ®© – was launched: later it became the Swedish colour standard (SIS).

1981

The Public Complaints Board became an independent authority.

1983
ROT-
programme
(Repair,
Reconstruct,
Retrofit) was
introduced

The programme involving new loan possibilities was introduced to make it possible for some of the shortcomings of the Million Programme to be addressed. An underlying reason was also the need to provide employment for the unemployed building workers who had lost their jobs when the pace of the Million Programme had slowed down.

One main aim of Swedish Design during the 1980s was to increase society's recognition of the importance of design. In 1983 the annual design prize, Excellent Swedish Design, was started, the first winner being Jonas Bohlin with his concrete chair 'Concrete'.

1987
Planning and
Building Law
(PBL)

The Planning and Building Law (1987:10) came into force on 1 July 1987.

1989
Environmental
labelling.

A swan, the official Scandinavian eco-label, was created by the Nordic Council of Ministers. Its purpose was to make it easy for consumers to find eco-friendly products and for businesses to produce them.

1991
Boverket

The Planning and Housing Agency changed its name to Boverket, which remains its name.

1995

The Furniture Institute moved to Jönköping, ran into economic problems and went bankrupt six months after the move.

1997
EU and EN

Following Sweden joining the European Union, the Swedish kitchen standard was replaced by EU standards, which had actually been inspired and influenced by the Swedish standard.

2001
SIS, Swedish Standards Institute.

All standardization work in Sweden was brought together in SIS, the Swedish Standards Institute. A couple of years later, ECC Sweden (which gives consumers free advice about consumer rights with regard to cross-border trade within the EU, Iceland, Norway and Great Britain) became part of the Consumer Agency.

2005
Design Year.

The Swedish Government designated 2005 as Design Year in order to emphasize the role of design in society and to recognize that much of what we use every day is a result of good design. The government invested fully 60 million kr. in the project and the campaign was run by Swedish Design. The Design Year resulted in no fewer than 1,600 projects across the country.

The first blogs about interior design and design in general in Scandinavia (including my own) began in 2005. Blogs were to become an important influence on consumption in this field.

2006
Design S.

The journal Råd och Rön (Advice and Results) was sold to the independent organization Sweden's Consumers.

Together with Svid (Swedish Industrial Design) and the Swedish Advertising Association, Swedish Design created Design S – the foremost and widest distinction in the country. It replaced the earlier Excellent Swedish Design. It is aimed at professional designers, architects, individual practitioners, producers and businesses working in the area of design in its widest sense.

2010

The Scandinavian Colour Institute AB changed its name to its present name NCS Colour AB. In the same year, the Furniture Facts label was given broader relevance and now included eco-credentials and social sustainability as well as just quality.

2011
The creation of FMI

The trade organization FMI (Colour Furniture Interiors) was formed by the amalgamation of Swedish Furniture Dealers Association and the Swedish Paint Dealers Association. The ambition is that you, the consumer, should be able to feel safe when dealing with the shops and online traders who are members of FMI. Should a legal problem arise, the trader has access to judicial help from FMI and that is also advantageous to you as customer.

2015
Consumer guidance for private individuals.

Hello Consumer was launched, a guidance service specifically for private individuals.

2016

ARN, the Public Complaints Board, broadened its function in order to take in all kinds of consumer disputes. A new platform for EU citizens makes it possible to lodge complaints free and electronically about purchases made online and across national borders. New, privately financed trades councils replaced ARN in some areas.

2017
Furniture Design Museum

The Furniture Design Museum in Stockholm was opened by its founders Lars Bülow and Kersti Sandin Bülow in November 2017.
   During their careers, both Kersti and Lars have worked for the Furniture Institute, Konstfack (University of Arts, Crafts and Design) and Swedish Design. In their younger years, they also cooperated closely with IKEA and with the Cooperative Union. Given their background as designers, design entrepreneurs and educators, they recognized that there was a lack of a specifically design-oriented museum in the capital of Sweden and decided to set up the Furniture Design Museum using their own collection of design furniture from the early twentieth century to the present as a basis.

2020
Furniture Facts 2.0

Furniture Facts 2.0 was launched with the ambition to become the leading labelling system for Scandinavia and trendsetting for Europe as a whole. Furniture Facts Sweden AB is a profit-driven company, majority owned by IVL Swedish Environmental Institute and run in cooperation with the Timber and Furniture Companies TMF. TMF is the trade and employer organization for the whole of the timber refining and furniture industry in Sweden. They represent about 650 member businesses.

Boverket and its predecessor, the Planning and Housing Agency, which regulates housebuilding in Sweden, has published many papers and collections of regulations over the years. These affect the nature of our housing and how we plan our design. They've been given all kinds of titles, everything from directives to general advice and suggestions. They have sometimes included binding rules that have to be followed; sometimes it's a matter of recommendations. Frequently it's been a matter of details to clarify and to make more precise the criteria necessary and how certain functions may best be achieved. Revision and updating are an ongoing procedure and you can keep yourself up-to-date by following the Boverket homepage, boverket.se

Planning Measurements and Concepts

Furnishing a room is not just a matter of aesthetics, it also involves a certain amount of mathematics. When interior designers and architects are working out how much space various different arrangements will need as a minimum, they work from these four factors: the measurement of the piece of furniture, the measurement of the piece when in use, the space necessary for cleaning, the space necessary for getting past it.

This may all sound very obvious, but it happens more often than not that, when we leaf through magazines or look at the photos on social media, we see houses and flats that are far too over-full or foolishly furnished. In this chapter I intend to run through some of the points that will help you work out how the furniture will fit into the space you are furnishing.

The space when in use

When planning the furnishing or when trying to decide on a purchase in the shop, it's all too easy just to measure the pieces of furniture in their 'unused state'. Don't forget to think about the radius necessary to open doors and drawers and to measure the amount of free space you need in front of the item when it's in use. You also need to estimate the amount of space your own body will occupy when you are pulling drawers or trays out to their full extent, or using carousels or wardrobe doors. These are by no means the least important aspects to be considered when you are deciding on which items to choose. These spaces may actually overlap, but they must not bump into any of the fixed parts of the building. And remember that you yourself take up different amounts of space when using one and the same item of furniture – chests of drawers, for instance: you take up less room when opening the top drawer compared with opening the bottom drawer.

Opening radius

It's not just the moving radius of the piece of furniture you have to think about, there is also the radius of fixed parts of the structure. How, for instance, do the outer and inner doors open? And the balcony doors and windows? How much space will you have to allow for them?

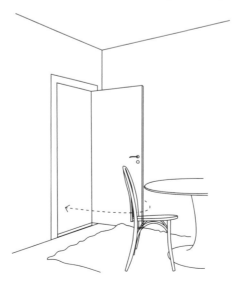

A common mistake is to forget to consider the radius of the opening of the door: you've measured the room but forgotten that the door needs to open. You can end up creating a annoying – and unnecessary – daily irritant if the edge of the carpet catches or a chair has to be moved every time you open the door.

PASSING ROOM IN MILLIMETRES

Normal level	Raised level	Lower level
Basic accessibility	Increased accessibility	No need for accessibility
800 short passage past items of furniture	900 short passage past items of furniture	600 short passage past items of furniture
900 between furniture and wall	1000 between furniture and wall	900 staircase indoors or main passage
1100 between walls	± 1300 between walls	

Passing measurements

Designers reckon that the average adult measures *c.* 60 centimetres elbow to elbow. Therefore, it is recommended that trafficked passageways in a home should be at least 100 centimetres wide to allow two people to pass one another without problems. Residences are designed with this in mind, but the occupants frequently create bottlenecks in the places where space is needed most.

Fixed restrictions

Small but important details can affect the furnishing of a room: wall-mounted radiators, pipes, electric sockets, for instance, and skirting boards if you are choosing a cupboard that stands against the wall.

Space for movement

In the section on anthropometrics I mentioned the distinction between static and dynamic body measurements. In certain rooms we need to allow a little extra room not just for our bodies, but also for whatever items we are setting in motion: in the hall, for instance, we need to think about the amount of space necessary for the heavy jacket or cape to hang as well as for the movements involved in donning them; in the bathroom there is the space needed for the towel and for us to move while drying ourselves; in the kitchen it's probably not only our body and our elbow width, but also the tray we are carrying and which we need to find space for on the way to the table. And wherever there is cleaning to be done, we need to be able to reach in and move round with the vacuum cleaner; and we'll want to be able to bend the vacuum tube down so that we can reach under the bed, the cupboard, the coffee table or the sideboard, while still leaving room for ourselves.

Furnishability

The furnishability of a home doesn't just depend on how big the rooms are, it depends just as much on the proportions and on the positions of the windows and doors. Big windows that run from ceiling to floor, or those with low sills, are common in current homes and allow a glorious amount of light in, but they can also make the room difficult to furnish since they reduce the available length of wall. It can be difficult to find space for bookshelves and wall-mounted TV screens – in the latter case also because of the way the light falls and is reflected on the available walls.

Many doors opening into a room can have a negative impact on its furnishability, partly because you will need to take account of the space for the doors to open and partly because it will be difficult to arrange for a smooth traffic flow through the rooms.

You also need to take account of 'softer' aspects that it may not be possible to draw on the plan. I'm thinking, for example, of the fact that certain parts of the room may have disruptive characteristics such as draughts or strong evening light or dazzling sunlight. And there is also the need to ensure safe distances from fireplaces or other heating units when you are working out the furnishing.

Keep things close

In planning the location of the various modules in a kitchen, we often work on what planners' jargon refers to as 'keeping things close'. Everything should be located as near its zone of usage as possible. The dishwasher should be near the sink in order to have access to running water to rinse off dishes before they go into the washer; saucepans and other pans should be kept no more than a step away from the stove and oven so that you don't have to cross the whole room to fetch a heavy frying pan. This basic principle should be used all over the house when you are furnishing it: what needs to be close to the piece of furniture you are positioning; what kind of situation is likely to arise that demands proximity; do you store things close to where you are likely to need them; do you have to go far to pick up or put things away in their proper place?

ANS-principle

There is a well-known furniture warehouse that works on the principle that has come to be known as the ANS-principle. The abbreviation stands for Activity, Need, Solution. Designers schooled in this methodology always start their planning process by establishing which activities will take place in the environment to be furnished, the needs that will result from that and the solutions that should be in place in the specific room.

Room design, shapes and zones

Room design is the shape of the room in plan, section and size. When architects and designers use the phrase 'room design', they include the geometric basic shapes (square, rectangular and so on), the physical and mental barriers that may arise or be experienced because of differences of level, distance and the positioning of the furniture. A big bulky bookcase or a wall-length media system can change our experience of the proportions of the room. And, similarly, freestanding furniture, curtains and screens can define different spaces in large, open-plan rooms.

When planning your furnishing, particularly in open-plan spaces, it may be helpful to start thinking in bubbles or bubble diagrams in order to plot which activities will take place and where before you move on to make concrete choices about exactly which model of sofa or armchair you want. You may find that you arrive at quite different solutions if, rather than the furniture, your starting point is the different zones of the room and which activities will take place where – and only then move on to which furniture will be necessary to fulfil those thoughts.

When computer game designers are creating environments, they make use of the basic principles as to how we read and orient ourselves in new spaces.

Organizing the rooms

What we mean by organizing the rooms is how the more public areas of the home and the private spaces relate to each other. We can, of course, furnish our home just as we like, but we usually feel that the more private parts, such as the bedroom, should not have to act as a passageway to the living room or the dining room. The idea that a home should have separate social and private parts already existed in the 1800s. Well-off families were much concerned with entertaining guests in their homes and this affected the planning of multi-apartment buildings: the drawing room and the formal rooms were placed at the front, facing the street, whereas the more private rooms were located at a suitable distance from them, facing the courtyard at the back.

The apartments built during the Million Programme (see p. 292), however, were built to a different concept: their ideal was what was called 'neutral communication', which meant that all the rooms should be approached from the hall or from a corridor.

In the 1980s, planning in Sweden took a different turn. The earlier building norm that insisted on a separate kitchen was changed in 1985 and replaced with a policy emphasizing that 'it should be possible to separate the kitchen from the living room in the future'. This led to the first open-plan solutions: these were popular with building firms, which saw the possibility of putting up more homes with a smaller area.

In the last couple of decades many people have taken to renovating older apartments and houses according to their own ideas, not necessarily paying any attention to the need for room organization. But if you do have the possibility of affecting the layout of the room by your choice of furniture, it may well be an idea worth keeping in mind.

Axiality

According to Ola Nylander, a researcher at Chalmers Technical University in Gothenburg, axiality is a concept of significance for the unmeasurable values of a home. He describes it as '[. . .] a line that connects two interesting points. An axis runs through and involves two or more rooms. An axis can also create the possibility of transparency and through-views in a home.'

The more rooms the axis cuts through, the more clear-cut it becomes. If the architect had axiality in mind, it would, of course, be silly of us to move into the place and proceed to furnish it in a way that destroys the experience by having bulky furniture that disrupts the view between rooms or the outlook to the outside. Anyone living in a house may find it interesting to note what there is at the ends of the axial lines. Is there a colour or a detail you can pick up in your choice of furniture, and is there anything you can do with the actual view out, with what can be seen on the other side of the window?

Enclosure

This refers to your experience of a room's sense of enclosure or openness. Studies suggest that we need both if we are to feel good in our homes. Just as in the case of axiality, it becomes meaningless if we work counter to the architect's underlying idea about enclosure when renovating or furnishing our home. We should avoid disposing of or over-emphasizing the variations and possibilities of enclosure too much.

Daylight and shadows

When setting about the furnishing of a new room, it's really worthwhile to study the way the natural light flows. How does the light move around the room in the course of the day? Apart from direct light – the rays of the sun coming in through the window – it is also worth taking account of the indirect, reflected light, the shadows made by various fixed parts of the structure of the building, and how you experience the colour of the light in the room. Daylight is often referred to as indirect light, i.e. global radiation from the sky, sunlight reflected in the atmosphere and not to be confused with direct sunlight.

What effect sunlight or direct light has on the temperature of a room can vary depending on compass direction, time of day and season of the year. Generally speaking, in our hemisphere, rooms in the north have colder light whereas rooms in the south have warmer light. A simple explanation is to think of the sun as a lamp that heats up during the day the longer it stays on. Warm light tends to reinforce warm and clear colours, whereas a colder light tends to reinforce cold colours – it's worth bearing this in mind when you are choosing the colours of your furniture and positioning various items that may reflect the light in the room.

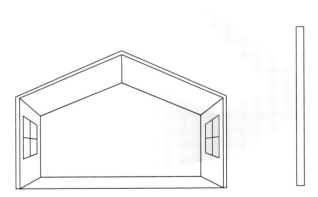

Is there anything in the external environment that may affect the colour of the indirect light that falls into the room you are designing?

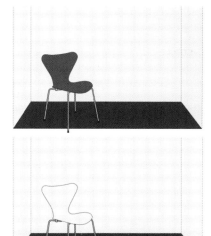
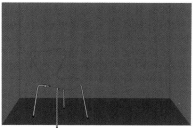

Do you want your designer chair to stand out clearly? Choose a colour that will contrast with the colour of the wall and the surroundings. In *The Interior Design Handbook*, you'll find more about how to perform magic tricks with focus points.

The colour of indirect light indoors depends on many other factors than just the colour of the sky at that moment. The light coming in, for instance, may first bounce off or be filtered by surrounding buildings that affect the colour of the light before it reaches your room. If the window faces a wall of orange tiles which the incoming light is reflected off, it is likely that the colour of the light will be warmer, irrespective of the direction or the season of the year.

Contrast effect

I get questions every day from people who want advice about various colour choices for their furniture (or walls). *Should I go for black chairs, or grey, or wooden? What do you think of this colour code for my living room?* It is actually impossible to give good advice without knowing what kind of contrast effect you want to achieve.

Do you want the furniture (or the wall) to stand out and be seen? In that case choose a colour that contrasts with the background (or the foreground) against which it will stand. Do you want to create a sense of harmony and coherence? In that case choose walls and furniture

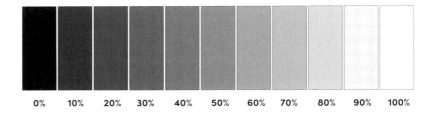

0% 10% 20% 30% 40% 50% 60% 70% 80% 90% 100%

that tone in with each other. Sounds obvious, but it's easy to forget when you're worrying about making decisions.

Light reflectance value

When choosing colours for furniture or when lighting or painting or choosing flooring for the room, light reflectance value (LRV for short) is a concept worth checking out. Interior designers use it, for instance, when they are working out how many and what kind of lamps a room will need, but it is also helpful when you are trying to create pleasing contrasts between different surfaces.

To have sufficient light and contrasts in a room is a matter of health and well-being, not just preference and taste. The LRV shows how much daylight and artificial light is reflected back from a surface measured on a scale from 0 to 100, whereby a mirror scores 100 per cent, a white-painted wall usually about 85 per cent and a black wall 0 per cent. The LRV is given in the specifications of paints for walls and ceilings and also in those for various types of wooden and vinyl flooring.

LRV in brief

- Walls, floors and ceilings with a high LRV help to spread light efficiently around the whole room. The higher the LRV of a surface, the greater the effect achieved by the same fixture or level of daylight admitted.

- Furniture and surfaces with higher LRV demand less illumination, which means less energy usage.

- Colours with an LRV rating less than 50 per cent absorb more light than they reflect.

- Since LRV is a universal scale for measuring the relative values of light and dark, different varieties of wood and different colours may have the same LRV. So, when choosing wall and floor colours, it makes sense to go for intermediates in order to avoid everything merging together. The recommendation for public spaces is that there should be at least 30 per cent LRV difference between floors and walls and between doorposts and walls. This is to make it easier for people to find their way round.

- Public spaces are covered by guidelines about having contrasting markings/signing for such things as outside doors, in order to make things easier for the visually impaired, for those with intellectual disabilities or dementia, and for anyone who has difficulties with orientation. There should be marking in public buildings and in the common areas of apartment buildings, but it is not necessary to have it in private apartments. It could, however, be useful to know the guidelines if you have family members or elderly relatives with any of the above. Contrast markings can be achieved by making distinctions in colour or in choice of materials: a contrast in terms of lightness of at least 0.40 on the NCS® Natural Colour System between the markings and the surrounding surface makes it very much easier for the visually impaired to notice the markings.

- If you take black-and-white photos of the room you are designing, you will quickly see where contrasts are lacking or how the environment will be experienced by the visually impaired.

Labelling in the Furniture Trade

There are many different quality, environmental and sustainability labels used in the interior design and furniture trade. Some of them have been thought up by the manufacturing or marketing companies themselves, whereas permission to use certain others is subject to checks and controls by independent third parties and has to be applied for. In this section I have put together a very brief collection of the quality, environmental and sustainability labels I think it's currently worth being familiar with in the furniture and interior design trades.

Blå Ängeln/Blue Angel/Blauer Engel is a sustainability label organized by the German government for the protection of the environment and the consumer. *www.blauer-engel.de/en*

Bra Miljöval (Good Environmental Choice) is the label of the Swedish Nature Conservation Association (Naturskyddsförening). It is what's known as third-party certification, which means that it is certified independently of both seller and buyer. The label is the only one in Sweden run by an environmental organization. *www.bramiljoval.se*

CE (Conformité Européene – approved by an EU directive). The CE label is a product label stating that the product fulfils the basic demands with regard to health, safety, function and environment, and that the prescribed checking procedure has been followed. The CE label is necessary to gain permission to sell a product within the EU. *www.sis/se/standarder/ce-markning*

FSC, the Forestry Stewardship Council, is a certification system stating that timber products must come from forests that are exploited responsibly from environmental, social and economic points of view. *www.fsc.org/se-sv*

GOTS, Global Organic Textile Standard, is one of the biggest international environmental labels for textiles. The label is only available for natural fibre products, such as cotton and wool, but some admixture of synthetic material is permitted. The GOTS standard has two levels:

- Level 1 – organic, means that more than 95 per cent of the textile fibres are ecological.
- Level 2 – made with organic – means that more than 70 per cent of the textile fibres are ecological.

The certification is carried out by approved certification bodies and is then followed up by random checks on the producers. The GOTS label covers the whole process from cultivation to finished product. *www.global-standard.org*

ISO, International Organization for Standardization, develops global standards in a wide range of different areas. *www.iso.org/home.html*

Möbelfakta (Furniture Facts) is a reference and labelling system run by Möbelfakta Sverige AB, a non-profit-making company. Any piece of furniture that lives up to Möbelfakta's three parts meets the market's environmental demands, is manufactured according to ethical guidelines, and follows international specifications for quality. Möbelfakta aims to be there to assist the producers, purchasers, designers, architects and any others who use or work with furniture. *www.mobelfakta.se*

PEFC, Programme for the Endorsement of Forest Certification Schemes, is a certification system to guarantee that products come from forests that are used in a responsible environmental, social and economic manner.
https://pefc.se

RDS, Responsible Down Standard, is a global standard for down which makes high demands in terms of animal welfare and traceability. The labelling ensures that the down does not come from breeders who use force-feeding or who pluck birds while they are alive. The label also guarantees that the birds are properly fed and watered throughout their lives and that they are not subjected to unnecessary stress. Moreover, all the down comes from birds mainly bred for food, which means that the down is actually a by-product of the food industry.
www.textileexchange.org/standards/responsible-down

REACH, Registration, Evaluation, Authorization and Restrictions of Chemicals is an EU regulation that came into force in 2007. Its purpose is to protect human beings and the environment from the risks of chemicals. The European Chemicals Authority, ECHA, is responsible for the REACH regulation at the EU level. The Chemicals Inspection has the main responsibility for the REACH regulation in Sweden.
ec.europa.eu/environment/chemicals/reach/reach_en.html

SIS, Swedish Institute for Standards, the Swedish member of ISO and CEN.

SS, Swedish standard is determined by SIS.

SS-EN is an EU standard which has been introduced as a national Swedish standard.

Svanen (the Swan) is the official Nordic environmental label. The state-owned company Miljömärkning is responsible for the Swan label in Sweden. Miljömärkning Sverige works to the instructions of government, with no interest in the line of business or profit. The same company is also responsible for the EU Flower, the European Union's common environmental label. The Swan is a Type 1 (ISO 14024) environmental label, which means that the products pass the environmental demands laid down by an independent third party, that those demands are continually being sharpened and that they are developed with a life-cycle perspective. After passing approved checks, a company receives a licence that gives it permission to use the Swan label on their products for a limited period of time, at the end of which the company must re-apply.
www.svanen.se

ÖKO TEX/OEKO-TEX® is a world-leading, global labelling standard for textiles and textile-like products. It sets the limits for a number of substances known to be dangerous both to health and to the environment. Many of these substances are already regulated by European legislation, but in some cases OEKO-TEX® Standard 100 makes higher demands. In addition to that, it lays down the limits for a number of health and environmentally dangerous substances not yet covered by legislation.

- Standard 100 by OEKO-TEX®
- OEKO-TEX® MADE BY GREEN
- OEKO-TEX® LEATHER STANDARD
- STeP by OEKO-TEX® stands for Sustainable Textile and Leather Production
- OEKO-TEX® DETOX TO ZERO
- ECO PASSPORT by OEKO-TEX®
www.oeko-tex.com

Afterword

When I changed the focus of my blog and started to write more about interior know-how than about current trends, it caused many of my readers to raise their eyebrows. Especially when I went out on a limb and criticized the kind of inspiration I had been a part of sharing for a considerable time.

But the more I learned about furniture-making and design principles, the more awkward it felt to continue praising quite ridiculous pieces and interior solutions – just because they looked good in photos. 'I don't understand your philosophy and positioning in the industry,' wrote a well-known interior designer, somewhat annoyed, when he found me blunt and questioning.

Well, I hope that this book clarifies my point of view. Not all furniture that's available today is made with the same focus on quality and comfort and they are not always compatible with each other in a practical sense. Yet consumers are offered very little guidance in this, apart from suggestions about what will look nice together.

My aim with this book is for it to work as an eye opener.

I want to offer advice and support on how to create a home that on top of being a nice display is also a home where you really want to stay.

Frida

Sources and acknowledgements

List of furniture illustrations

P. 20 (a/l) Lilla Åland. Designer: Carl Malmsten. Company: Stolab.

P. 20 (a/r) Spade Chair. Designer: Faye TooGood. Company: Please Wait to be Seated.

P. 20 (b) Family Chairs. Designer: Lina Nordqvist master's thesis. Company: Design House Stockholm.

P. 29 Åkerblomstolen. Designer: Bengt Åkerblom/Gunnar Eklöf.

P. 31 Norrgavels wooden chair. Designer: Nirvan Richter. Company: Norrgavel.

P. 44 (a) Spindle armchair. Designer: Nirvan Richter. Company: Norrgavel.

P. 44 (b) Woven chair. Designer: Hans Wegner. Company: Carl Hansen.

P. 45 Ton Chair no.14/02. Designer: Michael Thonet. Company: Ton.

P. 46 Beetle Chair. Designer GamFratesi. Company: Gubi.

P. 49 (m) Orchestra chair. Designer Sven Markelius.

P. 51 Concrete. Designer: Jonas Bohlin. Company: Källemo.

P. 54 (ö) Spin. Designer Staffan Holm. Company: Swedese.

P. 55 Stepladder stool. Bröderna Lindqvist AB Motala. Idag LQ Design.

P. 68 EA 217 and EA 108. Designer: Charles and Ray Eames. Company: Vitra / Herman Miller.

P. 90 (a/r) Pernilla 3. Designer: Bruno Mathsson. Company: Bruno Mathsson International.

P. 90 (b/l) Egg chair. Designer: Arne Jacobsen. Company: Fritz Hansen.

P. 90 (a/l) Lamino. Designer: Yngve Ekström. Company: Swedese.

P. 90 (b/r) Anonymised safari chair.

P. 95 Egg chair. Designer: Arne Jacobsen. Company: Fritz Hansen.

P. 96 J16 Rocking chair. Designer: Hans Wegner Company: Fredericia Furniture.

P. 104 (l) Sjuanstolen. Designer Arne Jacobsen. Company: Fritz Hansen.

P. 104 (r) Wishbone Chair/Y-stolen. Designer Hans Wegner. Company: Carl Hansen.

P. 107; p. 108 Sjuanstolen. Designer Arne Jacobsen. Company: Fritz Hansen. (The tables are anonymised sample furniture)

P. 117 Mi 901, Designer: Bruno Mathsson Company: Bruno Mathsson International.

P. 121 (a) Hejnum. Designer: Kristian Eriksson. Company: G.A.D.

P. 121 (m) Flower mono. Designer: Christine Schwarzer. Company: Swedese.

P. 121 (b) Tati coffee table. Designer: Broberg Ridderstråle. Company: Asplund.

P. 158 Snö. Designer: Thomas Sandell. Company: Asplund.

P. 170 (ä) Anonymised example.

P. 170 (b) Shelf brackets. Designer: Nirvan Richter. Company: Norrgavel.

P. 175 String-shelving (c). Designer: Nisse Strinning. Company: String®.

P. 185 Hall furniture Designer: Nirvan Richter. Company: Norrgavel.

P. 186 Nostalgi hat shelf. Designer: Gunnar Bolin. Company: Essem design.

P. 220; 224 Sebras baby and junior bed.

P. 305 Sjuanstolen. Designer: Arne Jacobsen Company: Fritz Hansen.

Anonymised example furniture: p. 20 (b/r); 32, 34, 38, 47, 48, 49 (r), 53, 54 (u), 56, 59, 62, 63, 65, 68 (b), 70, 72, 79, 84, 89, 94, 98, 102, 106, 115, 125, 127, 128, 131, 132, 134, 135, 143, 147, 150, 152, 162, 163, 164, 165, 169, 176, 181, 182, 183, 197, 6, 207, 208, 210, 212, 215, 217, 298.

Acknowledgements

My grateful thanks to all those who contributed their knowledge and advice:

Anders Lindholm, bed expert, SOVA

Benny Hermansson, bentwood expert, Gemla Fabrikers AB

Björn Nordin, timber expert, Svenskt Trä

Emma Olbers, furniture designer

Jakob Sjögren, upholstered furniture expert, O.H. Sjögren

Johan Dahlin, spiral spring expert, Starsprings Sweden AB

Kersti Sandin Bülow, architect, designer, founder of Furniture Design Museum

Lars Bülow, architect, designer, founder of Furniture Design Museum

Maria Holmberg, investigator Konsumentverket (Consumer Agency)

Markus Gotting, wardrobe and sliding-door expert, Pelly Group

Martin Johansson, furniture expert, Stolab Möbel AB

Mikael Kuurne, furniture designer

Nirvan Richter, architect and furniture designer & Tomas Fröding, cabinetmaker at Norrgavel

Patrick Nyberg, leather expert, Leathermaster Scandinavia AB

Pernilla Norling, linoleum expert, Forbo Flooring

Rebecka Ullholm, ergonomics expert and interior designer, Ergodesign

Sami Kallio, furniture designer

Thomas Thorsson, bookcases expert, Taras Hallgren & Son AB

Tomas Ekström, standardization expert, SIS-TK 391 Möbler (Furniture)

Victoria Tengstrand, project leader for SIS/TK 391 Möbler (Furniture)